A High-speed Flash, Clarifying a Whirling Blur, Reveals What the Eye Never Sees

Using 1/5000 part of a second, the author took this picture with electric-flash apparatus. By freezing motion in midair he proved flight techniques which he had only suspected. This male **Eastern Cardinal** unlimbers landing gear on approaching feeding station on Cornell campus. Feathers of the rounded wing, which here start the downward stroke, are overlapped to catch maximum air. (See "A New Light Dawns on Bird Photography," page 21.)

STALKING BIRDS
WITH COLOR CAMERA

By ARTHUR A. ALLEN, Ph.D.

Emeritus Professor of Ornithology, Cornell University
Honorary Director, Cornell University Laboratory of Ornithology

and others

Foreword by GILBERT GROSVENOR

President, National Geographic Society, 1920-1954

---

331 color photographs, showing 266 species of North American birds

---

National Geographic Society

WASHINGTON, D. C.

Contents

Arthur A. Allen Studies Birds Above Ithaca Falls, New York

In his articles in the NATIONAL GEOGRAPHIC MAGAZINE beginning in July, 1934, Dr. Allen has told millions of readers about American bird life. His expeditions, many of them sponsored by the National Geographic Society, have recorded the portraits and voices of vanishing species as well as those of hundreds of common birds from California to Florida and from Mexico to Alaska. Thousands of students have learned about birds under his tutelage as Professor of Ornithology at Cornell University, and many have become distinguished ornithologists.

Foreword

By Gilbert Grosvenor

President, National Geographic Society, 1920-1954

THE members of the National Geographic Society will recognize in the author of this volume a friend of many years. Dr. Arthur A. Allen's first contribution to the NATIONAL GEOGRAPHIC MAGA-ZINE, "Blackbirds and Orioles," appeared in 1934. Soon thereafter, The Society encouraged him to begin a series of natural color photographs of North American birds and substantially aided him in his efforts. Results of great scientific interest from this close cooperation through the years are revealed in the pages of this beautiful book of birds, the first to be profusely illustrated by natural color photographs.

Of the 331 color illustrations, 264 were made by Dr. Allen. In all, they portray 266 North American species in their natural habitats—an unrivaled photographic and ornithological accomplishment. Names of photographers other than Dr. Allen are printed under their contributions.

Dr. Harold E. Edgerton, the ingenious Professor of Electrical Measurements at the Massachusetts Institute of Technology, and two distinguished naturalists of the Denver Museum of Natural History, Robert J. Niedrach, Curator of Ornithology, and Walker Van Riper, Curator of Spiders, contribute the remarkable chapter, "Freezing the Flight of Hummingbirds."

That public interest in birds and bird life justifies this tremendous labor often has been demonstrated. An example was the Nation-wide publicity accorded Dr. Allen's discovery in June, 1948, of the nesting place of the bristle-thighed curlew in the Alaskan tundra.

Accounts of the dramatic struggle to capture the nomination for president at the Republican National Convention in Philadelphia were monopolizing the front pages of the newspapers on the morning in June, 1948, that I received a telegram from Dr. Allen in Alaska. It read simply: "We have found the curlew's nest." The next morning the bristle-thighed curlew rivaled the convention in news interest. Stories with two-column heads on the front pages of the New York Times, the New York Herald Tribune, and the Washington Post, for example, gave graphic descriptions of the bird, the importance of the find from an ornithological standpoint, and an account of the expedition in the Alaskan wilds. The Editor of the Washington Times-Herald, Mr. Frank Waldrop, discarded his comment on national politics and substituted a two-column dissertation on the bristle-thighed curlew, Dr. Allen, and the National Geographic Society. The weekly news magazines took up the subject with gusto, even to the extent of coining puns on the bird's unusual name!

For nearly six decades Dr. Allen has been associated with Cornell University. With the aid of his roommate he made his first bird photograph, of a ruffed grouse on its nest, when he was an undergraduate in 1904.

In 1912, the only year of his career when he forsook Cornell, he went to Colombia to collect specimens for the American Museum of Natural History. The first bird he took in the Colombian jungle proved to be an ant thrush, unknown to any collection in the world.

On an expedition into the Santa Rita Mountains of Arizona in June, 1939, he discovered the first trogon's nest ever found in the United States. Scientists had been searching the area for 30 years, vainly attempting to find the nesting place of this brilliantly plumed tropical bird.

Through his photographs, Dr. Allen was the first to determine that drumming grouse produce their reverberating sound by beating their wings on the air alone. Previously, naturalists believed the birds either struck a log with their wings or beat upon their own breasts.

In recognition of his early work for his alma mater, Dr. Allen became the first professor of ornithology in the United States. Among the thousands of students he has taught at Cornell are numbered some of the Nation's most widely known ornithologists.

For 30 years the author and his Cornell colleagues have engaged in a series of expeditions with camera and microphone to film in motion the behavior of North American birds and to record their songs and calls. Many of these expeditions have been sponsored by the National Geographic Society, and reports of their achievements have appeared in the NATIONAL GEOGRAPHIC MAGAZINE (page 307).

Publication of this book adds another important contribution of the National Geographic Society to its educational purposes— the increase and diffusion of geographic knowledge. Most of the color plates and articles first appeared in The Society's NATIONAL GEOGRAPHIC MAGAZINE, which assumed the cost of the original color engravings and manuscripts over a period of years. Preparation of 331 color engravings and the 93 in monochrome exclusively for the limited edition of this book would have been so expensive as to make the price of a volume prohibitive. Nevertheless, 72 new color plates never before published are included.

The Society is happy and proud to make available to bird lovers in a single volume at a nominal price this magnificent collection of Dr. Allen's natural color photographs and his fascinating narrative of his studies and experiences.

Stalking Birds with Color Camera

FOR YEARS I had dreamed of making natural-color photographs of birds, but the slowness and costliness of the film, the unsatisfactory results from short exposures, and the evanescence of the colors warned me not to begin.

Even in black-and-white photography, where because of modern ultraspeed films one is not handicapped by weak light, many technically perfect negatives are ruined by the motion or poor position of the birds. In color, action shots seemed out of the question.

Then suddenly all this was changed. The Eastman Kodak Company perfected a color film which was nearly half as fast as the black-and-white films with which I had started bird photography 25 years before. Moreover, since the final image was composed of stained gelatin instead of silver particles, it would stand great enlargement without showing the grain that is the bane of the darkroom artist working with black-and-white negatives.

The National Geographic Society offered to give me the color film and generous cooperation. Here indeed was a chance to capture the charm of birds in action in living color.

Looking out of my study window at Ithaca, New York, early in the summer of 1938, I was greeted by a little flock of purple finches, as well as by chickadees, nuthatches, and blue jays that had frequented my feeding station all winter and spring.

Birds Can't Count; Hence the "Go-awayster"

The finches were good subjects to start on, but the light close to the house and under the mulberry tree was too dim for a color camera. Therefore I moved the automatic feeding device farther from the house, next to the garden, and set up one of our grass-mat blinds near by, so the birds would become accustomed to it.

Almost as important as setting up the blind the day before the pictures are to be made is the need for an accomplice to walk away from the blind when all is in readiness for the photographer.

Birds apparently cannot count, and if one person leaves, even though two were present a moment before, they are well satisfied that danger is past. My son David served as my right-hand man in most of the photographic undertakings and was officially known as the "go-awayster."

Birds are so active while feeding that exposures of a mere fraction of a second are necessary, and with color film the lens must be wide open to admit enough light in that brief wink of time. In fact, I had learned from sad experience that the correct exposure for close-ups of birds feeding in bright sunlight was exactly $1/60$ of a second when the diaphragm was set at F:4.5, its largest aperture. At that stop there is little depth of focus, so the birds must come to exactly the right spot and stand more or less in profile before the lens.

To accomplish this, I set up, near the automatic feeder, a slender post with a cross board on top less than two inches wide and six inches long. On the middle of this strip of wood I fastened a small pan to hold sunflower seed. In this way all the action would take place squarely in front of the lens—that is, if I remembered to empty the food from the adjacent automatic feeder before going into the blind with my camera.

The tin seed container was not artistic, so I camouflaged it with flowers from the garden. A couple of milk bottles hung to the post served as concealed vases for the flowers and kept them from wilting.

I am afraid my love of color and zeal for giving the Kodachrome film a real test often got the better of my judgment, with the result that many of the earlier pictures resembled an old-fashioned nosegay with a bird stuck in the middle (page 87) or a glimpse of women's Easter bonnets on Fifth Avenue in the gay nineties.

Later in the season I provided a section of a log and fastened the feed pan to the back of a projecting piece of bark where it could be concealed by the floral arrangements. The resulting pictures seemed a little less artificial and fully as colorful (page 33).

Finches Get Bright New Suits

By this time the purple finches were molting, and though the portraits were interesting for showing progress of feather change, the birds were not at their best.

After molting, however, some of them were much improved, particularly young males of the preceding year. They resembled their brown-streaked mothers until July and then gradually acquired pinkish feathers. By the last of August they were rosy red all over, somewhat more intensely so on crown and rump. The change from this pale rose color to the deeper crimson of the old males is accomplished without molting by a curious type of feather wear for years not understood.

Rarest Bird in North America

In early colonial times the **Ivory-billed Woodpecker** was not uncommon in southern swamps as far north as the Ohio River. Today, if not extinct, it is North America's rarest bird. This male bird was photographed by the author near Tallulah, in northern Louisiana, in 1935.

without changing the shape of the feathers. As the red shaft and barbs become more conspicuous, the birds seem actually to change color, becoming much brighter. The color film accurately registered some of these changes.

Many Subjects in Sight

It must not be thought that I spent all my time in the grass blind in the garden, though I enjoyed watching the birds at close range and prayed for sunshine between 8 and 9 in the morning so that I could make a couple of snaps before speeding to the campus to hold my classes.

My graduate students began telling me about some of the birds' nests they had been observing. A grouse was incubating out by the rifle range; a kingfisher (page 290) was feeding young in a sand bank not far away; a veery had a nest by the path in some near-by woods; and so on. There were obviously plenty of subjects upon which to try out the color film. Whenever the sun

It was formerly thought that new pigment had to be introduced into the feathers to brighten them. We now know that in many birds the acquisition of new finery consists in wearing off the whole tip of a feather, which is frequently gray or rusty, thus exposing the color underneath. The English sparrow (page 17), for instance, acquires a trim black cravat in the spring by this sort of feather wear, and snow buntings (page 20) change from brown to white merely by wearing off the rusty edges of their white feathers.

With the purple finches, on the other hand, the feathers are not edged with gray, and there is no apparent change in their shape by feather wear. The fact is, the red pigment exists only in the shaft of the feather and in the main branches, or barbs. This color is more or less concealed by the gray secondary branches of the barbs, called barbules, which wear off

shone, therefore, I planned to make hay by slipping out of the laboratory and into a blind that I had set up near some nest the evening before.

When a person sits quietly in a blind for two or three hours, he not only learns a great deal about the birds he is observing and photographing, but he likewise locates by their songs the territories of the other birds in the vicinity.

While waiting for the grouse to return, for example, I located the nests of a scarlet tanager (page 86) and an indigo bunting (page 92), while the kingfisher led to a chestnut-sided warbler's home (page 62).

Nests Amid the Roses

At various times I sought other subjects that would make good compositions for the color camera. About the first of July, for

3

Braking Hard, a Female Duck Hawk Sweeps In for the Lure

Her trainer holds the piece of meat in his gloved hand. Several American hawks, including eagles, have been trained in falconry, sport of kings, but the duck hawk, the nearest American kin to the peregrine falcons of the Old World, is the most spectacular. Its wind-tossed jesses, or leather straps, by which the bird is secured when not at liberty, mimic the position of its wings.

instance, the Cornell rose garden was at its best, and what could be more desirable than the combination of beautiful roses and interesting birds in the same color film?

A search of the garden revealed several nests of robins, chipping sparrows (page 101), and song sparrows, the deserted nest of a spotted sandpiper, and, most remarkable of all, the nest of a purple finch. Every purple finch's nest I had ever found previously had been in the top of an evergreen tree; hence, what an opportunity was this!

When I discovered the nest in the top of a Lady Gay rose arbor, the male was incubating. Unfortunately for the color film, he was still in immature plumage; this, among the pink roses, was rather dull.

He showed his immaturity and lack of sophistication in other ways also, because, in spite of all the visits I made to the garden, I never saw the female bird. Apparently he had accepted the entire responsibility for hatching the eggs and rearing the family. This he proceeded to do in a highly efficient manner, paying little attention to the fearsome camera and tripod fastened conspicuously to the top of a tall stepladder.

"Happiness" on Hollyhocks

Some of the other nests in the rose garden were even more colorful, such as a chipping sparrow's nest in a rambler vine and a song sparrow's nest in a General Washington rosebush. The nests, for the most part, were

4

A Barn Swallow, Preferring Man's Abodes, Strikes a Phone Wire with a Wing Tip

In summer, barn swallows are found from Alaska to Mexico. Winter sees some migrating as far as Argentina. Having adopted man's buildings as their own, they have become subjects of fanciful tales. Contrary to legend, they do not hibernate in the mire on pond bottoms, but they do build nests of mud (right).

beneath the plane of the flowers, so that, in parting the branches to expose the nest for the camera, I had to be careful not to move all the flowers out of the picture.

The desire for colorful combinations often required ingenuity and days of most patient and careful watching in order to be on hand when the birds and flowers were both at their best, or to arrange a setting appropriate to the species concerned.

Years ago I saw a bluebird perched on a pink hollyhock in a neighbor's garden. Ever since, I had carried that picture in my mind, hoping that I could some day reproduce it with a camera.

Finally the opportunity arrived when some young bluebirds were about to leave their nest box on one of the University buildings, and the hollyhocks, not too far away, were in

their prime. Both the box and the flowers had to be moved to get the birds to perch on the hollyhocks when returning with food for their youngsters, but the resulting pictures seemed worth the effort and no harm came to the birds when the box was returned to its former position (page 42).

Nestlings Guarded Against Sunstroke

In working with birds' nests in the bright sunlight required for action pictures on color film, one has to be extremely careful not to leave young birds exposed to the direct rays for many minutes at a time.

Ordinarily, a nest is well concealed and shaded by the surrounding foliage, which must be carefully bent aside when a photograph of the parents feeding the young is desired. Naturally, one cannot run out of the blind

On the Downstroke a Robin's Feathers Overlap and Grip the Air

On the upstroke, the high-speed camera shows, they open by turning edgewise (page 6). These sleepy nestlings are too young to have acquired good vision. They do not recognize the home-coming parent until his feet have touched the nest, a bowl of mud, grasses, and weed stalks. A little later they'll sit up and take more notice. (See "A New Light Dawns on Bird Photography," page 21.)

and part the leaves every time one hears the bird coming with food. Indeed, the parents will usually not return at all so long as they know one is anywhere around.

After bending aside the obstructing leaves, one must devise some convenient method of shading the young while waiting for the parents to return.

An indigo bunting's nest, for example, I covered with a large piece of bark. To one end of the bark I tied a thread with which, from my position in the blind, I could pull away the covering. I don't know which surprised the mother bird the more, to find her nest concealed or to see the bark slide off the nest and her youngsters' heads pop up like veritable jack-in-the-boxes.

The female indigo bunting is a plain brown sparrowlike bird with just a tinge of blue on her shoulders, and, for the sake of the color, I particularly wanted her brilliant blue mate to come to the nest. This, unfortunately, he refused to do, spending all of his time singing and challenging another equally vociferous male to invade his territory.*

Goldfinch Proves Camera-shy

Though the male scarlet tanager visits the nest infrequently while his mate is incubating, and never broods the youngsters, he busily supplies them with food. I snapped him as he left for the second course of an all-day meal, but since the sky was somewhat overcast, the resulting picture was rather dark (page 86).

* See "The Bird's Year," page 69.

Papa Robin Opens the Shutters of His Own Venetian Blind

On the wing's upstroke each flight feather turns on edge to minimize resistance of the air. A racing oarsman uses the same technique in "feathering" his oar. Normally the male robin's head is darker than the female's, but this does not always hold true.

The male goldfinch persisted in coming to the back of the nest to feed the female instead of to the branch at the side, which was in sharp focus. More annoying, however, was the fact that, after once seeing the lens and hearing the shutter click, he would not return to the nest at all. Instead, he called her off and fed her on the fence hard by. Indeed, I had to move my blind to another nest even to get a picture of a male goldfinch feeding its young (page 102).

Since there are so many things that can go wrong, it is remarkable that one ever gets exactly the picture planned.

Of course, if one can be satisfied with pictures of incubating or brooding birds, time exposures are feasible. The brooding wood thrush, for example, was given an exposure of six seconds. She kept perfectly still, but

I had to brace the tree to keep it from swaying in the slight breeze (page 38).

The branch on which the hummingbird's nest was built had to be anchored securely in two places with ropes tied to pegs in the ground, for the day was both windy and cloudy.

Many persons have difficulty in finding the nests of meadowlarks. However, knowing what a colorful addition this species would make to my collection of color portraits, I drove my car to the edge of a field where I had heard the larks calling and watched from the driver's seat.

Birds are not afraid of cars, and in less than half an hour one of the larks appeared on a small tree at the far side of the field. I could see with my binoculars that it had something in its bill. Within a few minutes it flew down

Arrow Points to the Alula, or False Wing; the Worm Is Aimed at Gaping Targets

Clarified by the speed flash, the alula and the rudimentary primary just back of it are shown extended. One explanation is that these break the air flow and destroy its lifting power (page 39). These baby robins are a few days older than they were as shown on page 5. Now that the eyes focus, they give mother a rousing welcome. See pages 22 and 23 for end of robin sequence.

into the meadow, and a quick rush on my part flushed the bird directly from its nest of four young.

It was more difficult to get the picture I had conceived, of a meadowlark standing on a rock with its brilliant yellow breast toward the camera, because neither of the parents seemed to like the boulder which I set up back of the nest. They accepted the blind all right and sometimes even alighted on top of it; but they walked all around the boulder, quite disdaining it.

Even when I covered the nest with my hat, they crawled under the brim to feed the youngsters instead of getting up on the rock to inspect the hat.

Not until I placed the young birds in my hat right beside it did I succeed in getting one of the parents to pose on top of the stone (page 84).

After feeding their young the parents have the habit of cleaning the nest. Since the excrement is contained in a mucous sac, it can be carried away without difficulty. I was interested to see, now that the youngsters were in my hat, whether the parents would be as careful in cleaning it as they were in protecting the nest.

A Bittern Sounds Like a Man Driving a Stake

They apparently believed in returning good for evil and were just as scrupulous about my hat as if it had been their own home. Such is instinctive behavior.

One evening I set my blind in a marsh near

the nest of an American bittern and returned the following morning with Mrs. Allen as a "go-awayster." The young were about a third grown, but I had been working with small birds so long that I did not realize the size of the adult bittern and placed my blind too close.

When the bird came sneaking back through the cattails to its nest, I had to content myself with photographing its head and shoulders; I could not get the whole bird on the film (page 138). The full profile view of the bird on page 137 was made some years later.

About the size of a domestic fowl, the American bittern stalks frogs, tadpoles, and fish which it spears with its javelinlike bill. Its streaked brown plumage makes it inconspicuous in its marsh environment, and it "freezes" in stiff, awkward positions when alarmed, so that its general appearance becomes far from birdlike.

This marsh dweller, found in suitable places throughout most of the United States and Canada, is sometimes called "thunder pumper" or "stake driver" in reference to its strange "Boom-ka" note, suggestive of the sound of a hammer hitting a stake. It is really a species of heron.

How Baby Bitterns Are Fed

I had hoped to take some pictures of its curious feeding performance. But the youngsters all crept off into the cattails, and the old bird fed them away from the nest where there were too many obstructions to the view of the lens.

However, there was a least bittern nesting about 50 feet away in the same marsh, and we next set up the blind some six feet from this nest (page 138). The least bittern is much smaller, so we had little difficulty in recording the whole feeding operation in both stills and motion.

With a gulping action the mother bird lowered her bill to the expectant youngsters, two or three of which grabbed hold of it from the side.

Then, as she opened her mandibles, one tadpole after another slid down the incline, each dropping into the extended maw of a youngster.

Although the young were little larger than sparrows, they would eventually become nearly the size of pigeons, but with much longer necks and bills, and their long down would be replaced by a neat plumage of tans and dark browns.

It was nearly the middle of August when David discovered a cedar waxwing's nest in an apple tree. Leaning a ladder against the branch, I climbed until I could look into the nest.

The horrible apparition was too much for the young waxwings, and they fluttered from the nest to the ground. We tried putting them back in the nest, but they would not stay; so we put them in a box deep enough to prevent their jumping out and fastened it in the tree.

Picking Goodies Out of the Air

It was quite a satisfaction to see the old birds within half an hour feeding the young ones in the box as if nothing at all had happened.

The next day I returned with the color camera. On the way I picked a spray of wineberries, thinking perhaps the old birds would like a local supply of food.

Perching the youngsters above the berries and in front of the grass-mat blind, I awaited with greatest curiosity the return of the parents, imagining how pleased they would be to find all the nice ripe fruit laid out at their doorstep.

As long as I was visible, the youngsters pointed their heads toward the sky and tried to look like dead leaves, but they lost a little of their dignity when one of the parents arrived.

At first it looked as if the old bird had brought no food and would welcome my offering. But the waxwing is an expert prestidigitator and carries quite a bag of tricks in his throat, for, presto, up came a cherry and down it went into the gullet of a youngster.

For a moment the old bird watched the berry go down and then with another gulp brought up a large insect with wings, like a fly. I was reminded of the old gag about the "alternating currant pie"—"first a currant, then a fly." Well, these youngsters were having their pie brought to them from a distance and not once during the whole morning did any of them notice the wineberries (page 43).

Bird Behavior at Arm's Length

As the photographic season closed, I had taken, in natural color, satisfactory still and motion pictures of some 25 species of birds. Best of all, I had renewed that intimacy of observation which one gains from a photographic blind and which is so essential to correct interpretation of bird behavior.

One who observes birds at a distance through binoculars as they flit through the trees has many a thrill as he makes new acquaintances or hears new songs. But the one who watches them for hours at arm's length, at the nest or even at a feeding station, acquires a fund of understanding of bird life and bird instincts that can be gained in no other way.

9

Photographed near Ithaca, New York

"What's Going On Here?" This Red-headed Woodpecker Seems to Ask

One youngster, dodging into the nest, collides with excited brothers and sisters. For a moment the traffic jam interrupts the flow of fruits and insects. Red, white, and bluish-black attire of adult **Red-headed Woodpecker** is familiar in much of North America east of the Rockies. Even in winter the birds seldom stray south of the United States.

10 Photographed near Mount Diablo, California

These California Woodpeckers Live in a Two-family Flat and Share the "Acornary"

Two pairs use the nest hole to the right. Parents combine forces to drive jays and squirrels from the acorns which they store in holes drilled in the bark. Here two female **California Woodpeckers,** indicated by black bar separating scarlet crown from white forehead, and a handsome male (upper left) bring food.

Photographed in southern Arizona

⋏ Rare Visitor from the Tropics

The author discovered the first trogon nest in the United States in the oak forest of the Santa Rita Mountains in Arizona in June, 1939. The **Coppery-tailed Trogon** (male shown) is related to the quetzal, worshiped by Maya and Aztec (page 265).

He Digs His Home with His Sharp Beak →

Belying its common name, highhole, this **Southern Flicker** (right) has drilled its nesting cavity in a lowly fence post. Often seen on the ground probing for ants, it is found throughout the United States and Canada east of the Rockies. The adult female lacks the black patch below each eye.

Ⓒ National Geographic Society

Photographed by S. A. Grimes near Jacksonville, Florida

← **This Avian Carpenter
Carries His Own Kit**

With a head like a hammer and bill like a chisel, feet like pincers, and prop tail, the woodpecker leads a highly specialized existence. This is a male **Northern Downy Woodpecker,** found in Canada and northern United States, principally east of the Rockies. Barred outer tail feathers are concealed. The female lacks the red cockade.

Hairy Woodpecker, →
Larger Copy of the Downy

Though the two species resemble each other almost feather for feather, the **Eastern Hairy Woodpecker,** less common and usually wilder than the downy, has a longer bill and no black bars on the white outer tail feathers. Except in the far north, neither strays far from the locality where it was raised.

Photographed near Ithaca, New York

↗ ## Humans, Beware This Fighter, the Pileated Woodpecker!

So strong was this male's parental instinct after the eggs hatched that it might have knocked Southgate Hoyt, the author's assistant, to the ground had he not been roped to the tree. The **Northern Pileated Woodpecker** is found in broad woodlands through northeastern United States and Canada. It ranges only three or four miles from its nest. The northern pileated woodpecker is replaced by a slightly smaller subspecies in southern States. Both birds are similar in habits and calls.

Flicker Brings Home the Groceries →

No aspen grove in the Rocky Mountain region is complete without a family of these noisy **Red-shafted Flickers.** Members of the woodpecker family, they occasionally drill through weatherboarding to nest in barns or deserted buildings. If the entrance hole of the bird box is too small, they enlarge it to suit their needs.

Photographed by Alfred M. Bailey and Robert J. Niedrach
in Colorado High Country

Southwest Woodpeckers
Wear Jaunty Bellhop Caps

The **Golden-fronted Woodpecker** (upper left) rooms in a huisache. The **Gila Woodpecker** (upper right) shares the gila monster's arid domain; it may dig a nesting hole in a cactus. The **Red-bellied Woodpecker** (lower left) shows more red on head than belly. This one wears the Fish and Wildlife Service's numbered anklet.

Upper left: Photographed by S. A. Grimes near Brownsville, Texas; lower left near Jacksonville, Florida

Upper right: Photographed by R. J. and Florence Thornburg in Santa Catalina Mountains, Arizona

15

⋏   **Long-tailed Bird Builds**
Home on the Range

In courtship, male **Scissor-tailed Flycatchers** flutter over treetops, working their forked tails like shears. This female nests in Texas. The birds are common also in Oklahoma and southern Kansas.

⋎   **He's Not Too Gay**
to Share in Family Chores

The **Vermilion Flycatcher** of the Tropics and the Southwest, like most other bright male birds, lets the dull-plumaged female build the nest and hatch the eggs, but he does cooperate in feeding the young.

Photographed near Ithaca, New York

Flycatchers All Have Their Minds on the Same Thing—Food

The **Least Flycatcher**, or chebec, watches for insects to fly past within range and quickly darts out to catch them. This alert bird (upper left) is found along roadsides, in orchards, and in wood borders in northern United States and Canada.

When the four eggs of the **Alder Flycatcher** (lower left) hatch, the young will be fed on the insects that frequent the woodland borders and alder thickets of northern United States and Canada.

The **Northern Crested Flycatcher** (upper right) has just placed a large moth down the throat of the nearer baby, who immediately dozes. Hungry and alert, the other little one is ready at any disturbance to open its mouth and stretch its neck.

Never a Housing Shortage for These Versatile Artisans!

English Sparrow (upper right) shows considerable ingenuity in the selection of "building blocks." This male uses a lucky find of string and cotton. Grass, weeds, or any easily obtained material may go into the nest. House sparrows, English immigrants, were brought to the United States a century ago to war on cankerworms.

Lower right: The **Eastern Phoebe** builds a mud-plastered nest of moss and vegetable fibers. Early spring's sunny days find this cheerful bird searching watercourses for dancing gnats and other insects. Phoebes are named for their familiar call, "Fee-bee! Fee-bee!"

Below: The **Least Flycatcher** weaves a compact cup of shredded bark and cotton-like materials. This winged flytrap is a denizen of orchards and woodland fringes. It often visits dooryards, crying "Chebec! Chebec!"

17

Photographed near Ithaca, New York

18

Photographed near Ithaca, New York

↑ A Kingbird Sits on a Regal Throne—
Crows and Hawks Take Notice!

One of the largest of the flycatcher family, the **King-bird** derives its name from its habit of attacking big birds. This fearless warrior, an avid insect hunter, wins the farmer's favor by harrying hawks and crows from chicken yards. It is a spring and summer resident of many States.

↓ "Who's There?" Acadian Flycatcher
Eyes a Backdoor Caller

Woodland solitude is preferred by the **Acadian Fly-catcher,** found from Massachusetts to Nebraska and south to the Gulf States. Its nest, carelessly constructed of Spanish moss, shredded bark, and weed stems, is found in saplings or lower branches. This bird is broader of bill than its relative, the least flycatcher.

Photographed in Summerville, South Carolina

↑ Wood Pewee's Call Is a Plaintive Sigh

Soft, wistful notes from the **Eastern Wood Pewee,** calling "Pee-a-wee," have a plaintive quality. Deep woodland is this bird's natural habitat, though it often may be found in shade trees near houses. Its lichen-covered nest resembles a knob on the branch.

A Prairie Horned → Lark Harkens to a Chorus

Small but hardy, the **Prairie Horned Lark** prefers open ground, where it nests, sleeps, and seeks food. The flight of this bird is hesitant except in mating season, when it may mount to great heights and sing joyously. North America counts no fewer than 16 horned lark subspecies.

Photographed near Ithaca, New York

20

∧ **Hudson Bay Natives Go "South"**
to Snow Fields of New York

Even when temperature drops below zero, **Eastern Snow Bunting** (left) and **Hoyt's Horned Lark** do not seem to mind, provided they can find weed seeds or food supplied by man. Horned larks owe their name to black feather tufts which they can erect above the eyes.

∨ **A Hoyt's Horned Lark Awaits**
Quadruple "Blessed Event"

The four eggs of **Hoyt's Horned Lark** are olive-gray. It nests from the west shore of Hudson Bay to the mouth of the Mackenzie River and winters chiefly from Ohio to Nevada. A relative of the European skylark, the horned lark is North America's only true lark.

A New Light Dawns on Bird Photography

IT ALL happened so quickly I could not see what occurred; yet here it is before me as clear as the printed page.

First, I had heard the distant call of a female Cooper's hawk and seen the answering excitement of her youngsters six feet in front of the blind. A darting shadow, a flash, and the mother bird stood there glaring at me with fire in her eye. One foot grasped the branches of the synthetic nest we had built at the base of the tree; the other held a plucked starling.

But so quickly had the hawk come that I had no mental image of her in the air. I could not tell how she held her wings or tail as she approached, or whether her talons were withdrawn or fully extended. I did not even notice that she had food in her bill. I might have supposed she carried it in her claws, for she certainly had it in her foot when her image finally fixed on my retina.

Speed Flash Reveals the Unseen

A little experience with the speed-flash camera had trained my fingers to press the shutter release at precisely the right instant, so that the resulting flash of 1/5000 of a second's duration occurred when the image of the bird was passing the middle of the film. And behold, here is the whole story as I should like to have described it, and as you can now see for yourselves in natural color: the frozen action of a predatory hawk returning to her young with a plucked bird in her bill (page 190).

Caught is the look of expectancy and hunger in the eye of one of the youngsters; one sees the strength in the pinions of the old bird, and the powerful talons reaching out to grasp the nest. The colors are natural and true.

A few years ago, when I wrote the preceding chapter, we would have branded such a photograph a "nature fake," impossible for any camera to produce; but today it is fast becoming commonplace.

Dr. Harold E. Edgerton, of the Massachusetts Institute of Technology, first brought to the attention of eager naturalists and wildlife photographers the wonders of the new high-speed flash apparatus with his book *Flash!* and later with his marvelous hummingbird photographs in the NATIONAL GEOGRAPHIC MAGAZINE for August, 1947, and again in August, 1951 (page 297).

Dr. Donald R. Griffin showed the possibilities of Edgerton's apparatus in photographing bats for the July, 1946, NATIONAL GEOGRAPHIC, and Ernest P. Walker and Edwin L. Wisherd used a similar portable speed flash in making the phenomenal photographs of flying squirrels in the May, 1947, NATIONAL GEOGRAPHIC. In March, 1948, the NATIONAL GEOGRAPHIC published a series of high-speed color photographs by Dr. Edgerton and Mr. Wisherd freezing the action of circus acrobats in the ring, on trapeze and high wire.

My Cooper's hawk project was one of several interesting experiences during the season of 1947 when I applied the new light to old problems in bird photography.

Steve Eaton, a graduate student at Cornell, found the hawks' nest 65 feet up in a white ash tree in a dense wood lot about 10 miles north of Ithaca, New York.

The tree was the tallest in this part of the woods, so there was no possibility of placing a blind in an adjacent tree.

When the eggs hatched the first of July, it occurred to me to test a new method of study which, if successful, would permit us to get a more or less complete record of what and how a Cooper's hawk feeds its young, and to reveal each rapid action by high-speed flash photography.

Accordingly, with the help of an expert climber, Paul Shepard, a student in the summer session, I built a dummy nest in a bushel basket and hung it beneath the real nest when the young were about five days old.

Hawks Lowered from Tree in Basket

The hawks paid little attention to this innovation, so we transferred the young to the basket. A few hours later, the female flushed from the basket at our approach.

Next we built a blind on the ground, covering a framework with burlap. Then, during the next week, we lowered the basket 10 feet a day until it was fastened to the trunk of the tree 10 feet from the ground.

Perhaps the hawks were surprised at the rapid settling of the foundations of their home, but they continued to feed and brood their young with no apparent misgivings.

Later we successfully substituted for the basket a less conspicuous potato crate.

To complete our preparations, we rolled a stump against the base of the tree and built a dummy nest on top. Thus, when we were ready for our observations and photography, we had only to move the youngsters from the crate to this new bungalow in front of the blind.

Even when we added a 4-foot-square light-blue backdrop behind the nest, the old birds continued to feed and the youngsters

Robin's Eye Winks, Not in Flirtation but in Automatic Self-preservation

As the bird lands, the high-speed flash shows the nictitating membrane half-drawn across the eyeball. This device protects the eye against jabbing beaks as well as earthworm slime. As a protection against dust, it functions frequently (page 27 and opposite).

to behave in their characteristic domineering manner. We could see at close range the kinds of food the old birds brought; we learned (with patience) how long the youngsters had to wait between meals; and we were able to record with the speed flash the home life of these interesting predatory birds.

Two Birds a Day per Youngster

The youngsters apparently never suffered from hunger, because there always was unused food on the nest whenever we arrived. They grew normally, and the last of the three left home when it was 31 days old.

Observations were made on 11 days, during which two assistants and I spent a total of 58 hours in the blind at various times between 6:30 in the morning and 7:30 in the evening.

During the period they were under observa-tion, the young hawks were fed 28 times on 10 species of birds or small mammals, including one meadow mouse, two chipmunks, eight robins, five English sparrows, two starlings, four flickers, two meadowlarks, two young red-eyed vireos, one young song sparrow, and part of one white leghorn pullet.

This was at the rate of a little more than two birds a day per youngster.

The old birds apparently were not alarmed by the flash, although they became alert and departed at any movement made in the blind, such as that of changing plateholders.

Altogether, the experiment proved successful, and in the resulting photographs others can now view incidents in the home life of a hawk (page 190) without the inconvenience it caused us, and, incidentally, without the same degree of excitement or satisfaction.

Father Robin in Blinders Shows the Opaque, Lifeless Eye of a Statue

Here the nictitating membrane is fully extended. Other birds use such a shield; so do most reptiles and many mammals, including dogs and cats. The robin touches the back of his nestling's tongue with the worm to start throat muscles working; otherwise the dinner might crawl out (page 27 and opposite).

We next turned our attention to a bird which is the antithesis of a Cooper's hawk— a friendly little chickadee with no allergies to people or to cameras.

"Tooth to Nail" with a Chickadee

"Don't close your eyes, Dolly," I admonished my daughter as we tried for photographs of the chickadee flying to her lips to take a peanut from her teeth.

The first series of pictures we had made were ruined by tightly closed eyes, though neither of us had noticed at the time that, no matter how interested Dolly was in having a friendly little bird perch on her chin, she unconsciously closed her eyes when she saw it approaching her face.

The camera had caught all the eagerness and anticipation on the face of the chickadee,

but Dolly had reacted in a most natural, but nonphotogenic, manner.

So this time I constantly reminded Dolly to keep her eyes open. With conscious effort she partially did so, giving added charm to the photograph of a truly wonderful experience —that of meeting a wild creature face to face (or tooth to nail, as Dolly puts it) with a natural expression of confidence (page 29).

An ordinary robin provided a real test of the new speed flash for a study of wing and feather action in flight. The bird had very considerately accepted for its nest site a movable shelf we had fastened to the laboratory window casing.

When the young were well grown, we lowered the shelf to a convenient height from the floor, fastened a blue backdrop behind the nest so that the photographs would not

Allan D. Cruickshank
from National Audubon Society

↑ Dixieland Favorite— the Mockingbird

The female mockingbird builds her rough nest in a thicket or orange tree. The male, with professional boldness, sings conspicuously from chimneys and ridgepoles. His repertoire, in addition to his own melodious phrases, may include the calls of 50 other species.

← Unwelcome European Immigrant—the Starling

Introduced into New York City in 1890, the starling is now the commonest bird in eastern United States and Canada, and it has reached California, Mexico, and Hudson Bay. Native birds seem unable to compete with the adaptable and aggressive "foreigner." This arresting picture shows the bird alighting at a food shelf (pages 55 and 94).

24

Silent as the Night Is the Flight of the Screech Owl

The soft edges of the primaries with no hooklets show well in this speed-flash photograph, as the feathers are turned on edge so as not to catch the air when the wing is lifted. The enlarged pupils of the eyes indicate that it was dark when the photograph was taken at 1/5000 of a second.

appear as if made at midnight, and set the sealed-beam flash tubes at the right heights and angle inside the laboratory.

Color film is so slow that the lens diaphragm had to be set at F:5.6, even with the lights two feet from the subject; so there was very little depth of focus. Indeed, one could not get wings and body equally in focus except when the wings were held straight back (page 39).

Black-and-white film, however, provided sufficient speed to use a stop of F:22, and the resulting series of clear pictures of the wings in their different positions gives one a new notion of the flexibility of the feathers (pages 5 to 7).

Improved Edgerton speed-flash lamps now provide sufficient light so that, with two lights set at two feet from the subject, the correct exposure for Kodachrome is attained by shutting the diaphragm to F:16. There is the possibility that at some time in the future new types of reflectors will be developed which will permit the lights to be set at greater distance from the subject. This cannot be done now without opening the diaphragm wider to compensate for the increased distance.

Wing a Wondrous Mechanism

There is the upstroke, for example, when not only is the wrist joint bent so that the wing as a whole offers the least resistance to the air, but the individual primaries and secondaries are all turned on edge, so that the wing opens up like a Venetian blind (page 6, and above). One sees the robin's body right through the wing, and the wing is lifted with practically no air resistance.

On the downstroke, however, the flight feathers are beautifully imbricated, or overlapped, to give the greatest possible resistance to the air (page 5).

In photographs of the robin about to alight, we see the group of feathers borne on the thumb, and known as the alula, standing out at almost right angles to the wing. The

No Welcome Mat! A House Wren's Door Bristles with Spines to Discourage Visitors

To feed seven youngsters, the pair made an astonishing number of trips daily; yet the male still found time to sing. Other busy male wrens have been known to run two households at once. Here the speed flash lights up the wren's rounded wing and the foot's flight position (opposite and page 28). Cargo is a caterpillar.

tiny rudimentary first primary, which is found in all thrushes and for which there is still no satisfactory explanation, likewise stands out from the rest of the wing (pages 7 and 39).

Can it be, as my colleague, Dr. Paul Kellogg, suggests, that these feathers, acting in conjunction, serve like the spoilers on the front edge of the wing of a plane, to break up the smooth flow of the air and destroy its lifting power? This would allow the bird to alight more accurately.

The number and relative lengths of the flight feathers in different individuals of the same species of birds are always the same, as are the actual lengths, to within a few millimeters. Indeed, all the species in a bird family, such as the thrushes (Turdidae), which include the robin, show remarkably little variation.

In the robin photographs, for example, one sees a tiny first primary followed by four long primaries of about equal length, followed in turn by five gradually shortening primaries and six secondaries, giving the appearance of a more or less square-ended wing.

If one were to examine the wing of a wood thrush or a bluebird, or almost any one of the 304 species of birds found all over the world that make up the thrush family, one would find the same rudimentary primary, the same four long primaries, etc., making up the same shaped wing. There would be few exceptions.

On the other hand, if one examined any one of the 63 wrens that make up the family Troglodytidae, one would find, as in the photograph of the house wren (above), a wing in which the primaries gradually lengthen from the first to the fifth and then shorten again as the body is approached, giving the appearance of a rounded wing.

Similarly, in all the swallow family, the Hirundinidae (page 4), the first primary is the longest, and the flight feathers shorten very abruptly toward the body, giving what is called a pointed wing.

The number of functional primaries (those borne on the modified hand) of an ordinary bird is always 10, except in a relatively few families of perching birds, where the number is nine. The number of secondaries (those borne on the forearm), however, varies considerably in different families of birds, from the six (plus two tertiaries) of the thrushes to as many as 37 in the excessively long-winged albatrosses.

Birds in Flight Identified by Wings

Indeed, length of the wing in birds is usually gained by increasing the length of the forearm with its secondaries, rather than increasing the number or relative lengths of the primary feathers.

The different shapes of the wings of many small birds are shown in color photographs in this book. One familiar with birds in flight can often identify their silhouettes against the

Banded and Released, a Sora Rail "Runs" Through the Air as He Would on Land

In spite of their weak wings and awkward-appearing take-off technique, some soras cross the Caribbean, to winter in Venezuela and Peru. In the Atlantic States the rails are considered game birds. Each fall they run a hunters' gantlet in the tidal marshes (page 28).

sky by characteristic wing action and resulting steadiness or undulations in the course of flight.

It would take many photographs, however, and a careful study of the use of the different feathers to work out the correlation between wing shape and wing use, as practiced by different species.

Of course, certain relationships are obvious, such as the long, narrow wing of gulls for gliding, the broad, rounded wing of buzzards for soaring, and the short, rounded wing of grouse for quick bursts of speed. The numerous minor variations, some of which are manifest in accompanying photographs, will require much study before they are fully understood.

Speed Flash Quicker than a Wink

Another action which is too quick for the human eye, but which is recorded by the speed flash, is the movement of the bird's inner eyelid, or nictitating membrane, as it is called. This translucent membrane flicks across the eyeball to remove dust or to give protection to the cornea whenever it might be necessary.

When a robin feeds its young, the membrane naturally draws across the eye to keep out the bill of the youngster or to keep the sand on the worms from lodging where it should not.

An examination of photographs of the robin shows the eyelid halfway across the eye when the bird's feet touch the nest (page 22) and completely across it during the act of feeding (page 23). The young bird's eye is protected in the same way.

The position of birds' feet in flight and upon landing has given naturalists cause for conjecture and argument, and taxidermists and bird artists are frequently in disagreement. The tremendous forward swing or extension of the legs of hawks and falcons upon alighting or pouncing on prey is seldom credited or shown with accuracy in paintings or in habitat groups of mounted birds.

The work of two Cornell students, Heinz Meng and Steve Collins, in training hawks gave us an opportunity to record leg action as well as wing action when the birds pounced upon dead mice or returned to their owners' fists (pages 3, 191, and 194).

It is remarkable how obedient these birds become when properly handled, celebrated though they are for their wildness.* Captured when fully adult, and knowing only the fear of man and the ferocity of killing its prey in mid-air, a duck hawk (page 192), also known as peregrine falcon, becomes gentle after a few months of training and flies to its trainer's hand at the proper whistle.

* See, in the NATIONAL GEOGRAPHIC MAGAZINE: "Life with an Indian Prince," February, 1942, and "Adventures with Birds of Prey," July, 1937, both by Frank and John Craighead.

Tossed into the air, given his liberty to go where he pleases, he waits on the pleasure of his trainer and circles about until the whirling lure tells him there may be food at his owner's feet, if he strikes the imitation bird from the air.

In striking as in alighting, the hawks extend their legs to the utmost, so that the weight of their bodies in bending the tibiotarsal joint will drive the sharp claws into the victim or about the perch where the hawk alights. With the larger hawks the trainer must wear a heavy glove.

Photographs of the hawks (pages 190 and 191) do not show where the feet are carried during normal flight, but with binoculars they are easily seen under the tail as the birds circle overhead.

The long legs of herons and cranes (pages 141-144 and 263) trail out behind and are easily seen at considerable distance, but how does a small bird hold its feet in flight? Many photographs in this book, both in color and in black-and-white, are of birds about to alight, when the legs are being let down like landing gear. The house wren, however, still has his feet tightly pressed against his breast (page 26), and others are apparently dropping their legs from a similar position rather than from beneath their tails.

The ridiculous posture of the sora rail (page 27) is due to the fact that when rails take off on their weak wings they continue to claw the air with their long toes as if they were still running over the mud flat. It is only when they get well under way that their legs trail out behind like a heron's.

At First, Camera Caught Only Tails

Wing shooting with a shotgun, whether at quail, grouse, ducks, or clay pigeons, is usually not very successful for the tyro. It takes years of experience before one can confidently place a 3-foot circle of shot on the exact spot where the flying target is expected to be at a somewhat uncertain fraction of a second later, depending on the distance, the speed, the wind, etc.

In like manner, with the high-speed flash of flying birds, if one waits until the bird is at the desired spot before pressing the release, one will photograph a blank every time or at best get only the bird's tail on the film.

The first time any of us used high-speed apparatus we focused on a spot that chickadees and nuthatches were expected to pass in coming to a feeding station. They passed the spot, but so rapidly that out of 12 shots fired by three of us the resulting bag of bird photographs was three chickadee tails.

The photographer has to learn from experience his personal delay in reaction from the moment he says to himself, "Shoot," until the message is conveyed to his finger tips with the resulting flash, and he has to estimate how far the bird will travel during that delay.

Of course there are no cripples if he does not center his birds, but there is considerable disappointment and loss of face when an otherwise perfect photograph emerges from the darkroom following processing to show only the tail of a bird.

Naturally, the operator has no control over the position of the wings of the bird he is photographing. Many a dud results, even when he becomes expert at centering the bird, because the wings are far forward, concealing the bird's head, or in some other awkward position.

Practice Shots at Feeding Station

We began our practice shots with the high-speed flash at a feeding station for birds, where their comings and goings could be somewhat regulated. It is necessary to have the apparatus set up in advance, with lens and lights trained on a definite square foot of space where the action is to take place. In addition, the action has to occur on a very narrow stage, for the depth of focus is only a few inches.

Therefore, I trained the birds to feed in front of our blind on a shelf about six inches long and two inches wide, and I placed a convenient perch about two feet from the shelf on which the birds were expected to alight before flying to the feed.

Eighteen inches, I discovered, was my delay in reaction. That meant I had to push the shutter release the moment the bird left the prepared perch if I wished to catch him in the center of my film, which was focused on the square foot 12 inches distant.

Even after all these preparations, I sometimes photographed the blank blue background which I had set up behind the food shelf to avoid the blackness of most flashbulb pictures. The reason for this was that the birds occasionally changed their minds after leaving the perch and flew to the ground or to the top of the set—and, after all, I was no mind reader.

Particularly was this true of the little chickadees, which became allergic to the flash after a few experiences. Even though they could see no motion or other indication of my intentions in the blind, they would change their course in mid-air and flit in some other direction just before the flash consummated my delayed reaction.

It was a good setup, however—like shooting skeet in preparation for the duck season—and resulted in many interesting photographs of wings in action.

Face to Face with →
a Chickadee

For bait, the author's daughter, Dolly Allen, holds a peanut in her teeth. Of the two, the bird performed more easily. When the **Black-capped Chickadee** darted toward her chin, Dolly blinked, spoiling a series of photographs. (See "A New Light Dawns on Bird Photography," page 21.)

Photographed near Ithaca, New York

← Food Put Outside a Window Attracts This Little Fellow

The **Black-capped Chickadee** is a winter visitor at suburban feeding stations where it finds suet and sunflower seeds. It is a permanent resident except in the most northern parts of its range, which extends from Alaska to Newfoundland and southward into the United States.

© National Geographic Society

↗ ### Air Wardens for
Nuisance Raids

Because they keep down mosquitoes and other pests, **Barn Swallows** are encouraged to build their feather-lined nests of mud pellets and straws inside our barns. They winter in South America and return in April.

← ### It Comes as a
Harbinger of Spring

Northern Cliff Swallows nowadays are cliff nesters only in the West. Elsewhere they build under eaves of buildings. They winter in Brazil and Argentina and breed as far north as central Alaska.

Purple Martins Choose → Homes in Cavities

The **Purple Martin** (female, right) likes human neighbors. In the East she may occupy a man-made box or a brightly painted gourd. Sparsely settled areas in the West find her nesting in hollow tree, cliff, or between rocks.

↓ Iridescent Blue Back, Snowy Breast Mark Tree Swallow

For its home it picks an old woodpecker hole or a cavity in a dead tree or rocky cliff, but many adopt bird boxes. **Tree Swallows** assemble on telegraph wires in the fall before migrating southward to Florida marshes.

31

Photographed by S. A. Grimes near Jacksonville, Florida

Photographed by the author near Bergen, New York

Something of a Hermit Is the Rough-winged Swallow

It does not nest in colonies like other swallows, but uses the deserted burrow of a kingfisher, a crevice in the cliff, a drainpipe, or a tunnel of its own. In summer the **Rough-winged Swallow** ranges the United States as far north as southern New York and New England, and in winter goes south to Mexico and Central America.

Photographed near Ithaca, New York

It Keeps Its Treasures in a Bank

The **Bank Swallow** is found in colonies during the summer throughout most of the Northern Hemisphere wherever it can find sandbanks in which to dig its burrows. It returns to the Southern Hemisphere for the winter. In England it is known as the sand martin.

Christmaslike Bands Identify This Nutcracker, Whose Home Is at Crater Lake

The fondness of **Clark's Nutcracker** for meat, suet, peanuts, and other handouts makes a camp robber of him. Crowlike in action, this western mountaineer is as much at home on the ground as in the fir trees, and normally consumes large numbers of grasshoppers and big wingless crickets.

33

A Blue Jay Adopts the Gold Standard

The bold individual in the shining blue coat readily came to the feeding station even though it had been surrounded with goldenrod. The aluminum leg band, acquired on a previous visit, may eventually show how far the **Northern Blue Jay** wanders and how long he lives.

Photographed by the author near Ithaca, New York   Photographed by S. A. Grimes near Jacksonville, Florida

"Well, This Looks Appetizing!" Nuthatch (Left) Discovers a Free Lunch of Peanut Butter and Sunflower Seeds

Topsy-turvy nuthatches defy gravity by strolling headfirst down the trunks of trees. Strong claws anchor them to the bark. To vary an insect menu, these birds crack nuts with their sharp bills; hence the common name. An unusual "sandwich spread," applied by the author to a tree trunk near his home, attracted this female **White-breasted Nuthatch.**

Center: The **Brown Creeper** uses its tail as a brace when climbing. It feeds on tiny insects and insect eggs hidden in the bark. Usually its wrenlike nest is built behind loose bark of a dead tree as shown here. Brown creeper is an Old World bird that journeyed to North America.

Upper right: Chickadees, though unable to climb perpendicular tree trunks, often hang upside down from a twig or small branch. They perform yeoman service in helping to preserve the balance of Nature. As many as 454 plant lice have been found in the stomach of a single chickadee. This is a **Carolina Chickadee** family of southeastern United States.

34

Cattails and Sedges Are a Marsh Wren's World

The **Prairie Marsh Wren** (left) is unhappy except in a marsh; it has no use for bushes or trees. This bird is familiar throughout the United States and Canada. The opening in the side of the nest is sometimes concealed. Bumblebees often use nests for rearing their young.

Short-billed Marsh Wren (below), like its cousin, may build dummy nests to mark its territory. Man seldom sees it, so rarely does it fly. Its "Dee-dee-dee" sounds like two stones tapped together.

Photographed near Ithaca, New York

35

36

Photographed in Summerville, South Carolina

⋏ Mother Wren Built Her Nest in a Dark Woodshed

Nesting wrens often invade the abodes of man. This **Carolina Wren,** entering the shed through a rat hole, picked a cardboard box for a homesite. An eastern bird, it frequently cries, "Teakettle, teakettle!"

⋎ A Breadwinner Wings Home to a Painted Gourd

Newly hatched young await this **Eastern House Wren.** The female's fussy, shrewish disposition little resembles that of England's mild-mannered "jenny wren," though the popular name is applied to both.

Photographed near Ithaca, New York

⚵ "Just Try to Find My Home!"

David Allen, son of the author, sat on a rotten stump for half an hour, watching this **Eastern Winter Wren** and trying to discover its nest. Meanwhile, the nest was beneath David! It had been so cleverly concealed in the side of the stump that it virtually defied detection.

Only a Mouthful →
Stills This Mimic

Fair weather may find the **Eastern Mockingbird** singing all day and most of the night. It is a gifted mimic not only of birdcalls but of many other familiar sounds. The mockingbird's own song is a beautiful, never-to-be-forgotten melody.

38

These Sentinels React Differently to Man

The **Brown Thrasher** (upper left) defends his nest courageously, sometimes hurling himself at intruders. As a singer, he ranks a close second to the mockingbird. Not a true thrush, he is the "merry brown thrush" of children's books.

The **Wood Thrush** (lower left) is quite tame. This daydreaming mother bird was brooding her young six feet from the ground in a grove on the campus of Cornell University. When the wind blew, the cradle would rock; so, to get this picture, a time exposure, the author had to brace the little chokecherry tree to keep it from swaying in the breeze (page 6).

Unlike the old-fashioned good child, the **Catbird** (upper right) is heard more than it is seen. It likes to hide its bulky nest of twigs and rootlets in briers and undergrowth. Brilliant, deep-green eggs contrast sharply with the parent birds' inconspicuous coloring. Often berated for its raids on strawberries and other fruits, the catbird destroys enough insects to pay for its "keep."

Father Robin Spreads Wing Feathers Like the Ribs of a Fan

Here the speed flash exposes a tiny, rudimentary primary feather and the ear-shaped alula, or false wing, seen just back of the head. These feathers, standing almost at a right angle to the wing at the instant of the flash, are borne on the thumb of the bird's modified hand.

Ornithologists have not been able to agree on Nature's reason for providing the alula. Analysis at 1/5000 part of a second suggests that this process, acting like the spoiler of an airplane wing, shatters the air's smooth flow in the interest of a shorter, more accurate landing.

This cheery **Eastern Robin,** caught with an earthworm in his beak, considerately nested on a window shelf, where he made his brood a perfect camera target. (See "A New Light Dawns on Bird Photography," page 21.)

Photographed near Ithaca, New York

39

40 Photographed by Walter Meayers Edwards in Bethesda, Maryland

"Sweet Ad-uh-line, It's Dinnertime!" Noisy Trio Strives to Influence Mama and Win Food

But tired mother robin seems deaf to their clamor. Each fledgling **Eastern Robin** will consume its own weight in food daily until full-grown. If a growing boy had a bird's appetite, he would eat two sheep or a small calf each day. This robin built its nest on the photographer's bedroom window sill.

41

Photographed in Ithaca, New York

∧ America's "Nightingale" Poses with a Hunting Trophy

Deep in woodland solitude dwells the **Eastern Hermit Thrush,** our finest songster. Fortunate indeed is the person who hears the exquisite soaring notes of its flutelike voice. A true hermit, it is extremely shy, rarely singing if it suspects man's presence.

∨ To Hear This Singer You Must Visit Canada

Migrating from South America, the **Gray-cheeked Thrush** passes through eastern United States late in May. However, it does not sing until it reaches Canada's spruce forests. Wild fruits and berries in the fall spice an insect diet.

Photographed at La Tabatière, Quebec

42 Photographed near Ithaca, New York

Bluebird and Pink Hollyhock Create a Midsummer Idyl

An early harbinger of returning spring is the **Eastern Bluebird,** whistling its wistful refrain, "Dear, dear, think of it, think of it." Maurice Maeterlinck, the Belgian poet, used the bluebird as a symbol of happiness in his play of that name. Only too often, however, the bird of fantasy stays but a short time with one person. The bluebird of orchard and garden is a summer-long resident of the northern States and eastern Canada. Knowing the fondness of this bird for cutworms and caterpillars, orchardists attract it by placing boxes on fruit trees (page 4).

43 Photographed near Ithaca, New York

Like a Magician, the Cedar Waxwing Produces Food Out of Empty Air

A moment ago there was nothing in his bill. Now from his distended throat the **Cedar Waxwing** whisks up insects and ripe cherries until he has fed the whole family. Though the branch of wineberries was provided as an extra food supply, they were ignored, since the parents always returned with full market baskets. Sometimes called "cherry birds" because of their liking for fruits, waxwings breed in southern Canada and in most of the United States. The bird is an unpredictable migrant, some winters remaining in the northern States in great numbers, in others going as far south as Central America (page 8).

44 Photographed near Mountain Village, Alaska

ʌ   This Visitor from China
      "Wigwags" as She Walks

Like other members of the wagtail and pipit family,
the **Alaska Yellow Wagtail** has a way of flipping its
tail up and down when promenading. It breeds in
northern Siberia and Arctic Alaska, but winters in
China. Wagtails apparently prefer the Eastern Hemisphere. In the male the yellow extends to the bill.

ⱽ   A Crevice in the Rocks Is a Pipit's
      Home on the Shores of Hudson Bay

But the rocks must be near the Arctic or on some high
mountain where conditions are similar. The **American
Pipit,** like Shelley's famous skylark, sings as it soars,
its song drifting down from such heights that the music
comes "from Heaven, or near it." The song ended, the
bird descends with direct flight.

Photographed near Churchill, Manitoba

Birds on the Home Front

"WHEN Jerry was shot down and by a miracle landed safely in a New Guinea jungle," remarked his dad, "his interest in bird life helped keep his morale high the 10 days he was lost."

It was strange, during those war-torn years, how boys infected with bird lore didn't mind where they were sent or how hazardous the journey if they could count on seeing new birds. For, once the vaccination had "taken" and the avian antibodies had become well established in the blood stream, it took more than a blitzkrieg to destroy the impulse to look and listen when a feather floated by.

Students who early in 1942 gathered on Monday evenings in the ornithology seminar to discuss research problems and check over the birds seen about Ithaca, New York, a few months later were scattered in training camps all over the country and on many fighting fronts. Letters they wrote back were filled with notes of the new birds they had seen.

Mentions of Birds Betrayed Stations

Sometimes the boy's whereabouts would be deleted by the censor. Only by references to birds could we guess where he was. A letter would come from San Francisco, but we knew the "goonies" mentioned do not nest east of the Hawaiian Islands. It was a pretty sure guess that Jim was on Midway or stopping on some lesser island on his way to the Solomons.

Tinamous are Latin American; sand grouse are Asian and African; broadbills are mainly Indian; honeysuckers, Australasian; birds of paradise are confined to New Guinea and near-by islands; and so on. The distribution of birds took on a new significance for us during the war.

On the other hand, my older son, who never became sufficiently infected with the bacillus of bird study to master the principles of classification and distribution, was unable to tell us anything of the natural history of his island. We could not guess within a thousand miles of where he was stationed, for coconuts and oranges and sharks and jelly-fish and even "wild chickens" are widely distributed throughout the Tropics.

However, it is not with the birds of the battle fronts that this article is concerned but rather with the birds the boys had left behind them. They offered us stay-at-homes an excuse for getting out into the open country, enjoying the new sport of pedestrianism, and building up a reserve of pleasant experiences.

Now once again we may enjoy the sport of touring for birds. Even during the war years and the attendant rationing of gasoline and tires, bird study was enthusiastically pursued, first in suburban backyards and city parks within walking distance; then, after exhaustion of near-by possibilities, by bus and streetcar that dropped us off near lake shore or woodland or marsh for a few hours in a different environment.

Birds Working on Home Front

We did not feel unpatriotic because of our continued interest in bird study, for every hour spent in the field convinced us of the need for encouraging bird life. The birds were working on the home front just as assiduously for the protection of our forests and crops as if we had supplied them with hoes and spray guns.

We watched a least flycatcher in the sycamore by the roadside (pages 16 and 17). In ten minutes he darted from his perch eight times to snap up passing insects, and he kept this up all day.

There was a yellow-throated vireo (page 56) nesting in the next tree. Without so much as the loss of a single phrase of its song, it gobbled up one cankerworm after another at the rate of two a minute.

With watch in hand, we timed a chickadee (pages 29 and 34) bringing food to its hungry youngsters in the hollow of a stump. In 30 minutes it returned 35 times—not with a single insect each time, but with a whole bill full. Indeed, there is a record of a house wren that was watched continuously for 15 hours and 45 minutes of daylight, and in that interval it fed its young 1,217 times!

Some of the insects birds eat we recognize as deadly enemies; others we are not so sure about. Still, the birds keep right on eating, and few crannies go unexplored.

Variety of Insects Fair Game for Birds

There are insects that live on the bottom of ponds. Others burrow in the soil, crawl on the surface, or infest the grass and lower vegetation. There are insects that eat up our crops and defoliate our trees and go flitting from one farm to another. There is no bird that feeds on all kinds of insects wherever they may hide, but, fortunately, we have many kinds of birds of many different habits.

We have the grebe (pages 127-129), which dives to the bottom of ponds; the meadow-lark and upland plover (pages 84 and 231), which probe in the soil or glean from the surface of the ground; warblers, vireos, and orioles (pages 55-67 and 77-80), which scan leaves and small branches; nuthatches

Heinz Meng

The Author Climbs High to Photograph a Cooper's Hawk Treetop Home

Once he smashed his camera and sprained his ankle in a plunge from an ancient apple tree. Another time he suffered a broken arm in a fall from a tree near Ithaca. A third time he buried his head in the hood of his Graflex on a branch some 20 feet high as he made a picture of an oriole's nest. Just at that moment the branch broke and down came photographer, camera, and all!

Screech Owls Serve on the Night Patrol

Since some insects are nocturnal, it is fortunate that these birds do their hunting after dark. Here a mother has returned from a raid with a large hawk moth to feed her youngster. The weird cry of this bird has been regarded by the superstitious as an ill omen; but it predicts death for none but the vermin and insects it eats (text below and page 280).

and creepers (page 34), which examine crevices in bark; woodpeckers (pages 9-14), which dig into the heart of trees for borers and carpenter ants; and flycatchers and swallows (pages 15-19 and 30-32), which dart back and forth over field and forest to catch them on the wing.

The adaptations among birds for varied activities and methods of finding food are well illustrated in the photographs in this book. Some of these species are more valuable than others, and some work for the good of man more continuously or more effectively. But each has its place in the scheme of things and at times proves itself indispensable to the common good.

Birds Battle Insect Invaders

There are times when we feel that we could get along with fewer doctors, or that there are too many lawyers. Certainly in the emergency of war some college professors were a luxury. Normally, however, each group serves a useful purpose, and we need them all. Even in peace we maintain a standing army at heavy expense.

Thus it is with many birds. We do not realize their usefulness, we even denounce them as robbers when they vary their diet with a few cherries; but we are always glad to have their services when emergencies arise and pray for more of them to do a better job of exterminating some insect pest that is out of control.

As a matter of fact, it is a wonder we are not continually besieged and run off the earth by any one of a thousand species of insects, so great is insect reproductive capacity.

Students of entomology and arithmetical progression tell us that the offspring of a single plant louse at the end of one year, should they all live and reproduce at a normal rate, would weigh more than the combined weight of the population of China. And that the Japanese beetles in this country just a few years after their introduction far outnumbered all the people in Japan.

Of course, not all birds—the hawks and owls, for example—eat insects. Only the smaller species, such as the sparrow hawk and the screech owl, take an appreciable number of insects, and these are mostly of large size, such as grasshoppers, hawk moths, and beetles, (page 280). Some of these predaceous birds eat other valuable birds, but the food of most of them consists largely of small rodents.

Orchardists who have lost hundreds of trees from girdling by meadow mice should rejoice when a flock of short-eared owls locates in the vicinity. They should be glad to save

John E. Davis

A California Woodpecker's Well-stocked Pantry

Often working in groups, the woodpeckers drill holes in trees or telegraph poles, where they store acorns for future use (page 10). These acorn-storing woodpeckers are found in the Pacific coast region from southern Oregon to southern California. They have no counterpart in eastern United States.

such as the magnificent peregrine falcon, or duck hawk, on page 192, have been held in high esteem since ancient times by those who thrill to the wild stoop of the falcon. Certainly the grandeur of Taughannock Falls, in New York State, is enhanced by this glorious bird. It would be a shortsighted policy to destroy it because it sometimes strikes down a slow-flying pigeon from the adjacent countryside, or a wild duck from the migratory hordes that pass through the Finger Lakes on their way north and south.

Weed Destroyers, Scavengers, Game Birds

Some birds, such as sparrows and doves, get most of their food from the seeds of weeds and serve man as weed destroyers; others, such as the vultures of the southern States and the gulls of our harbors and seashores, serve best as scavengers; still others serve best as game.

There was a time when any bird large enough to provide a bite was considered a game bird. Robins and meadowlarks and sandpipers furnished out the table of many a nimrod in this country, but that day is past. Today we reserve the name "game bird" for those species which are not more valuable as destroyers of insects or whose esthetic appeal does not overbalance the bit of meat they might bring to our tables.

A game bird must be prolific to withstand the strain of hunting in addition to the many other destroying factors. Some birds, such as the snipe and the woodcock and the dove, normally considered game, are having difficulty maintaining their normal numbers because they lay so few eggs.

The ruffed grouse (page 198), however, is an ideal game bird. Possessed of amazing

one hollow tree for a screech owl to make her home, for the owls are Mother Nature's mousetraps.

The horned owl shown on page 278, was incubating three eggs when the photograph was made from an adjoining tree. When it flushed, I could see a large Norway rat stored on the edge of the nest. The bird apparently had caught more than it could eat the night before.

The rat, more than any other rodent, harbors the fleas that carry endemic typhus and spread bubonic plague. Other small rodents which hawks and owls destroy harbor the fleas and ticks that spread spotted fever and tularemia. We should not begrudge them an occasional bird or chicken.

Even those species that feed largely on birds,

skill in eluding gunners, it lays a normal complement of 7-16 eggs, sufficient to maintain its numbers under any reasonable hunting pressure. It is only when disease suddenly strikes, or the ax destroys its coverts, that it is in danger. On the other hand, the upland plover (page 231), which formerly was an abundant bird on the prairies and hayfields of northern United States and southern Canada, was so depleted by excessive shooting that 30 years ago it was thought to be on the verge of extinction.

Only today, after years of complete protection, has it begun once more to be a familiar bird over part of its former range. And even now, since it lays but four eggs and never has a second brood, haying operations alone sometimes prevent whole colonies from rearing young. This is disastrous, because its long migration to Argentina is so hazardous that many are lost and some young must be reared each year if it is to maintain its numbers.

Elsa G. Allen

Parental Devotion Overcomes Timidity

This little American redstart flew right into the child's lap to feed his young. The bird is an untiring hunter of spittle insects, tree hoppers, and leaf hoppers. So vivid are its colors that Spanish imagination has coined for it the name *candelita,* "little torchbearer" (page 67).

The Canada goose (page 162) is one of the few nonprolific game birds that seem to be able to hold their own in spite of the millions of shotguns. This ability is due perhaps as much to its own sagacity as to the protective laws surrounding it. Spring and fall their wavering "V" formations traverse the heavens as these birds make their way back and forth between the southern States, where they winter, and northern Canada, where they rear their families. It takes a canny hunter to bring one to bag.

Canada Geese Mate for Life

Unlike most birds, Canada geese mate for life, and the little families stay together on their southward migration, even when they have joined dozens of other families. Who knows what knowledge the youngsters may get from their parents about the ways of wily hunters beyond that with which their instinct endows them? It is said that if one of a pair is killed the survivor never remates, but I think this is a little old-fashioned even for geese.

But why try to put a dollars-and-cents value on every bird we see? Certain it is that many of them affect man's pocketbook very slightly, if at all. It seems like trying to evaluate a sunset or a glimpse of a mountain lake among the spruces. Many of us would go a long way and put up with much hardship and expense to get the view from some high mountain.

Personally, I would not trade my experience on the Quebec coast with the quizzical puffins (page 260) or my first view of a flock of yelping black skimmers (page 254) in a

A Black and White Warbler Fills the Bill

But the baby at the end does not want to be forgotten. This warbler builds a cup-shaped nest under the edge of a bank or at the base of a sapling, but it spends most of its days climbing around tree trunks and large branches, like a nuthatch, in its search for insects. This is a male; the female has only faint streaks on the sides of its breast. Summering in the northern States or southern Canada, these warblers winter in northern South America or the southern regions of Florida and Texas.

Florida lagoon for any number of night-club adventures or spectacular melodramas that cost me good money. When I see a Virginia rail (page 203) sneaking through the cattails or hear a clapper rail (page 203) sounding his approach through the salt marsh, I do not ask, "How much are they a dozen?" or "What right have they to live?" Instead, I feel with Sidney Lanier:

> As the marsh hen secretly builds on the
> watery sod,
> Behold I will build me a nest on the
> greatness of God.

I marvel at the shades of brown and gray by which the rail fades into the background when occasion demands; at the long toes that distribute its weight on the floating vegetation; and at the slim body compressed for slipping easily through the dense vegetation. Perhaps the rails do some good by picking up the larvae of obnoxious horseflies that breed in such places, and perhaps they even destroy mosquito larvae. But it little matters; they are reason enough for their own existence.

And so it is with the pert Florida gallinule, or "water chicken" (page 205), and the mysterious pied-billed grebe, or "hell diver" (page 129). The gallinule is sometimes classed as a game bird, but the grebe is not even good to eat or pretty to look at. Yet there is a fascination in both these marsh-loving birds.

It is amusing to watch a pied-billed grebe when it hears an enemy approaching its nest, and see how deftly it covers all its eggs with the loose debris it has gathered about itself while incubating.

The Submersible Grebe

With no less speed the bird itself dives from sight and seems never to reappear. Of course it cannot get along without air for more than a minute or so, but it is adept in poking its bill above the water or in rising slowly in the floating vegetation, so that it is seldom observed.

When the eggs hatch, the youngsters almost immediately climb upon their mother's back, where they are brooded beneath her wings. They even ride around this way, like little jockeys, with their heads peeping between her wings. Then if she is disturbed, she merely clamps down her wings upon them and dives to the bottom, carrying them off to the shelter of the sedges or brush before surfacing again.

Often, instead of diving headfirst, the grebe merely submerges like a submarine so gradually as to leave scarcely a ripple.

The grebe's legs are located far back near its tail, and the long toes are edged with lobes

Laurence M. Huey

"Open Your Mouth Wide, and I'll Give You a Juicy Red Squawberry!"

This phainopepla, or silky flycatcher, likes mistletoe berries also. Most clumps of that parasitic growth are started on desert trees from seed scattered by these birds, who thus plant their own food crop.

so as to make it an expert swimmer and diver. On the other hand, this fact makes it practically helpless on land; so it never comes on shore intentionally. Certainly the pond that shelters a pair of grebes is more interesting because of their presence.

So also one's walk through the wood lot becomes more exciting if one hears the distant thump-thump-thump of a drumming grouse, or if one comes upon the actual drumming log itself, even though the bird be not there.

It takes a master woodsman to sneak through the woods so quietly toward the drumming sound that he can finally see the drummer at work. The photographs of the ruffed grouse on page 198 were made from a blind which was set up near a drumming log for a week until one day before dawn the author crawled into it with his camera to await the coming of the bird.

Use Same Drumming Log over Years

The drum of the grouse takes the place of song. It is the bird's challenge to other male grouse to keep out of that corner of the woods, and it is his announcement to the female that he is back at the old stand.

Many of these drumming logs are used year after year, and the birds are such creatures of habit that they stand on the same spot on the log and always face in the same direction.

Though Audubon described the performance, he could not have observed it, for he said the bird "beats its sides with its wings in the manner of the domestic cock." As a matter of fact, it merely pounds the air.

With forward and upward strokes of its concave wings it strikes with such force that the sound can be heard for half a mile on a quiet day. That is, it can be heard by most human ears for that distance, but the sound is one of very low frequency and it seems no louder at 50 feet than at 50 rods.

Horned Owl Has High-frequency Ears

It was always a mystery to me how the drumming grouse escaped its archenemy, the horned owl (page 278), for the drumming logs are sometimes within hearing range of a horned owl's nest and the grouse very often drums during the night when the owls are hunting.

The mystery was solved several years ago when Ernest Edwards, a graduate student at Cornell, tested the hearing of a captive horned owl and discovered that it could hear high frequencies very acutely, but that its lower hearing range did not extend downward to the 40 vibrations a second produced by the wings of the grouse (page 181).

The display of the grouse is as interesting as the drum, but is stimulated usually by the presence of another bird. To obtain the photograph of the ruffed grouse (page 198), a captive female was put in a small cage by the log, and the show the male put on for her benefit was magnificent.

Spreading his tail and drooping his wings, he raised the frill of glossy black feathers that a moment before had been quite inconspicuous until they formed an Elizabethan ruff.

Next, shaking his head from side to side, at first slowly and then more and more rapidly, he made a short run in her direction and struck the pose captured in the photograph. With each shake of his head he uttered a "Chug," the sounds coming closer and closer together until at the time of the last run they slid together into a prolonged hiss.

At a little distance the performance sounded like a far-off locomotive getting under way.

In most of our training centers during the war the boys were kept so busy that they didn't have time for birds, but always there were some that demanded attention.

In Florida it is the snowy herons that line the roadside ditches; in Louisiana and Texas it is the great flocks of geese that go honking overhead. One does not have to be very observant to see a Bullock's oriole (page 80) or a vermilion flycatcher (page 15) if one is stationed in the Southwest, though neither bird goes out of its way to make friends.

The vermilion flycatcher is really a tropical species that reaches the northern limit of its range along our Mexican border and is much more common farther south. When you approach its nest, the male flutters up into the air like a little ball of flame, its feathers all puffed out until it is practically spherical, with a little wing vibrating at each side. It does not come very close to the nest, however, until the eggs have hatched, but leaves the earlier domestic chores to its dull-brownish mate.

Every Spring Sees a Bird Invasion

The Bullock's oriole is found west of Brownsville, Texas, to the Pacific coast and northward to South Dakota, and it is very conspicuous in the acacia trees of the Southwest, where the foliage is sparse. In the East its place is taken by the closely related Baltimore oriole (page 78).

As often as the month of May rolls around in eastern United States and Canada, two great armies meet in the parks and woodlands. One army is that of the migratory birds invading us from the south.

The other is the army of bird observers, mustered from every walk of life, who get out early in the morning, not to repel the invasion but to cheer it on its way. If April has been cool so that the leaves do not obscure the

branches, the warblers are conspicuous as they feed about the opening buds.

To the beginner, the warblers seem an endless array of provocative color combinations and confusing sounds, while their restless habits are his despair. There are really only 41 species that migrate through eastern United States, but they seem twice as many because with most species males and females have different color patterns, though their shapes and sizes and idiosyncrasies are alike.

Additional species found in western United States bring the total up to 55, which is about a third of the whole family, but the spring rush of warblers is nowhere else so conspicuous as in the eastern half of the United States.

The family of wood warblers to which ours belong is strictly one of the New World, with resident species in Central and South America, where ours go visiting in winter.

Some Wood Warblers Travel Far

Some warbler species are greater travelers than others. The myrtle (page 59) and yellow-throated and palm, for example, winter in southern States, while others, such as the oven-bird (page 66) and chat (page 65) and hooded (page 64), go south into Mexico, and the chestnut-sided and cerulean (page 62) to Panama. The Canada (page 64) and golden-winged (page 58) seldom stop short of Colombia or Venezuela, while the black-poll (page 63) continues on to the Guianas and Brazil. Some, like the oven-birds and water thrushes, are terrestrial, seeking their food on the ground. Others, like the black and white, search out the crevices in bark, or, like the chestnut-sided and yellow-breasted chat, live mostly in low vegetation. Still others, like the Blackburnian and Tennessee, keep mostly to the treetops.

Some, like the prothonotary (page 58) and hooded, stop off in the southern States to nest; others, like the yellow (pages 60 and 61) and redstart (page 67), fly on to northern States.

The black-throated blue and Canada nest in southern Canada and only in the mountains farther south; the Wilson's and black-poll continue on to the northern spruce forests.

On migration a single flock may contain a dozen different kinds feeding in different strata in different ways and aiming toward different destinations, but all traveling together and landing in one's garden overnight, to the delight of the bird lovers of the neighborhood.

If you really wish to feel content with your lot, enjoy a trip to the park, a drive to the country, or a visit to a neighbor's garden, seek out a bird-loving friend as you would a doctor and get an injection of "warbleritis" or "thrushmania." If it "takes," you will be looking at birds the rest of your life.

53

Photographed near Aurora, New York

↑ Half the Family Is Still Hungry;
Young Shrikes Complain

Well-fed, two adolescent **Migrant Shrikes** turn their backs while a less fortunate pair clamor for their turn. The adult bird looks discouraged; a billful of insects doesn't go far when the young are this size. Migrant shrikes inhabit central and eastern States, sometimes preying on mice and small birds.

↓ "Butcher Birds" Feed Chiefly
on Grasshoppers

Loggerhead Shrike earned its nickname from its habit of impaling prey upon thorns or barbs. This shrike, being smaller than its northern cousin (page 54), is less inclined to kill and eat other birds. A devoted parent, it builds a bulky nest in thick bush or leafy tree.

Photographed by S. A. Grimes near Jacksonville, Florida

Photographed near Churchill, Manitoba

54

Evidently Still Hungry, a Tiny Shrike Tells His Father What He Thinks of the Food Shortage

The dapper parent of this family of **Northern Shrikes** fed his seven youngsters the bodies of smaller neighbors. Redpolls and longspurs were his quarry, captured by surprise attacks from the rear when they were busy eating. In winter the shrike carries on its solitary, nefarious activity as far south as North Carolina.

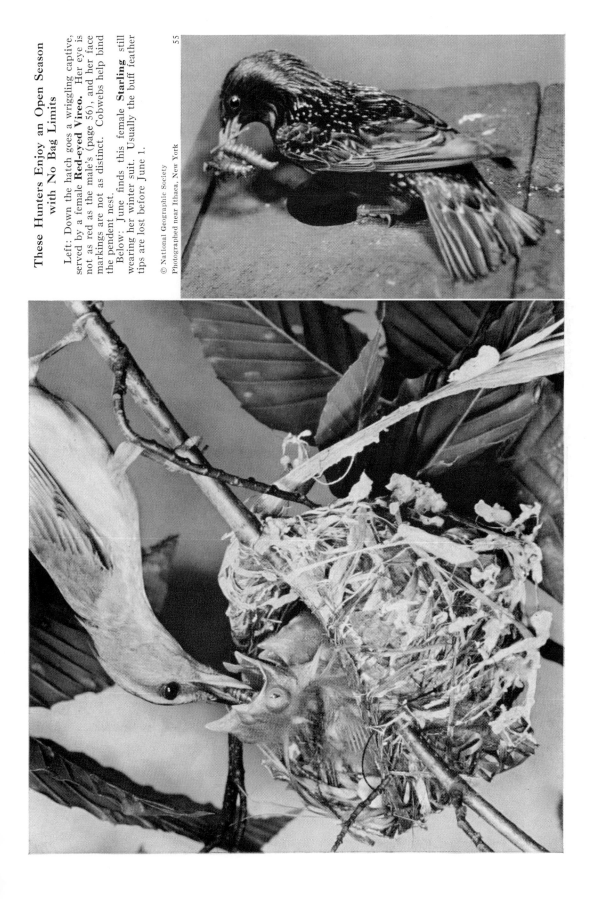

These Hunters Enjoy an Open Season with No Bag Limits

Left: Down the hatch goes a wriggling captive, served by a female **Red-eyed Vireo.** Her eye is not as red as the male's (page 56), and her face markings are not as distinct. Cobwebs help bind the pendent nest.

Below: June finds this female **Starling** still wearing her winter suit. Usually the buff feather tips are lost before June 1.

© National Geographic Society

Photographed near Ithaca, New York

Vireos at Home: Father Guards the Nest . . . A Youngster Wonders, "Can I Fly?"

Red-eyed Vireo (male, left) is often called "preacher bird" because of its talkative ways. It says, "Look up—
way up—treetop!" **Eastern Warbling Vireos** (right) are summer residents east of the Rockies.

© National Geographic Society   56   Photographed near Ithaca, New York

Battle-scarred, an Avian Hero Carries On

The loss of one leg did not prevent this **Yellow-throated Vireo** from building its pendent nest and rearing a
family. In summer it is found east of the Rockies and in winter from southern Mexico to Venezuela.

Brave or Trusting? →
This Bird Often Disdains
to Fly from Man

Remarkably tame, the **Blue-headed Vireo** seems more curious than alarmed at man's approach, sometimes even permitting itself to be stroked while on the nest. Ordinarily it winters in Gulf States, migrating in early spring to northern United States and southern Canada. Cool depths of evergreen forests shelter it in summer, accounting for its other name of "solitary vireo." A voracious enemy of the caterpillar, it is one of our most useful forest guardians.

Center: Moist wood and shady ravine are preferred by the **Kentucky Warbler.** There its sweet song may be heard all day. It ranges from Hudson Valley westward to Nebraska. Winter may find it in Colombia.

Upper: photographed by the author in Ithaca, New York. Center: photographed by Hal H. Harrison in western Pennsylvania

↓ "Whose Turn Is It, Children?"
A Mother's Dilemma

Usually the youngster which can stretch its neck the farthest and open its beak the widest wins the mother bird's attention. However, these "twins" are well matched, posing a problem for the adult **Black-throated Green Warbler.**

This warbler species nests in southern Canada and throughout the northeastern United States. Farther south (to Georgia) it builds only in mountainous terrain.

Photographed near Bay Pond, New York

Swamps and Streams Are Near When You See This Warbler

Prothonotary Warblers fly across the Gulf of Mexico to winter in Nicaragua and Colombia. Both parents do their share in providing for the young. The male shown here is considerably brighter than the female.

On Golden Wings He Comes to Us from Northern South America

After enjoying the winter in the tropic air of the republics to the south, the **Golden-winged Warbler** returns to the northern and eastern States and southeastern Ontario in early May to nest on the ground.

Wings Spread Like a Parasol, a Myrtle Warbler Shields Her Young

Hot sunlight, filtering through an Adirondack forest, prompted this pose. While wintering in southern States **Myrtle Warblers** wear dull plumage. A spring molt brightens their feathers before the April migration to Canada.

Room with a View: This Warbler Built Near the Grand Canyon's Rim

Nesting in a cedar, it sang repeatedly for tourists. **Black-throated Gray Warblers** seldom stray east of the Rockies. However, one visited the author's New York home on a mid-November morning in 1932.

60 Photographed near Ithaca, New York

Why the Two-story House? To Oust a Social Parasite

A cowbird laid an egg in this **Eastern Yellow Warbler's** nest beside one of the owner's. Refusing to be imposed upon, the warbler added another nest, burying the cowbird's speckled contribution where it could not hatch. The warbler then laid eggs in the second-floor nursery and here busily cares for triplets (pages 62, 77, 81, 82, 83, and 86).

61

A Much-traveled Yellow Warbler: It Flew from South America to Hudson Bay

In a stunted willow near timber line at Churchill, this **Yellow Warbler** stops at last and builds its cottony nest of Arctic pussy-willow down and lines it with ptarmigan feathers. This "summer yellow bird" breeds from northern Georgia to Alaska, some individuals flying much farther than others for reasons unknown.

62

Photographed near Ithaca, New York

↑   Cerulean Warbler Tenderly Cares
for a Greedy Imposter

↓   Maternal Solicitude Keeps Her Close
Until the Baby Is Quiet

A parasitic cowbird laid an egg in this nest. Mother **Cerulean Warbler** hatched it. Her own offspring have been smothered or crowded from the nest by the fast-growing young cowbird. Many parent birds are thus victimized (pages 60, 77, 81, 82, 83, and 86).

Chestnut-sided Warblers build rather flimsy nests in low bushes in clearings or near woods. Their summer range extends from southern Canada to northern United States east of the Rockies. The male has a larger chest-nut stripe and brighter crown.

63   Photographed near Churchill, Manitoba

ʌ **End of a 10,000-mile Hop**

This little **Black-poll Warbler,** incubating five eggs in a dwarf spruce at timber line near Churchill, Manitoba, must have traveled at least that far since leaving its home the previous August. Every year these birds make the round trip from the Hudson Bay area to Venezuela and Brazil.

ᴠ **A Slim Meal for a Warbler**

The **Northern Yellow-throat,** one of the warbler family, is found in several forms throughout the United States and Canada. It usually frequents tangles of weeds and low bushes near swamps, though it sometimes nests farther from water. The male has a conspicuous black mask.

Photographed near Ithaca, New York

64

↑ **Red Mouths Gape for May Flies Brought Home by the "Old Man"**

The male **Canada Warbler** performs his paternal duties in deep gloom, for not a sunbeam penetrates the Adirondack forest where his hungry offspring are concealed. The speed flash lights the darkness like a midday sun.

↓ **"Where Did You Get the Quaker Lady's Bonnet?" Ask the Babies**

Only the male **Hooded Warbler** has markings resembling a bonnet fastened under the chin. Nests are placed low in small saplings. These birds may summer from Florida to New York and winter from Veracruz to Panama.

65

↑ Time Out for a Chat During
the Lunch Hour

The **Yellow-breasted Chat,** largest of our warblers,
in summer frequents dense thickets and woodland borders throughout the United States and southern Canada.
It is noted for its jumbled outpouring of whistles and
clucks on clear nights.

↓ "Are They All There?" Returning, a
Warbler Checks Her Eggs

Her sunken nest is built among dwarf cornels *(Cornus
canadensis)* growing beneath spruce trees in a Quebec
clearing. **Wilson's Warbler** winters in Central America and nests from northern Maine to tree-line limits of
northern Canada.

Photographed in New York State

66

Warblers Never Face a Housing Shortage. These Versatile Artisans Use Plant Fibers as Building Blocks

Avid insect hunters, these homemakers help preserve the balance of Nature. The female **Canada Warbler,** shown on an insect foray (upper left), builds a bulky nest of leaves and grasses, which it places by a mossy bank or log. **Oven-bird** (upper right) sings "Teacher! Teacher!"—hence the synonym, teacher bird. **Mourning Warbler** (lower left) does not grieve; she's happy with her four beautiful eggs. **Magnolia Warbler** (right) prefers spruce tree to magnolia.

Redstarts Pack Boundless Energy in Their Tiny Frames

Gaily darting through the forest, **American Redstarts** appear to be the spirit of motion. They are among the daintiest of the warblers, a family beloved for its cheery ways and usefulness in destroying insects. Redstarts prefer the eastern States, though some inhabit western areas.

Males refuse to help in nest building and egg hatching, but assist their mates in feeding the young.

Left: The female wears distinctive yellow patches. Lower: The male prides himself on reddish-orange beauty marks.

© National Geographic Society

Photographed near Ithaca, New York

67

68

A Handsome Envoy Flies In from South America

After wintering in Brazil and Argentina, the **Bobolink** (male, above) migrates to northern United States and southern Canada. The birds feed their young on grasshoppers, cutworms, and other insect pests. In July when the young are full-grown and all bobolinks are yellowish brown like the female, they start southward. (See "Ambassadors of Good Will," page 97.)

The Bird's Year

THERE is a cardinal in our neighborhood that has caused mixed emotions. To a former mayor, Arthur N. Gibb, and his family he was a gift of color and cheer when he came to their feeding station at the window or sang from the top of the maple. To the Lloyds, who lived across the road, he was a troublemaker.

No sooner had the cardinal cracked a few sunflower seeds at the Gibbs' feeding station than he would dash across the road and fly headlong against one of the Lloyds' windows. He did this for nearly three years, and the Lloyds spent much of their time washing glass.

Especially unpopular was the bird half an hour after sunrise, when he was known to fly against the window fifty times without stopping, or with just sufficient interval to permit the dreamer to drop off again.

Shadowboxing His Own Reflection

To this particular cardinal the Lloyds' home was full of rivals. It never occurred to him that the intruders were only his own image reflected in the windowpanes. Going from one window to another, he would drive each bird back where it belonged, thus preserving the neighborhood for himself and his mate.

During the spring season, at least, the female was not averse to helping him, perhaps not in actual combat but with flattering whistles or even a complete song. The cardinal is one of the comparatively few species whose females can sing.

After the second year of window washing, the Lloyds sent me an ultimatum, threatening to trap the bird and carry him off into the country. As a pacifier I fastened a mirror outside the window of their guest room, where the cardinal could find an image really worthy of his prowess and where he could concentrate his attentions without being so objectionable.

The mirror was an immediate but temporary success (pages 70 and 89). Eventually Sam Lloyd had to put up window screens long before the fly season, just to destroy the reflections that made the cardinal see red.

This is not the only cardinal with such antisocial behavior. As long ago as 1599, Ulissi Aldrovandi, the great Italian naturalist, told of one that had been transported from America to a garden at Pisa and spent most of its time fighting its reflection.

At my own home in Ithaca, New York, a female cardinal has taken the part of Don Quixote tilting with a nonexistent foe. The male aids her efforts by bringing her sunflower seeds already cracked, so that she need not cease her chivalrous defense of their chosen estate.

Cardinals along the northern limit of their range seem much more given to this "shadowboxing" than those farther south, where the species is much more numerous and therefore accustomed to having close neighbors.

Perhaps these northern pioneering individuals are endowed with a greater flow of hormones, as well as increased vitality. This has caused them to push onward into new country, just as our own ancestors did, and at the same time has made them intolerant of their kind.

This behavior of the cardinal is not at all exceptional in the bird world. I have known many robins, catbirds, wrens, song sparrows, orioles, and even indigo buntings to fight their own reflections when some offending window happened to be included in the area which the bird claimed as its nesting domain and which ornithologists have come to call the bird's "territory."

There are a few birds, such as the bank swallow, cliff swallow, and purple martin, that nest in colonies and seem to enjoy close neighbors. They do not appear to object to a friend even peering into the nest occasionally. But most birds are strictly "territorial" during the nesting season and will not allow another male of their own species to approach within a certain self-determined distance of their headquarters.

Defense of Territory Falls to Male

It is usually the male's job to defend the territory, but in some species the female will not permit another of her sex to enter the sacred precincts. My militant cardinal is a good example of these fighting females.

In cases where the females are not territorial, several may occasionally settle down in the territory of one aggressive male, and thus polygamy results in some normally monogamous species. House wrens, orioles, starlings, red-wings, meadowlarks, and robins have been found fathering two or more families at the same time, although most individuals of their kind are strictly one-family males.

There are records of two female robins having the same mate and occupying the same nest, or two nests touching each other, yet with the birds apparently on good terms. I have even heard of two female cardinals occupying the same nest; but this is most irregular, and the resulting confusion caused the eggs to get broken.

Love-blind Cardinal Brooks No Rivals. He Fights His Own Image in a Mirror

The author's scarlet neighbor announces by singing that he has claimed a territory. He stakes out its limits with a series of song perches. Now a glandular stimulus robs him of reasoning power. He ignores birds of other species, but another male cardinal makes him see red (pages 69 and 89). Nature may have intended his brilliant color to lure marauders from the nest. The incubating female needs to be less conspicuous.

In one case of bigamy, where two robins built nests side by side, the eggs in one nest hatched the day the young in the other nest were about ready to leave. The stimulus of the wide-open mouths and insistent food calls of the clamoring large youngsters was so strong for both females that the small young were entirely neglected and therefore perished.

Two Keys to Bird Behavior

In general, a bird's behavior throughout the year is controlled by two major forces, and these allow little opportunity to use what we might call intelligence.

First, there is the physiological control from within the body. It tells birds when it is time to migrate, to stop migrating, to select a territory, to sing, to fight, to mate, to build a nest and lay eggs, to incubate eggs, to feed the young, to assemble in flocks, and so on.

In a healthy bird these cycles of instincts follow one another with clocklike regularity. If there were no such things as weather or accidents, each species would probably leave its winter home on a definite date, pass through Washington or some other way station on the same day each year, and arrive on its nesting ground and lay its eggs with equal predictability.

Indeed, some birds that are not much affected by the weather—for example, the cliff swallows of San Juan Capistrano, in California, or the puffins of Quebec—do exactly this. One could plan his journeys years ahead so as to arrive at Capistrano with the swallows or on Perroquet Island in the Gulf of St. Lawrence on the same day as the puffins (page 245). But if all bird behavior were so predictable, bird study would lose much of its zest and charm.

The other major force comes from without and is in the form of an intricate series of releasers, as they were first called by that brilliant student of bird behavior, Konrad Z. Lorenz. Most of these are visual, but many are auditory and a few are tactual or perhaps even olfactory, though the sense of smell is very poorly developed in birds.

For instance, a bird might fail to breed if its surroundings did not look, sound, feel, or possibly even smell right. Its normal behavior pattern would not be released.

Glands May Turn Sissy into Bully

The physiological control is apparently governed by the activity of the pituitary gland and the secretion of certain hormones which in turn control the activity of other glands.

During the winter, for example, the reproductive glands are quiescent and all the activities connected with the breeding season are entirely suspended.

Elsa G. Allen

The Author's Triumph: Ruffed Grouse Raised in Captivity

It was long considered impossible to rear captive grouse. The author found the trouble lay in lack of sanitation, chicks infecting one another with their droppings. Chicken-wire flooring solved the problem, saving 85 percent. Birds were friendly toward their keeper, but the mating season started vicious fights among males. Hand-reared, they bred freely, whereas wild-trapped birds refused (page 198).

Most species do not sing, or, if they do, they have a different song from that given on the nesting ground.

If they fight, it is entirely irrelevant to sex and merely for the purpose of establishing what has been called the "peck order"—determining which birds can peck and bully which others; and the dominant birds may be either male or female.

An established peck order is subject to many changes and even reversals as spring advances and a new cycle of behavior is ushered in.

In my flock of waterfowl, a few years ago, a snow goose lorded it over all the other fowls during the winter; but by April the mallards were passing into the breeding cycle while the snow goose was still quiescent sexually. As a result, one of the male mallards, which had submitted to the snow goose's brutality all winter, rose in the peck order to such an extent that he drove the snow goose off the pond and kept him away so successfully that he could hardly get a drink.

All the factors that control the pituitary gland are not understood, but it has been shown experimentally that the amount of sunlight or artificial light which the bird receives affects the activity of this gland and in turn the activity of the reproductive glands. It likewise affects all the secondary sex characters, such as color of bill, feet, and any "soft parts" that are normally subject to color change in the spring.

Sparrows, juncos, starlings, pheasants, grouse, crows, and other wild birds, as well as poultry, have been brought into breeding condition during fall or winter merely by giving

Allan D. Cruickshank from National Audubon Society

Beauty's Price Was Sudden Death

The filmy aigrette plumes worn by this snowy egret during the nest-building season caused its near extinction in the latter part of the 19th century. Milliners used the feathers to trim high-style hats or to fashion striking hair ornaments for wear with evening gowns. Under efficient protection, egrets have greatly increased in recent years. This bird was caught in active courtship display (p. 139).

Each spring these wildfowl went through the regular cycle of fighting, courtship, and mating, but there the cycle stopped; no nests were built and no eggs were laid. There was something in the environment I had supplied which did not release the proper nesting behavior.

After several years of this, I obtained some eggs from wild nests in Canada and hatched them under domestic hens. The redheads hatched well enough to give me a breeding stock, and when they were placed on the same ponds with the wild-trapped birds, they had no inhibitions whatsoever about building nests and laying eggs the very first season.

Uninhibited Birds Have Normal Behavior Pattern

These hen-raised ducks could never have seen or experienced a normal home or a redhead mother's attentions; yet the selection of the nesting site, building of the nests, the plucking of down from the breast of the incubating bird—in fact, their entire behavior—seemed perfectly normal for the species.

This experience has led me to believe that each species of bird has a normal annual cycle of behavior which it follows in detail when uninhibited, but which is often governed or modified by outside releasers, many of which are learned through the experience of the individual.

Thus the wild-trapped waterfowl were perfectly satisfied with my ponds for winter and mating quarters, but the ponds were found lacking in some detail when it came time to release the nesting behavior—a detail which they had acquired from their previous lives in the wild and which the hand-reared birds had never experienced.

When the birds come back to us in the spring, some continue on to the spruce forests

the birds in cages increased allotments of light, corresponding roughly to the lengthening days of spring.

Hand-reared pheasants, grouse, and quail will actually produce eggs in the winter; but birds trapped in the wild do not proceed quite so far, since nest building and egg laying are controlled by releasers which are not so easily supplied.

Waterfowl Homesick for Some Unknown Releaser

For many years I tried to induce wild-trapped canvas-backs, redheads, and other waterfowl to breed in captivity. They were pinioned and placed on fenced ponds where there was plenty of natural food and nesting cover in addition to the stimulating laying mash which I supplied.

Louisiana's Snowy Herons Submit to Crowding, but Each Defends His Small Apartment

Nests may almost touch; but let one bird step an inch across an imaginary line and a sharp peck puts him in his place. Territorial trespass is avoided by exact flight routes back to nests. On their feeding grounds the birds may post large territories against fishing by other herons. Once settled on their nests with their eggs, the birds no longer engage in courtship display (opposite page). Their plumes lie flatter and become less evident.

⋏   Dinner Hides in Mother's Throat

Regurgitated fruits, with insects for dessert, await mother's three star boarders. Using her esophagus as a basket, the cedar waxwing carries enough for all. The speedlight's stroboscopic flash, freezing motion, analyzes the wingspread (page 43 and opposite).

⋎ One Redpoll Bluffs Another from Chow Line

The two follow the flock's peck order, a feeding arrangement established by intimidation or combat. First bite goes to the prime bully, but if he loses his pep he will drop low in the queue. Winter visitors to Ithaca, New York, the redpolls flew out of the far north.

of Canada and some to the Barren Grounds of the far north before their nesting behavior is released. Local birds scatter to wood, field, or marsh, according to the experiences of their youth.

So insistent is Nature on having exactly the right combination of releasers that one seldom finds a nesting bird "out of place." True, the little clumps of spruce forest on the tops of the Appalachians may induce some Canadian birds to stop and nest as far south as Georgia; but, more often, wandering birds that stray from the established breeding range of the species, even though they find mates, do not breed because they do not find the proper releasers to nesting behavior. Through the ages the summer ranges of most birds show little change.

Local populations of wide-ranging species, like song sparrows or yellow warblers, may gradually develop slight variations. These may tend to be preserved until we eventually recognize a race or subspecies, dependent for its preservation on some releasers of breeding behavior which our crude powers of observation are unable to recognize.

In like manner, slight differences in songs and courtship displays may develop in different parts of a bird's range and help segregate the populations. But the remarkable thing is that there is such regularity in the behavior patterns of the thousands of individuals that make up bird species, and such blind insistence on the details of the releasers, that normally two species are automatically prevented from interbreeding.

Hybrids are not uncommon in captivity-reared waterfowl, and in pheasants or even songbirds that have not experienced the releasers of their respective species; but in normal wild birds hybrids are most uncommon. They occur principally along the borders of overlapping ranges, where apparently the sex ratio of both species is likely to be upset.

75

A Few Cherries Pay for Protection from Raiders

Although the waxwing has an unfortunate appetite for fruit, it makes up for its misdeeds by eating enormous quantities of destructive insects. It feeds its young by regurgitation, usually bringing back from a single foray enough food for the whole family. These birds sometimes perch in rows on a mulberry branch, where only the outermost can reach the berries, and pass each titbit back from one to the next (page 43 and opposite).

Staking a Claim and Choosing a Mate

When a male bird sets up a territory, therefore, he is responding to a series of releasers that indicate to him that the particular area where he is located is suitable for his species. If he is strong enough to defend it against other males of his kind, eventually a female will arrive that is similarly affected, and she will try to settle in the same territory.

At first the male may try to drive her away, for he may still be in the aggressive cycle of his behavior and may not be desirous or capable of mating.

The mating period in most wild birds is short, both in the male and in the female, and the entire pattern of their behavior in the spring is designed to bring together birds that are in exactly the same stage of the cycle, so that fertile eggs will ensue.

Since domestic birds have been bred away from this weak link in the chain of high productivity, we are likely to overlook its importance in the wild.

Probably every territorial male drives away many females, as well as males, before a female in the proper stage, or approximately so, comes along. Often the song alone of the male is sufficient to cause other males to move on. If they persist, he flies at them and gives an intimidation display.

In the case of the red-winged blackbird, or red-wing (page 85), the chip-on-shoulder act consists of puffing out his feathers and raising his scarlet epaulets every time he sings. This is enough to show his neighbors that he is ready to defend his territory.

In the white-breasted nuthatch (page 34), the black and white underwing and tail markings are usually not very conspicuous until he approaches an aggressor. Then he spreads his wings and tail so as to flash them in the intruder's face.

The ruffed grouse (page 198) droops his wings and raises his tail like a turkey cock, then spreads his ruff in true Elizabethan fashion and shakes his head rapidly from side to side, at the same time producing a sound like a miniature freight train.

Prairie chickens stamp and boom (page 197); sharp-tailed grouse spread their wings, lift their tails, and give a stiff-legged dance, their feet making quick, stamping sounds; flickers bow and twitch and display the golden linings of their wings and tails; and so on.

In fact, every bird has some method for appearing bigger and better than he really is at this stage of the breeding cycle. It serves to intimidate all rivals and, with slight variations, to stimulate the female that is trying to settle in his territory.

Male's Song Raises Female's Pulse

Just what the stimulation amounts to is difficult to measure. But when the late Samuel Prentiss Baldwin and S. Charles Kendeigh were studying house wrens, they put a cardiometer in the bird's nest and discovered that each time the male sang the pulse rate of the female increased.

The various displays of plumage and the cavortings of the males, of which the females pretend to be oblivious, undoubtedly have a similar effect. Eventually the two birds find themselves in exactly the same stage of the mating cycle, and fertile eggs result.

In the meantime, the female bird has not only accepted the male's territory but has felt the urge to build a nest, which must be completed in time for the first egg. It takes about six days for an egg to be formed and laid after the first yellow yolk is deposited about the ovum.

Since most birds spend about six days building their nests, we infer from this fact that the instinct to build usually starts with the formation of the first yellow yolk in the ovary. However, there are undoubtedly many exceptions to this rule.

Henpecked Male Phalaropes Keep House

It is usually the female's job to build the nest without any help from the male, though here again are many exceptions. The male of the common English sparrow (page 17), for example, is much more active in nest building than the female. So are male woodpeckers.

In the case of the phalaropes (pages 234 and 235), the sexes are entirely reversed. The males not only select the nest site and build the nest, but they hatch the eggs and rear the young while the females go off in flocks by themselves. These gadabouts do, however, deign to lay the eggs. Incidentally, they wear the brighter colors and are larger than their henpecked mates.

Males and females of many birds share equally the duties of incubation and care of the young. This is especially true of species in which the sexes are colored alike. Even among the plainly colored song sparrows, however, if the species is abundant and territories small, a male may feel that he should spend all his time singing and defending the territory rather than sitting on eggs.

In birds like the indigo bunting (page 92), goldfinch, and most warblers (pages 57-67), whose males are brightly colored and females plain, the males do not sit on the eggs at all, though they do help feed the young. The male rose-breasted grosbeak (page 90) is one dazzling male that does sit on eggs, but the ruby-throated hummingbird not only passes up egg sitting but disdains all household duties as well (page 295).

Every bird species lays eggs of definite size, shape, color, and markings. There is, likewise, a rather definite clutch number for each species, from which they seldom depart. Auks and murres (page 262) lay but a single egg; hummingbirds, 2; robins, 3 to 5; chickadees, 5 to 8; grouse, 8 to 15; and so forth. The number is probably an adaptation to the dangers to which the eggs and young are so often subjected.

Each egg has a definite incubation period, or time required for hatching. This ranges

A Sennett's Oriole Home Along the Rio Grande, Cunningly Concealed in Spanish Moss

The plain blue egg among the speckled ones was laid by a red-eyed cowbird (*Tangavius aeneus*), a bird which does not occur north of southern Texas. To obtain this picture, the author exposed the eggs by parting the moss. The **Sennett's Oriole** (female) can't decide whether to enter by the large new door or to slip in the old way. It finally decided on the latter. Speckled eggs in warbler's nest shown on page 60 were laid by the cowbird (*Molothrus ater*), found throughout the United States except in high mountains and southeastern corner, and in southern Canada. Male Sennett's oriole is shown on following page. (See pages 60, 62, 81, 82, 83, and 86.)

Orioles, Fashion Plates of the Bird World, Wear Striking Vests

The old adage, "Handsome is as handsome does," has been taken to heart by the **Baltimore Oriole** (male, upper left). A delight to the eye, it is also a good citizen, feeding on caterpillars, boll weevils, and many other insects. Its song is highly varied; one characteristic whistle says, "Come right here, dear!"

Baltimore orioles sport the colors of Maryland's founder; hence the name. They are summer residents in States east of the Rockies.

Texas is the only State frequented by **Sennett's Oriole** (upper right), which prefers Mexico to the United States. This male dwells in a yucca.

Left: The female Baltimore oriole weaves a hanging nest of string and milkweed fibers. Food, pushed far into the young bird's mouth, produces a swallowing reaction when it touches the back of the tongue.

© National Geographic Society

Upper left: photographed by the author near Ithaca, New York

Upper right: photographed by S. A. Grimes near Brownsville, Texas

Lower left: photographed by Hal H. Harrison in northwestern Pennsylvania

79

⋏   Spanish Moss Provides a Home

Orchard Orioles more often weave hanging nests of dried grasses in tree forks, but around Summerville, South Carolina, they use the epiphyte which here festoons wild cherry; this is the Spanish moss which interests northern human visitors as well as birds. The male never sits on the eggs, but helps in feeding.

⋎   Grasshoppers Make Delicious Salad

This is a female **Orchard Oriole;** the male appears above. When anything jars their nest, the young open their mouths for food. The species is familiar from Florida and Texas to Nebraska and Massachusetts, but is less common in the northern States where the orange-and-black Baltimore oriole ranges.

↑ "Down with Insects" Is the War Cry

Bullock's Oriole, a species of the Great Plains area and westward, replaces the Baltimore oriole of eastern United States. The hanging nest of Bullock's oriole usually is more firmly attached and does not swing so freely as the Baltimore's.

← Silence Is Golden for Unmusical Blackbird

Most blackbirds are a joy to hear, although their songs are fairly simple piping whistles. The **Yellow-headed Blackbird,** however, must depend upon its beauty, not its voice, for its charm. This one sings "Our cook skedaddled, our cook she-e-e-e!" while rocking on a rush in a Utah tule marsh. It seldom ventures east of Indiana.

Reflections on a Corn-fed Bronzed Grackle Gleam in Splendor

This male **Bronzed Grackle** is the common crow blackbird, familiar about parks, lawns, and cornfields throughout the United States and Canada, east of the Rockies and west of the Alleghenies. Along the central Atlantic coast is found its relative, the purple grackle; and in Florida, the Florida grackle. Male is more iridescent than female.

81

Photographed near Ithaca, New York

He "Follows the Horses" and the Cows

His gamble, however, is that his neighbors will take care of his children. This **Eastern Cowbird's** gray mate lays eggs in other birds' nests. Bird gets its name because it follows cattle for insects they attract (pages 60, 62, 77, 82, 83, and 86).

← **Caught in the Act!
Sneaky Mrs. Cowbird
Jettisons an Egg
in a Predawn Raid**

Bigamist and social parasite
—that's **Eastern Cowbird's**
shady reputation. Having lost
her homemaking instincts, she
lays eggs in the nests of
smaller birds. Foster parents
hatch the interlopers, feed and
raise them.

This extraordinary flashlight
Kodachrome is believed to be
the only color picture ever
made of a cowbird parasitiz-
ing a nest. Finding mother
warbler not at home, the daybreak visitor has deposited her
own egg. Now she tosses out
a warbler egg to make more
room. Other eggs she foists
upon different hosts.

Poultrymen play varieties of
the cowbird trick on barnyard
fowl—witness hens hatching
ducklings.

**Chestnut-sided
Warbler Adopts
the Bogus Egg** →

Some warblers floor over
foreign eggs by building sec-
ond-story nests. More often,
as in case of this **Chestnut-
sided Warbler,** they hatch
the foundlings. Rightful heirs,
usually smaller, fail in competition for food (pages 60, 62,
77, 81, 83, and 86).

Photographed by Hal H. Harrison in
western Pennsylvania

Mrs. Redstart Feeds the Destroyer of Her Children, a Greedy Cowbird Already Bigger than His Foster Mother

The young foundling, **Eastern Cowbird**, using his greater size to advantage, has grabbed most of the food and starved or smothered his nest mates. Now his prodigious appetite requires constant insect servings, and deluded **American Redstart** guardians wait on him endlessly (pages 60, 62, 77, 81, 82, and 86).

© National Geographic Society

Photographed near Ithaca, New York

Photographed near Ithaca, New York

"Who Wants a Fresh Grasshopper?"

An **Eastern Meadowlark**, resplendent in yellow shirt front, white coattails, and black cravat, looks around for possible danger before feeding his quadruplets. They repose, of all places, in the author's hat (right). The nest usually is found under the dried grasses of the previous year (page 7).

A Hatful and a Mouthful

Moved from their nest to the author's hat, four young **Eastern Meadowlarks** make themselves at home while mother brings two large green katydids. After each meal the old birds carefully carried away all excrement, keeping the hat as clean as if it had been their own nest (page 7).

84

"Something Tells Me I Am Not Alone"

From his perch among the sedges (carefully arranged by the author) a suspicious **Eastern Red-wing** surveys the blind before going in search of food for his young. The nestlings, out of sight below, are even nearer the camera. Only mature male has the bright red patch which gives bird its name.

Photographed near Ithaca, New York

85

"Looks Like Lunch to Me!"

A female **Eastern Red-wing** has brought home a cutworm for the youngsters, waiting in their cradle in the cattails. The female is somber compared with the male, which has bright scarlet epaulets. The red-wing is found from Canada to Mexico; relatives occur in South America.

© National Geographic Society

86

↑   "Good-bye, Daddy—Hurry Back"

The brilliant male **Scarlet Tanager** has just fed his youngsters, and now, while they look after him hopefully, starts his search for the second course of a meal that lasts all day. Well camouflaged, the young resemble their mother (below) rather than their dazzling dad. In October the birds will fly to Colombia or Bolivia to spend the winter.

↓   Which Child Is Hers?

A parasitic cowbird, unwilling to raise her brood, sneaked two eggs into the nest. Already the cowbird's offspring have kicked out one foster brother. Young tanager (middle) has a yellow mouth lining; the foundlings, pink. Mother **Scarlet Tanager** works hard to feed the babies, not realizing that two are impostors (pages 60, 62, 77, 81, 82, and 83).

87

Photographed near Ithaca, New York

⋏ "Framed" by the Photographer

A female **Eastern Purple Finch** is drab compared with her rosy spouse, so the author "said it with flowers"—a screen of larkspurs and four-o'clock to cover the feeding pan. The bird calmly lunches on a sunflower seed, never suspecting the camera in a blind three feet away.

⋎ Picnicking in Yosemite Park

A slice of watermelon attracted this **Western Tanager,** whose song is almost identical with the East's scarlet tanager. The author's food handout also lured western robins, black-headed grosbeaks, and blue-fronted jays. Anticipating a feast, they began to assemble while the melon still was being cut.

Photographed in Yosemite National Park, California

88

↑ **Cardinals at Home in New York**

During recent years **Eastern Cardinals** (male above) have extended their range northward and become common in central New York, Michigan, Wisconsin, and Minnesota, where formerly they were unknown. Few winter scenes are more impressive than a group of brilliant males feeding in the snow.

↓ **"My Turn Next"**

Mother **Eastern Cardinal** spells father in feeding hungry babies. Birds usually feed the hungriest youngster first, or the one with the longest neck and the widest mouth. When full, it subsides and the others get a chance. This nest is in a bower of wisteria. Bird is also known as Kentucky cardinal.

89 Photographed near Ithaca, New York

In Green-eyed Rage a Cardinal Fights His Fancied Rival

Cardinals brook no competition from other males in the territories which they select for their nests.

While flying through a garden, this **Eastern Cardinal** saw his reflection in a windowpane and convinced himself that he had spotted an interloper. Using beak, claws, and wings, he gave the "stranger" a good going over. When a mirror was placed on the window sill, the bird transferred his attentions. Undiscouraged by his failure to achieve more than a draw, he continued the battle for weeks.

Like other birds, the cardinal has no idea of the meaning of glass. In time of danger he may fly head on into a closed window. See "Pinkie," the grosbeak, on page 90.

Frequently nesting in the vines of a back porch, the cardinal performs in many lovable ways for the entertainment of his hosts. He also wins acclaim as a model husband—he often feeds his mate while she is on the nest. But it is as a father that he plays his most characteristic role, taking charge of the young when they leave the nest. It is Papa Cardinal who seems "to love the babies and hate to see them grow up." He is still trying to help his offspring get a good start in life, while the mother bird has started to build another nest and is preparing for the next brood.

The female cardinal has one great distinction: she is one of the few feminine singers in the bird world.

90

⅄   Albino Is One in Thousand   ⅄   "Don't Forget Me, Dad"

This bird is a freak **Rose-breasted Grosbeak;** below it is shown in normal plumage. Pursued by a hawk, it flew against a window and stunned itself. Although "Pinkie" had a cage in the Allen kitchen for years, he never showed affection for his human friends.

So this young **Rose-breasted Grosbeak** seems to beseech its father. The females, like the young, are brown and sparrowlike. The birds travel to Mexico and northern South America in winter. In summer they live from Mackenzie, Canada, to central Kansas and eastward.

Redpolls Are the →
"Linnets" of Far North

Nesting in willows and dwarf
spruces of timber line and tundra,
the **Common Redpoll** behaves
very much like the more southern
goldfinch.

In winter flocks are seen in the
northern United States, and occasionally redpolls visit northern California, Alabama, and South Carolina.

Older males have rosier breasts
than this yearling.

Photographed near Mountain Village, Alaska

Photographed in Cortland, New York

← Hoary Redpoll Likes
Northern Climes

Long Arctic days allow the bird
plenty of time to hunt alder seeds,
its favorite tidbit. The young are
fed by regurgitation. Always hungry, they grow more rapidly than
their southern cousins, the goldfinches.

Hoary Redpolls in winter gather
in flocks and wander southward,
sometimes as far as the northern
States.

A lichen-covered alder in the
Yukon Delta supported this Alaskan
family.

© National Geographic Society

91

92

Raucous Young Cowbird Demands Food from Devoted Foster Parent, an Indigo Bunting

This male **Indigo Bunting** and his mate unwittingly hatched a voracious foundling. Most of our small songsters are victims of the cowbird's parasitic ways. In Europe the cuckoo plays a similar trick on neighbors.

from the 10 days of a cowbird to the 78 days of a royal albatross, with the average around 12 or 14 days for small birds like robins and sparrows.

Some species, like most of the shore birds, the grackles, and warblers, regularly have only one brood in a season; others, like the doves, sparrows, and thrushes, may have two or three. Most birds, if the nest is broken up, will attempt to nest again.

Chiselers of the Bird World

There are a few birds, like the Old World cuckoos, the African honey guides, certain weaverbirds, and the New World cowbirds, that have lost entirely their parental instincts and have become social parasites. Laying their eggs in other birds' nests, they let the foster parent hatch the eggs and rear the young.

Some of the birds, like the wrens, catbirds, and robins, respond by throwing out the cowbirds' eggs. Others, like the yellow warblers, frequently bury the cowbirds' eggs in the bottom of the nest (page 95). But the majority of small birds just accept and hatch the eggs and rear the young cowbirds (pages 82, 83, 86, and 92). Often this costs them their own young, which are smaller, grow more slowly, and are eventually smothered or crowded out of the nest.

Sometimes the cowbird removes one of the foster parent's eggs from the nest to make room for her own (page 82); but usually she lays her egg when there are only one or two of the rightful eggs in the nest. Always she lays the foundling egg before incubation has started.

Birds do not usually commence incubating their eggs until the full complement has been laid, because otherwise the resulting young would be of different ages and sizes. This would have obvious disadvantages, as the larger ones would get all the food.

Own Brother May Swallow a Runt

In the few exceptions to this rule among the hawks and owls, there is sometimes a resulting runt in the family, and the luckless mite often gets swallowed by one of its big brothers or sisters when they all make a dive for the same piece of food.

Young birds fall into two general types. We ornithologists call these types precocial and altricial.

The former are like ducklings and chickens —covered with down, eyes open, and able to run around soon after hatching (pages 167, 199, and 230). Many of these, like young grouse and shore birds, have to find their own food from the start. They are dependent on their parents only for brooding and then only until their juvenile feathers retain sufficient heat so that they won't get chilled.

Altricial young, on the other hand, may be hatched entirely naked, like young woodpeckers and bluejays; but the majority have a little downy fluff on their upper parts (pages 55, 85, 91, and 138), and the juvenile feathers grow so rapidly that the nestlings are completely covered in 10 days. All of their food, however, has to be supplied by their parents, and many and varied are the ways of transferring it to the youngsters.

Most small birds carry the insects or fruit for their young in their bills, where one can see it (pages 84 and 85); others swallow the food and later cough it up (pages 74 and 98). Hummingbirds have tubular tongues and inject their youngsters with nectar* (page 292), while cormorants and pelicans merely open their mouths and let the children help themselves, cafeteria fashion (pages 130 and 241). It's not so bad for the first course, but they sometimes almost entirely disappear in reaching for the dessert.

The amount of food young birds require is almost unbelievable and gives an entirely different connotation to the expression, "appetite like a bird's." During their period of maximum growth they consume more than their own weight in food every day.

We once raised a black tern from his first day out of the egg until he finally flew away. When he weighed 31 grams one morning, he consumed 48 grams of earthworms during the day.

If Boys Ate Like Young Birds!

If a growing boy ate like that, he could gobble daily two or three lambs or a whole calf.

When young birds outgrow the nest, at from 12 days of age in red-winged blackbirds to six months in the case of albatrosses and condors, they practice using their wings on the edge of the nest before they flutter out into the near-by vegetation. There again they are cared for by their parents for variable periods, depending on the species. Sometimes the male takes care of the first brood while the female builds a new nest for a second brood.

Eventually the youngsters join others of their kind and form roaming flocks that start off in almost any direction in their search for food. Families thus become separated and dispersed long before it is time to migrate. Although some individuals may remain near where they were hatched, others of the same family may show up some time later hundreds of miles away.

* See "Freezing the Flight of Hummingbirds," page 297.

So it is that the following year a few of the young may return to the area where they were reared, while the rest will be scattered, with little chance for inbreeding. The majority will find suitable areas for setting up territories, acquiring mates, and rearing young of their own the first year, although some species require a longer period.

In general, the bird's year measures a generation. If the bird lives for three years, it has grandchildren and has accomplished as much biologically as the average human being in his allotted three-score and ten.

The Eagle and the Little Black Hen

A few years ago I was given a live bald eagle which had been captured as it pounced on a rooster near a farmhouse. I kept this bird for 15 days in a building 50 feet long and 15 feet wide without its eating a morsel of food.

I tried everything from fresh fish to rabbit, mouse, and chicken, to no avail. I went so far as to put a live bantam hen in with it, thinking that this might stimulate its predatory instinct.

When I peered through a crack in the door that evening, what was my surprise to see the little hen cuddled up on the perch by the side of the eagle!

For 30 days they lived together, the little black hen scratching out a living during the day and each night going to roost close beside the eagle.

Charles Del Vecchio, Washington Post   94

Uninvited Guests to the National Capital

Every winter tens of thousands of starlings settle down in Washington, roosting at night on the protected ledges and ornamental cornices of public buildings, where their noise and dirt make them unwelcome. Annually, old tricks to get rid of the birds are tried and fantastic new "gimmicks" are suggested. Here at the Archives Building even balloons once were used in an attempt to frighten the avian hordes. But the starlings refused to be frightened and continue to return to their haunts every year.

© W. V. Crich

Skyscraper Nest near Toronto Reveals Tribulation Caused by Cowbird

The side of this five-story yellow warbler's nest was cut away to show the extent to which a cowbird's persecutions can go. Every time the parasitic bird dropped an egg into the nest, the warbler roofed it over. Only by this strenuous labor could the warbler protect her young from the determined attempts of the cowbird to get a foster home for her brood (pages 60, 62, 77, 81, 82, 83, and 86).

Of All Roosts, Abie the Mockingbird Chooses a Bird Dog

Abandoned as a fledgling, Abie was adopted into a Maryland home. He paid off with song and cheer. At feeding time he strode the Irish setter's back; his friend tolerated every indignity. Attacked by wild birds while exercising outdoors one day, Abie was never seen again.

and hunt its food had suddenly been obscured and was being replaced by another entirely different. Until the adjustment had been made, even physiological functions largely ceased. By the time the adjustment had been made, the mental picture included the little black hen, not as an item of food but as a companion.

The same holds for the little black hen. She had been summarily removed from her companions and placed in a new environment with another companion the like of which she had never seen before. Because of its size she immediately conceded its dominance, and it mattered little if it had a more curved bill and larger feet than the roosters of her acquaintance.

When it grew dark, her social instinct required that she roost with the flock, and she flew to the perch and moved along until she was as close as she had been the night before to a less lordly fowl.

The relationship between them might have endured indefinitely had not something suddenly stimulated the killing reaction in the eagle.

Meantime, the eagle gave up its hunger strike and soon was eating any kind of meat I supplied it, including little black hens exactly like its companion.

Friends who saw the miracle of the "lion and the lamb" suggested that the eagle had lost its predatory instinct in captivity.

To test this, I introduced into the room a sister of the little black hen. I had scarcely closed the door before the eagle pounced on the newcomer and devoured her.

After a month of amiable companionship the eagle turned on the little hen that had roosted with it and gobbled her up!

During the 15 days of fasting the eagle was gradually adjusting itself to an entirely new environment. The mental picture of the habitat in which it had been accustomed to live

Falconers know that a bird in distress will lure hawks from a long distance, and a tethered pigeon that can be made to flop awkwardly is regularly used as a lure in catching wild hawks. For example, when searching for duck hawks migrating along Atlantic beaches, a falconer often will bury himself in the sand, tie a pigeon to his wrist, and conceal his head under a bushel basket. Upon seeing the pigeon, the hawk swoops down upon it, only to be seized in his turn by the falconer.

It may well be that the little black hen suddenly expressed alarm or helplessness and thereby stimulated the killing instinct that put the touching story to an end.

Ambassadors of Good Will

U P FROM the Gran Chaco they come, ambassadors of good will from our sister republics of South America. Spending the winter on the pampas of Brazil or Argentina, Bolivia or Paraguay, they recognize no international boundaries in their travels.

Over the vast forests of the Amazon they fly during February or early March. Delaying on the llanos of Venezuela, traversing the Caribbean in a single night, visiting in Cuba during late March, they arrive in Florida in early April.

When they appear over the clover fields of central New York in early May, we call them bobolinks; and many an eye dances at their carefree flight and many a heart throbs to their rollicking, banjolike song.

They are *our* bobolinks now, but soon again they will return to the land of their ancestors and become the *chambergos* of Puerto Rico and Cuba, or the beloved *charlatáns* of Brazil and Argentina.

Thus, year after year, they carry an unspoken message to our southern neighbors and return in the spring with their *felicidades*— feathered emissaries of international good will.

Envoy in Formal Black and White

As I sit by my camera in an observation blind planted in a meadow in the New York State Finger Lakes region, waiting for my bobolink to return to his song perch among the daisies and hawkweeds (page 68), I like to think of him as a special envoy sent from my friends in Argentina to bring me cheering news of their well-being, singing me their greetings and dispelling the distance between us.

And when, in late July, he changes his showy black-and-white clothes for a traveling suit of streaked yellow-brown like that of the rest of his family, he will bear my message back with him.

A new realm of international brotherhood lies in an understanding of birds and their migrations. In the words of Shakespeare, "One touch of Nature makes the whole world kin."

If you prefer the mountain forests of Colombia and Ecuador to the savannas of Argentina, let's call upon the red-eyed vireo nesting in the lilac bush by the porch (page 56).

The bobolink had been back in his fields a week before we began to hear the oft-repeated song of this little "preacher bird" with fire in his eye.

All winter he had been enjoying himself in the chocolate plantations of the Cauca Valley, in Colombia, flitting from one *madre de cacao** to another without a thought for his

friends plowing through the snow and ice of a northern winter.

Then, about the last of March, the tropical sun began to arouse his migratory instinct and implant the urge to return to his former home.

Returning Vireo Travels More Slowly

He did not follow the bobolink's short cut across the Caribbean and the West Indies, however, but took a somewhat longer route northwest through Panama and Central America, crossing the Gulf of Mexico to Louisiana from Yucatán.

After reaching the United States he traveled more slowly, for, although he arrived on the Gulf coast more than a week ahead of the bobolinks, he did not make New York until a week after they had taken over the meadows.

The red-eyed vireo is another good-will ambassador, and our greetings to Colombia and Venezuela go with him when he leaves for his winter home in September.

All winter the little hanging basket that he wove in the lilac bush, conspicuous now that the leaves have fallen, will be a vivid reminder of our tiny friend and our good neighbors to the south who are sheltering and feeding him during our long winter.

He will not travel alone, for hosts of our vireos, warblers, and thrushes spend the winter as far south as Colombia. Even the curious yellow-billed cuckoo (page 274), so shy that he seems but a phantom slipping through the undergrowth, will take wing in September and join the migratory hordes that have round-trip tickets to Colombia and Ecuador.

His lunch of hairy caterpillars he will not have to pack and take with him, for all along the route he will find these delicacies shunned by most other birds.

With the bobolink wintering in the Argentine, and the red-eyed vireo and the yellow-billed cuckoo in Colombia, we are led to wonder if there are not equally attractive places along the way.

Most migratory birds return to the land of their ancestors for the winter, and when the wood thrush (page 38) and the yellow-breasted chat (page 65) leave us, they will be well satisfied to winter in southern Mexico, Honduras, Guatemala, Nicaragua, or Costa Rica.

On the other hand, the eastern red-wing (page 85), the red-headed woodpecker (page 9), and the kingfisher (page 290) may be satisfied with our own southern States. Like many another fisherman, however, the king-

---

* Trees shading rows of cacao plants are known by the poetic name, "mother of cacao."

In Silent Appeal, Not Raucous Shout, These Blue Jay Babies "Open Wide"

Foot-loose blue jays are the very synonym of noisy chatter; yet this family carried on so quietly that its presence in the spruce next to the door almost escaped the author. There is plenty of action but no sound in this high-speed shot, which "froze" the parent's wing action at the moment of landing.

fisher can be lured farther and farther from home by bigger and better fish, until he reaches Trinidad or British Guiana.

As early as the last of March, tree swallows (page 31) reach the northern United States, while insects are still scarce. Indeed, during cold spells they eke out their existence with bayberries, which scarcely seem appropriate for swallows.

They come early, nearly a month ahead of other species of swallows, because they winter in Florida and even farther north, while the barn swallows (pages 4 and 30) go skimming over the West Indies and the Caribbean Sea bound for Brazil.

A Whirling Tornado of Swallows

It is a marvelous sight to watch 10,000 tree swallows go to roost in the marshes of the St. Johns River, in Florida. All day they skim over the river and dart over the saw grass in scattered formations; but as dusk approaches they all head for a common roosting place in the marsh.

Round and round the huge flock whirls, forming a gigantic vortex which from a distance resembles a cloud of smoke, as if the marsh might be on fire.

The longer they swirl the denser becomes the cloud, and for a few moments, as they are descending into the marsh, it resembles the funnel of a tornado. Gradually it changes to a wisp of smoke and then vanishes as the swallows settle to their perches.

If one returns at daybreak expecting to see the performance reversed, one will be greatly disappointed, for the morning awakening is much less spectacular. A few birds at a time rise and scatter to their feeding grounds. Nearly an hour elapses before swallows are skimming all over the marsh, and at no time can one imagine the vast convocation of the night before.

Indeed, after having viewed this pageant, one is almost ready to believe, as intelligent persons apparently did in the 18th century, that swallows throw themselves into the mud and sleep all winter.

In 1768, for example, Boswell wrote in his *Life of Johnson:* "He (Johnson) seemed pleased to talk of natural philosophy. That woodcocks fly over the northern countries is proved, because they have been observed at sea. Swallows certainly sleep all the winter. A number of them conglobulate together, by flying round and round and then all in a heap throw themselves under the water, and lie in the bed of a river."

Tiny Travelers Fly Thousands of Miles

After watching the behavior of the swallows on the St. Johns marshes, I could almost have written this myself.

So fleet of wing and so graceful in the air are the swallows, however, that we accept their lengthy migrations without wonderment, surprised only that any should prefer to stay in the United States during the winter when they

99

⌃ Chickadee Comes in for a Landing

Its claws extended to grasp the edge of the feeding tray, this chickadee is caught by high-speed flash as it prepares to alight. Rounded wing and strong rudimentary first primary would seem to make use of the alula unnecessary (pages 7, 25, and 39). Band on leg facilitates migration studies.

⌄ "Triple Play" in the Cardinal World

The photographer operated the camera, four feet from this scene, by remote control. The female bird showed no fear of its presence, but the male made his trips to the nest as brief as possible and passed food to his mate for final distribution whenever he found her at hand.

Ralph E. Lawrence

could so easily set their wings for that romantic land to the south.

But when we contemplate the tiny warblers, vireos, and hummingbirds, with their small wings and fragile bodies, that unfalteringly make the 7-10,000-mile trip each year, we marvel at their endurance and their love of home.

Happily for us in the United States, however, all birds are not migratory, and some bits of life and color remain to cheer us, even in our snowbound north. Lucky we are if one of the permanent residents is an eastern cardinal (frontispiece and pages 88 and 89), popularly known as the Kentucky cardinal.

We think of cardinals as belonging to the southern States and Mexico, but of recent years they have been increasing, and the younger birds have been pressing northward to occupy areas where our fathers never saw them.

Indeed, in the Finger Lakes region, cardinals have become almost as common in our gardens as scarlet tanagers and indigo buntings. It may be that similar invasions have occurred in the past, but if so the pioneering individuals left no progeny.

Today, feeding the winter birds has become such a popular pastime that it is much easier for southern birds to extend their ranges northward.

The cardinal is a prolific species, regularly laying three or four eggs to a clutch and having two or three broods a year. Thus, with fair success in protecting their eggs from red squirrels and their youngsters from cats, they should soon become established in most of the northern United States and southern Canada.

Another beautiful invader from Dixie is the the golden-yellow prothonotary warbler (page 58). A small colony of these dazzling southerners has come to live along Oak Orchard Creek, west of Rochester, New York. Each spring they return from their winter sojourn in Central America, and their number has increased to seven or eight pairs.

Cars Kill Many a Careless Bird

While the prothonotary warbler and the cardinal have been increasing during recent years, another attractive bird, the red-headed woodpecker (page 9) varies in abundance and has become less common in the East. There are still places in the Mississippi Valley where it is a familiar bird.

In some places it is one of the birds most commonly killed by automobiles along the highways, because it delights in perching on fence posts or telegraph poles and flying down for grasshoppers stirred up by passing cars. Whether this alone can account for its increasing scarcity is as yet unknown.

The drainage of marshes has caused birds such as the bitterns and rails to become rare in many localities where they once were common. But the red-winged blackbird, or redwing, as it is also known (page 85), which ordinarily nests in marshes, takes to hayfields or meadows when swamps disappear. There it fraternizes with bobolinks and meadowlarks, weaving its hanging basket in weeds.

Birds of Old and New World Origin Mingle in Our Melting Pot

North America has two major groups of bird families, one having its origin in the Old World and one in South or Central America. These birds, unlike the starling and English sparrow, came to this continent gradually and of their own free will, like the American Indians and later the white men, and they have been here so long we call them native species.

Indeed, most of them are native, for after many generations of separation from their forebears they have developed characteristics all their own. Our friendly little black-capped chickadee, for instance, is almost the exact counterpart of the European marsh tit; yet it is sufficiently different to be separated as a distinct species.

There seems to be little question that chickadees invaded this country several million years ago—prior to the Ice Age—by way of Siberia and Alaska, when this area was much more temperate than it is today.

That their invasion was more recent than that of other Old World families is indicated by the fact that only 42 of some 300 known species and subspecies belonging to the chickadee family are found in North America, and none of these has yet extended its range south of Mexico.

On the other hand, fully a quarter of the 400 varieties of crows and jays, another bird family of Old World origin, are now found in the Western Hemisphere, and some jays have invaded South America all the way to Argentina. The same is true of the woodpeckers, cuckoos, thrushes, and sparrows.

I don't suppose we shall ever be able to guess the order of their arrival. But for the most part we are glad they came. We are glad, too, that they now live peaceably with other birds which, though today considered native species, obviously came to us from tropical America, such as the hummingbirds, warblers, vireos, mockingbirds, and the New World orioles and flycatchers.

Our birds, like the American people, came from a variety of sources and have learned to play the game of life amicably together, each species filling a certain niche no longer claimed by others.

101 Photographed near Sacramento, California

⋏ Male Blue Grosbeak Gaily Clad

The blue grosbeak is found throughout the southern United States. It frequents the borders of woods and bushy places. Here a **California Blue Grosbeak** nests in a thicket of pigweed in the lower Sacramento. Both the female and the young are a sober brown.

⋎ Chipping Sparrow Prefers Bed of Roses

She built in a rambler vine, safe from cats and other pouncing foes. The **Eastern Chipping Sparrow,** sometimes called the hairbird, always lines her nest with horsehair. But the automobile age has left its mark; the lining is thin and straws show through.

Photographed near Ithaca, New York

← Mrs. Goldfinch Guards a Stolen Treasure

This pensive-looking female has carried off a piece of cotton to use as a substitute for thistledown in lining her nest. Most **Eastern Goldfinch** homes are built in the lower branches of shade trees; some are found in bushes, or on cornstalks, goldenrod, and thistles. Goldfinches, widely distributed, nest later than most birds. July and August are the preferred months.

↓ 14-carat Gold in Coat and Disposition

The male **Eastern Goldfinch** helps raise the young and brings food to his mate while she is preoccupied with incubation duties. These hungry fledglings are about to dine on seeds regurgitated from father's crop. Bright yellow feathers and black cap are worn only by the male.

102

Photographed near Ithaca, New York

↑ **Mother Arrives for a
Stint of Baby Sitting**

Youngsters, not yet aware of their
parent's silent approach, seem intent
on examining a strange new world.
Soon, however, mouths will be
stretched wide as mother **Eastern
Goldfinch** feeds them a cereal of
cracked weed seeds. This nest
occupies a honeysuckle bush on the
Cornell University campus.

**"See, Ma? I Can →
Do It Too!"**

To shade her offspring from hot
sunlight, the female **Eastern Goldfinch** stands on the nest with wings
partly spread. A venturesome
daughter, seeing how mother does
it, strikes a similar pose. Rapid
breathing through open mouths
helps them cool off.

103

Photographed near Ithaca, New York

Sunflower Seeds Lure Evening Grosbeaks (Left), Photographed Through a Window by Flash Exposure

Eastern Evening Grosbeak is a misnomer, the bird having been mistakenly described as a twilight singer. Upper right: The female evening grosbeak is less colorfully garbed than the male (left). **White-throated Sparrow** (lower right) hides its nest so cunningly that it virtually defies detection.

Baby Sparrows Demand Attention →

Both parents must make repeated visits with insects to satisfy their fast-growing young. Nests of the **White-crowned Sparrows** are found in willow bogs at 10,000-foot altitude in the Rockies and nearly at sea level in Hudsonian spruce forest of northern Canada. Ants, caterpillars, beetles, grasshoppers, and spiders are on the "formula" for these babies. While these birds also eat seeds and take bites out of small fruits, their destruction of insect pests outweighs their depredations on profitable crops. Looking at bunches of spoiled grapes, the grower may forget the sparrows' services.

Photographed near Churchill, Manitoba   © National Geographic Society

Photographed by Alfred M. Bailey and Robert J. Niedrach
in Colorado High Country

105

Where East and West Meet

←

East is East and West is West, but Kipling was not speaking for the bird world when he claimed that "never the twain shall meet." At Churchill two races of the **White-crowned Sparrow** have met, as is proved by the many intermediates like the fine fellow at left. Tiny white feathers among the black ones in front of the eye indicate a western Gambel's sparrow in his family tree. One of the first American sparrows to win scientific recognition, the white-crowned sparrow was described in 1772.

Photographed near Ithaca, New York

Is This Towhee Surprised! No Mouths to Feed; the Family Is Full

Towhee, chewink, joree, or ground robin, as it is variously called, is familiar in brushy gardens. This is the **Red-eyed Towhee** (male) of eastern United States and the South in winter. Resident Florida towhees have white eyes; those of Alabama and central Georgia, yellowish.

← A Different Story Here; Noisy Young Demand Food

Mountain and desert thickets are favorite haunts of the **Green-tailed Towhee** (left), a western bird. It scratches for a livelihood among the bushes, often running from intruders instead of taking wing. The nest is built in low shrubs or on the ground.

This bird, having fed her insect catch to the young, examines the nest for harmful mites or bird lice.

The green-tail's unusual color pattern led ornithologists to give it a separate generic name (*Oberholseria*) differing from that of the other towhees.

Photographed in Estes Park, Colorado

Junior's Hunger Cry Goes Unheeded as a Towhee Parent Scouts for Danger

Ten spotted towhee subspecies, similar in appearance and habit, are found in western North America. This representative of the family is a **Spurred Towhee,** photographed by the author in Mexico during a National Geographic Society ornithological expedition. Its summer range extends from Durango to Wyoming.

A Mexican Tourist →
Visits the
Grand Canyon

Bird watchers, viewing a crossbill for the first time, often assume that its beak is deformed. Nature, however, designed the powerful curved mandibles to remove scales from pine cones, the seeds of which are the bird's principal food.

A bird bath near the Grand Canyon's Nature Workshop attracted this **Mexican Red Crossbill.** It nests in pine-forested mountains in Mexico and Guatemala. Fond of wandering, it frequently visits the southwestern States. North America counts five varieties of the red crossbill, among them this Mexican good neighbor.

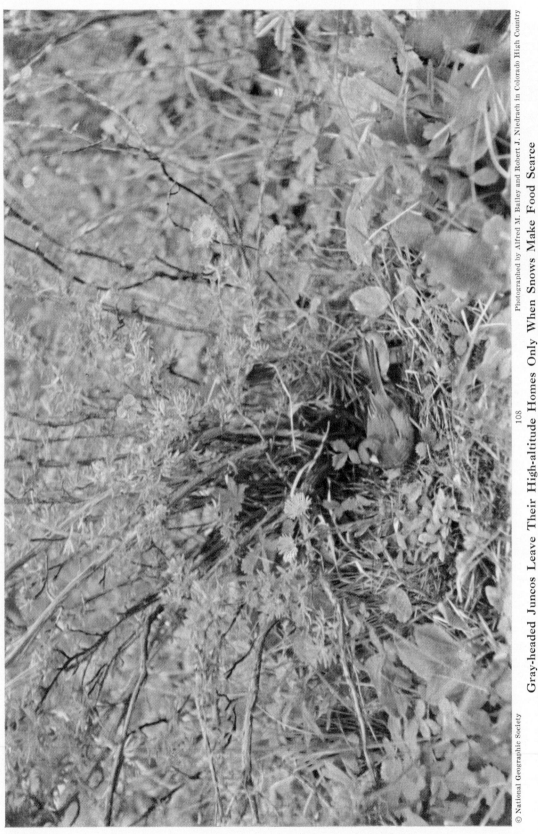

108

Photographed by Alfred M. Bailey and Robert J. Niedrach in Colorado High Country

Gray-headed Juncos Leave Their High-altitude Homes Only When Snows Make Food Scarce

Their nests usually are well hidden near the base of a wiry mountain plant, such as the cinquefoil above. When seeking food at lower levels in winter, large numbers of **Gray-headed Juncos** appear about cabins and wilderness camps. Several other junco varieties are found in the Colorado high country in winter.

"I'm Hungry!" Youth's Eternal Complaint Greets a Song Sparrow

In gardens and shrubbery the song sparrow responds to the warm sun with cheerful and melodious voice. So adaptable is it that 26 different races are recognized, among them this **Eastern Song Sparrow.**

Nesting time finds the male defending the "territory" while his mate builds their home. Later he brings food to the nest while the female sits on the eggs.

Plumage is alike in both sexes. The male determines the sex of a strange song sparrow by challenging it to a fight. If the newcomer is a male, it flees; if a female, it sits still and calls "Eee-eee-eee!"

© National Geographic Society 109 Photographed in La Tabatière, Quebec

Photographed near Ithaca, New York

"Foxy" Believes in Air Conditioning

With open bill and fluffed feathers, this **Eastern Fox Sparrow** endeavors to keep cool on a hot June day in Quebec. Chill weather finds it migrating to southern United States. Noticing the fox sparrow's habit of scratching among leaves, children coined a nickname, "brown digger." Sixteen North American varieties of the bird are recognized. Its plumage is brighter, its song more brilliant than that of the smaller song sparrow.

110 Photographed near Ithaca, New York

Pussy-willow Time Sends the Tree Sparrow North to His Hudson Bay Home

All winter the hedgerows of the northern United States tinkle with the cheerful notes of this gay little **Eastern Tree Sparrow.** Then in late March or early April he journeys north and builds with his mate a feather-lined nest in the base of a dwarf willow or spruce in the solitudes of timber line.

111 Photographed near Churchill, Manitoba

ʌ   **Wild Flowers Bloom in a Tree Sparrow's Dooryard**

Fond of weed seeds, the **Tree Sparrow** is rated a valuable ally of the farmer. This female awaits the hatching of her young near Churchill on Canada's Hudson Bay. Incubation requires two weeks. Tiny flowers are those of the dwarf andromeda.

v   **Domed Nest on Forest Floor Hides a Southern Family**

The **Pine-woods Sparrow** inhabits woodland areas of southern Georgia and Florida, cleverly concealing its home in the forest's wire-grass carpet. Preferring the ground, it seldom flies. A near relative, Bachman's sparrow, is found from Georgia to southern Ohio.

Photographed by S. A. Grimes near Jacksonville, Florida

112

Photographed in Lower Souris Refuge, North Dakota

↑　　A Concert Tenor Records
His Favorite Song

↓　　This Hardy Explorer Roams
Arctic Tundras

Birds like to be conspicuous when singing. Long-spurs, for instance, flutter high in the air to pour forth their melody if unable to find a suitable perch. This obliging artist, a **Chestnut-collared Longspur,** is a north-central prairie dweller.

Lapland Longspur builds a secluded nest in the tangled roots of dwarf rhododendrons and crowberries. Siberia, Lapland, and Arctic America know its tinkling summer song. It migrates in great numbers through the central States to Texas.

Photographed near Churchill, Manitoba

Birds of Timberline and Tundra

IT IS no secret today that during the war years the United States Government, co-operating in hemisphere defense, built an enormous airfield and set up an Army post at Churchill, Manitoba, a thousand miles north of Winnipeg on the shores of Hudson Bay.

It is not a thousand miles as the bomber flies, but it is at least that distance as the bulldozers and 3,500 workmen had to travel on the little one-track railroad through spruce forest, muskeg, and barrens to the mouth of the Churchill River.

Now the base is operated by the Royal Canadian Air Force and is used jointly by the U. S. Air Force and the U. S. Army for cold-weather training.

Back in 1944, however, it was such a tight secret that neither the Canadian Government nor the United States War Department would divulge a word in response to my inquiries about working at Churchill with cameras and binoculars in behalf of the National Geographic Society. Indeed, had it not been for a casual mention of a "restricted area" in a letter from the Hudson's Bay Company, I should never have guessed that permits were necessary.

As we approached Churchill, I became more and more uneasy as to the significance of a "restricted area" and how it might affect our work. When we stepped from the train and beheld an array of uniforms, my heart sank.

"I am Major Wilkins, in charge of the post here, and I have orders to expedite your work for the National Geographic Society to the best of my ability."

With these few direct words the handsome young officer who greeted us dispensed so much sunshine that I must have grasped his hand like an old friend.

"If you will come with me in my car," Major Wilkins added, "I will show you what you must not photograph and then I will give you the necessary permits to enter the re-stricted area."

Only the Birds Are Unchanged

A car at Churchill! There was no road a quarter of a mile long when I studied birds at Churchill 10 years before.

A broad gravel road led from the townsite three miles straight through the Barren Grounds to the edge of the timber, and then two miles east to the ridge overlooking Hudson Bay, with extensions leading as far again into the spruce forest. The area over which I had trudged so laboriously 10 years before was now covered in a few minutes.

We whipped around the post, sped down the mile-long airstrip, inspected the hangars and a modern hospital, had a bit of refreshment at the Officers' Club, and were back at the townsite in less time than I formerly spent in hiking to the area where I wished to work.

Still more auspicious was the sight of cur-lews and phalaropes, sandpipers and plovers all along the roadside, as if nothing had happened to their nesting grounds, which they too had traveled thousands of miles to find.

The Army's plans had been accomplished. The workmen had left, save for a maintenance crew; the airport itself was no longer active; and the wildlife of the country had taken the incident in its stride. Caribou left their hoof-prints in the sand at the roadside, wild geese swung low over the landing strips, and loons called from the ponds.

All seemed too good to be true, especially when we discovered that Mr. George Reid, proprietor of the little hotel, had a car in which he offered to taxi us each morning with our cameras and blinds to whatever spot we wished and to call for us at the end of the day.

Think of driving a car within sight of a nesting Hudsonian curlew, stilt sandpiper, or Harris's sparrow!

Railroad a Godsend to Naturalists

Only a few years ago the eggs of Harris's sparrow were entirely unknown and the nests of the other species had seldom been seen. If a naturalist wished to study these birds during their nesting season in June, he had to spend the winter with the Eskimos to be on the ground the following spring.

When in 1931, after 14 years of persistent labor, the Canadian Government completed the railroad to Churchill, it was considered a godsend by ornithologists interested in Arc-tic birds. It mattered not that the railroad was built to open up a shorter route to Liver-pool for the wheat crop of the Canadian prairies and that a huge wheat elevator had been erected at the mouth of the river. To them it was the open sesame to a new fauna.

Naturalists at last could get to the nesting ground of the golden plover, the stilt sand-piper, the parasitic jaeger, the Hudsonian cur-lew, and Harris's sparrow with a minimum of effort. They might have to walk only 5 or 10 miles to find these birds. And now we were driving right up within a stone's throw of many of them.

Of course, Churchill is not in the real Arctic; it lies 500 miles south of the Arctic Circle. But it was near enough for our work.

As one travels northward from Winnipeg and The Pas, one sees what are sometimes locally called the False Barrens, or the Little Barrens, 65 miles before one reaches Hudson Bay. An extensive area of spruce forest intervenes. Then the train finally leaves the last spruce behind and for some three miles chugs across the real Barren Grounds and into the station at Churchill.

The vegetation proclaims that this is near the real Arctic. Only creeping birches and willows and low, scrubby laurels lift their heads above the densely packed mosses and lichens that cover the rocks for miles.

But even here the Arctic is only beginning. Snow buntings, ruddy turnstones, black-bellied plovers, snowy owls, and whistling swans are not satisfied with these borderline conditions. They continue their sure flight on to the real North where thousands of miles of unbroken tundra make more of an appeal.

The borderline conditions, however, make for the greatest concentration of bird life and have made Churchill famous among ornithologists the world over. Many Arctic birds extend their ranges south to the border of trees, and some Hudsonian species extend theirs northward to the Barren Grounds.

Thus, within easy walking distance, one finds nesting such birds as the lesser yellowlegs, northern shrike, Bonaparte's gull, rusty blackbird, and black-poll warbler, all of which range to the southward, and others, such as the willow ptarmigan, golden plover, parasitic jaeger, and Pacific loon, which are commoner much farther north.

It was June 8 when my son David and I arrived. Sledges, so necessary during the long winter months, were now stacked against the frame houses, and the dogs, the trappers' proudest possession, were staked out for the summer where they would receive plenty of water and a generous chunk of whale meat every other day.

This was the season for whales—the white belugas that follow the fish up the river at high tide. When they come up momentarily for air, they look not unlike the icebergs among which they sport.

Whole Town Meets the Train

The citizens of Churchill are friendly people. They were interested in what we were doing and were always eager to be helpful. From all walks of life and from all parts of the country they had come, and all seemed to like the place and to have no immediate plans for leaving.

The town itself is still primitive in most respects. The winters are long and severe, the summers short and plagued with insects. Entertainments are scarce and diversions few except for the arrival of the train, which the whole town turns out to meet. Yet the people are well satisfied with their lot and, like the birds that frequent the townsite, they take things as they find them.

The Hoyt's horned larks trot along the streets; Gambel's sparrows and Lapland longspurs nest by the back doors; semipalmated plovers lay eggs almost anywhere on exposed patches of gravel, and no one knows why they come to Churchill each June to raise families (pages 20, 112, and 206).

Certainly on their migrations they see thousands of places where food is just as abundant, where natural enemies are no more numerous, and where their offspring would stand as good a chance of surviving.

Only Hardy Plants Survive

Early June shows little color on the tundra. The flowers that inundate the landscape later are still sleeping, their roots frozen in the ice a few inches below the moss. Indeed, ice never melts more than some 14 inches except in spots, and it takes a hardy plant to bloom and mature seeds under such conditions.

The grays and browns, the lavenders and golden greens of the mosses and lichens, however, have a charm that is never eclipsed even by the pinks, yellows, and purples that follow in such profusion in late June. At the height of the flowering season there remains a conservatism to the colors quite in keeping with the austere environment and not at all comparable to the garish hawkweeds, mustards, and goldenrods of more southern latitudes.

The evening was pleasant as we sat on the high ridge of Pre-Cambrian rock overlooking the bay. It was 9 o'clock, but more than two hours still remained before the sun would drop below the horizon, and then for only a couple of hours.

The ice had gone out of the river unusually early, clearing a space for several miles along the shore, but the open water was still filled with shimmering bergs that threw pale-green or rosy-pink reflections across the deep blue of the bay. Beyond stretched the unbroken ice toward Southampton Island, more than 400 miles to the north.

Off to the northeast one could see on the horizon misty cliffs which our maps told us were not there. The illusion was as real as the rocks on which we were sitting, so fallible is the human eye in the presence of a mirage.

"Go Back," Warns a Brusque Voice

"Go back, go back, go back," came a voice from behind a huge boulder. Then, with a loud cackle, the author of the sound flew into the air to make himself more conspicuous.

Landing about 50 feet from us, he revealed

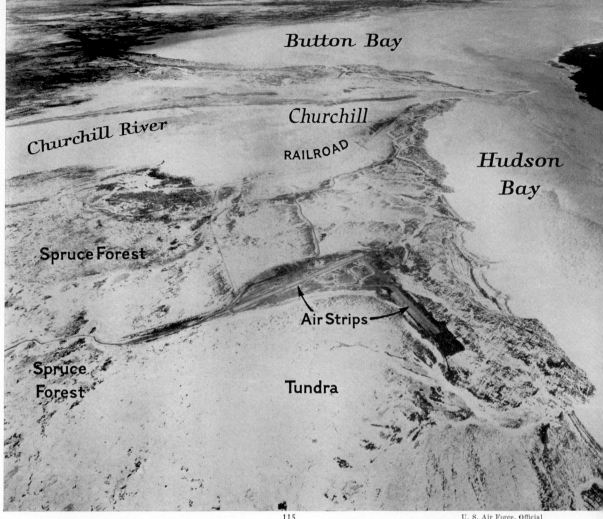

Button Bay

Churchill River

Churchill

RAILROAD

Hudson Bay

Spruce Forest

Air Strips

Spruce Forest

Tundra

 U. S. Air Force, Official

Churchill, Bird Paradise in Summer, Lies Grim and Forbidding under Winter Snow

Most of the photographs included in this chapter and many color plates of shore birds and northern nesting species were made in the area between the air strips and the Churchill River. A spruce forest stretches south of the town. Barren Grounds and Hudson Bay lie to the north (right).

himself as a willow ptarmigan, resplendent in the snow-white body plumage and chestnut-brown head and shoulders of the male in the breeding season (page 116). We had evidently seated ourselves in his territory and he was complaining in his vociferous fashion.

Somewhere within a hundred yards there must be a protectively colored female sitting on a dozen strikingly beautiful eggs—deep buff with strong black markings (pages 117 and 195). It would be David's job to find that nest and mine to make color photographs, for we had come these thousands of miles, under the auspices of the National Geographic Society, for the purpose of bringing back natural-color studies of the birds of timberline and tundra.

Much would have to be crowded into the three remaining weeks of June—tramping the tundra, wading the sloughs, searching the stunted spruces for the nests of those Arctic and Hudsonian birds which we in the United States know as transients for a few brief days

in spring and fall, or as hardy winter visitors. Among them are some of the world's greatest travelers.

Birds Fooled by "Go-awayster"

One gains considerable familiarity with birds by watching them through binoculars, but studying birds at arm's length gives real insight into their behavior. This is best accomplished from observation blinds set up near their nests, and for successful photography this procedure is essential.

Hence, strenuous but fascinating days lay ahead of us, with mile after mile of tundra to be covered before we could even locate a nesting pair of stilt sandpipers or golden plovers, to say nothing of the many other species (pages 207 and 211).

Next step would be to watch them from concealment until they should unwittingly give up the secret of their nests; then to set up a blind so made and so placed that it would not disturb them.

In Spring Dark Feathers Begin to Replace the Willow Ptarmigan's Winter White

Always wearing a cloak of invisibility, this bird of the North is all white in winter except for its black tail; in spring it blends with patches of snow and in summer it matches the tundra. Natives and Arctic animals prize the ptarmigan for food. Its winter bed is a snowbank.

The following day, perhaps, we could move it closer to the nest until it finally would stand within six feet of the birds' home; then we would have only to wait for a day of sunshine so that the colors would register accurately on the film.

Finally the day comes. I crawl into the low blind with the cameras, one for stills and one for motion pictures, and when all is in readiness David walks conspicuously away. If all goes well, the bird returns within 30 minutes, well satisfied that there is no one around, for he cannot count and is fooled by the disappearance of the "go-awayster."

However, he may not like the looks of that great eye, the lens of the camera, staring at his eggs; or he may not like the click of the shutter. Indeed, the reactions of no two birds are exactly alike, and the uncertainties of the game of life-history studies, with the fascination of watching unusual birds at such close range, give one all the excitement of a major sport. If "our team wins"—well, herewith are a few of the trophies.

In a small lake southeast of Churchill is a large boulder from which the frost has chipped a rectangular block, leaving a somewhat protected ledge that makes a suitable site for the nest of a herring gull (page 258).

I have seen herring gulls nesting on similar boulders in some of our Adirondack lakes. Between the Adirondacks and Churchill there must be thousands of such rocks. But every year a pair of herring gulls passes them all by, bound for the one in Isabelle Lake at Churchill. Ten years before, when I made my first studies of birds at Churchill, the rock was occupied, as it has been every year since.

Ten years before, too, I photographed a Pacific loon that was nesting at the end of a little peninsula jutting out into a near-by lake. The site was somewhat unusual, for all the other loons' nests of that region were on small islands where they were safer.

Loons Cling to Old Nest Sites

Imagine my surprise and pleasure, on revisiting the little peninsula after a decade, to find a loon's nest within five feet of the old site. The former home was now untenable,

In Manitoba a Mother Waits for Sextuplets or More to Hatch

A willow ptarmigan's family usually varies from 7 to 10, but as many as 17 eggs have been found in a single nest. The eggs are a rich buff with dark-brown markings which change with time to tan and black. Gulls often attempt to steal the eggs.

as the level of the lake had dropped several inches; so the bird, which ordinarily laid its eggs on the shore a few inches above the water without much pretense of a nest, had built up a platform of mud above the action of the small waves and was sitting with no cover at all about it (pages 125 and 126).

Still another loon, nesting on an island but similarly affected by the lowering of the lake level, had worn a channel like that of a musk-rat to its nest, which was now several feet from the present shore line.

Loons are practically helpless on land, because their legs are placed so far back, but they can propel themselves in very shallow water by a froglike jumping motion and a final leap to the nest. Rather than desert its chosen nesting site of the previous years, this loon had worn the channel and clung to the old site in spite of its clumsiness and the attendant dangers.

On an island in Rosabelle Lake we discovered about 20 pairs of arctic terns nesting (page 257). Here I found a dead tern with a band on its leg bearing the number 36-339172 and the statement, "Notify the Biological Survey, Washington, D. C."

I sent the band to my friend Frederick C. Lincoln, who at the time had charge of all the cooperative birdbanding work and was later Assistant to the Director of the Fish and Wildlife Service. He found that the bird was banded as a nestling at Churchill, perhaps on the same island, by Mr. Albert L. Wilk, of Camrose, Alberta, on July 10, 1937.

In the meantime, the bird had made seven round trips to the Antarctic by way of Europe and Africa. Each trip involved some 22,000 miles, making a total of 154,000 miles.

Odyssey of the Golden Plover

Just why this little tern could not be satisfied with the coast of Maine or Labrador, Iceland or Scotland, but had to travel possibly an extra 2,000 miles to Churchill; just why it could not migrate along the east coast of America instead of crossing the ocean before traveling south—these are mysteries that scientists have not yet satisfactorily explained.

The golden plovers, whose great speckled

20-20 Vision Is Not Enough to Reveal Downy Snipe at First Glance

Brown-streaked plumage serves as camouflage for Wilson's snipe in the grassy marsh or tundra where she nests. The two babies, flecked with dark brown and gray, look like bits of dead, moldy moss. Formerly considered game birds, Wilson's snipe were not sufficiently prolific to stand the hunting pressure. Since their removal from the game list, they have increased slightly. They nest from the northern United States to the edge of the Barren Grounds.

eggs we found in the tundra moss about the middle of June, leave Churchill in August and head eastward over James Bay and across the Labrador peninsula to Nova Scotia or Newfoundland. Here they grow very fat on the abundant "curlew berries" (crowberries) until they feel ready for the trip south.

Twenty-four hundred miles over the Atlantic they fly; over Bermuda, over the mangrove swamps of the coast of Venezuela, never stopping until they reach the lowlands of the Orinoco River.

Here again they rest for a while before taking the next big jump over 2,000 miles of Amazonian jungle to southern Brazil and northern Argentina.

Several months pass before they reach southern Argentina, so it is time to start northward again almost as soon as they arrive.

But they do not retrace their flight. Instead, they cross the high Andes of Peru and cut across one corner of the Pacific to the highlands of Honduras.

Then, when the urge to move again strikes them, they cross the Gulf of Mexico and enter the United States on their northward journey through eastern Texas and western Louisiana. It is March when they arrive here, and they are still in their winter plumage with gray breasts instead of black.

Slowly they journey up the Mississippi Valley, acquiring new black feathers on their underparts, and it is mid-April when they arrive in the vicinity of St. Louis.

There is no need of reaching Churchill before the first of June, so they loiter on their way, frequenting burned pastures and plowed fields wherever food is abundant. Thus, when they finally reach the breeding grounds, they are in their lustrous black, white, and gold liveries (page 207).

The golden plover is not a common bird at Churchill. In the 15 square miles of tundra where we did most of our hunting we located only six pairs, and these birds restricted their activities to patches of dry, moss-covered tundra where the grays, yellows, and blacks of the lichens made them very inconspicuous.

As with the herring gull, the loons, and the arctic terns, we found their nests not far from the spots that had been occupied by plovers 10 years before. The passage of 10 years, the passage of a thousand years, perhaps, produces little change in a land where man has not interfered with the balance of Nature.

The millions of miles traversed by golden plovers on their migrations, with the attendant

Six Inches of "Sandpeep" Cover a Large Nest

Smallest of shore birds, the least sandpiper is sometimes mistaken for its cousin, the semipalmated sandpiper (page 211). It breeds from northwestern Alaska to Newfoundland and is a familiar figure along the Atlantic coast. It is often observed as it trots along the shore, probing in the ooze for midge larvae and the like. Sometimes it will allow one to approach within a few feet without taking alarm.

A Black Tern's "Houseboat" on a Pond near Lake Ontario

This tern has built a floating nest of reeds and grasses. Great numbers of these birds appear in inland marshes from central Alaska to California, and as far east as central New York. Wintering off the coast of the Republic of Colombia, the bird's feathers are "winter white." Some of these white feathers still show, even though this photograph was made in June in New York. Later they will be replaced by the black feathers which give the bird its name.

Two Churchill Neighbors, a Snow Bunting (Right) and Lapland Longspur

Both breed near the top of the world, the snow bunting laying its eggs as far north as land is found. In migration or on winter feeding grounds the Lapland longspur often associates with this bunting.

hazards, serve to thin their ranks so that the suitable nesting spots never become over-populated; yet they continue to be occupied, generation after generation.

Not far from the tern island we found a little black-poll warbler nesting in a stunted spruce (page 63). It, too, must be conceded one of the world's great travelers, for although it was not banded and we cannot trace the exact route that it followed, we know that no black-poll spends the winter north of Venezuela.

Mighty Mite Flies 10,000 Miles Yearly

This little mite of a bird, therefore, weigh-ing less than an ounce, must have traveled at least 10,000 miles from the time it left Churchill the year before. Surely gasoline is not the last word in motor fuel.

Thus, as we hiked about the tundra and paid our respects to plover, curlew, and sand-piper, many of which winter in South America, we felt that we had come to a veritable ex-plorers' club and that we were the merest novices in the sport of touring. Not until we have our individual planes and hop from Churchill to Rio de Janeiro and Timbuktu can we qualify with these feathered denizens of the Barren Grounds.

There were, of course, birds like the ptarmi-gan that claim Churchill for their permanent home. These birds do not migrate more than

a few miles to find the buds of willows and birches projecting above the snow.

Others, like the tree sparrows (pages 110 and 111) that we found building feather-lined homes in bases of willows or little spruces, wander southward only as far as the northern United States. Indeed, with them we felt much at home, for every winter they come to our window for seeds, and when we put bands on their legs we find the same ones returning year after year.

I don't suppose any of the tree sparrows wintering at Ithaca actually nest at Churchill, but it gave us a friendly feeling to see them—like running across a prep school roommate in some unlikely spot thousands of miles from home.

Ubiquitous Starlings Discover Churchill

When Percy A. Taverner and George M. Sutton published a list of the birds of Churchill in 1935, they included 146 species which had been recorded from that area up to and in-cluding their visit. Of these, fewer than 100 are of regular occurrence, and the rest are more or less accidental.

Every year a few individuals of species found to the southward overshoot their migra-tion schedule and arrive at timberline, where they do not belong. If a careful observer lived at Churchill long enough, he could, with-out doubt, double the number on the list,

Like Ulysses, the Sanderling "Cannot Rest from Travel"

This migrant, here shown in fall plumage, nests in the northern Arctic islands. In early autumn it starts the wanderings which take it to the beaches on both the South African and Patagonian sides of the world. Its annual odyssey may include Australia and the Polynesian islands.

although some species might never be recorded a second time.

Nearly every ornithologist who visits Churchill adds one or two birds, and our trip was no exception. We added seven to the list, the most interesting, but also regrettable, perhaps, being the starling, four of which showed up on June 12.

By some accident their number was reduced to three in two days, and one of the survivors had lost its tail.

Starlings (page 55) were first introduced into North America from England in 1890 in Central Park, New York City, and have proved themselves so adaptable and so prolific that they are now the commonest bird in most places east of the Rockies. However, I believe this was the first record of their appearance so far north in the New World.

Other birds not on the Taverner-Sutton list that were seen at least once during our three weeks' stay were the red-wing, cowbird, song sparrow, house wren, alder flycatcher, and barn swallow, all common birds a few hundred miles farther south.

The robin, which was only an occasional bird ten years ago, had become in the meantime a very common species in the spruces at timberline, and a number of pairs were nesting about the town.

Indeed, the only species which seemed to be much less abundant was the ptarmigan, and it always has had its ups and downs. Apparently in 1944 it was again near the bottom of the cycle, for we saw fewer than 20 birds and found only two nests.

The Hudsonian curlews (page 214), once listed as on the downgrade, have again become abundant, and their tremulous calls could be heard in all directions.

As we tramped the tundra we usually had one or more pairs in noisy attendance, for it is their custom to fly toward an intruder, scolding loudly, and to escort him beyond the borders of what they consider their territory.

To find a curlew's nest, therefore, one has to conceal oneself beyond this area, wait for the disturbance to die out, and watch the birds through binoculars. Usually within an hour the curlew would return to its eggs. Since there are few landmarks on the tundra, however, it was even then difficult to walk to the exact spot where the bird had disappeared.

Honkers at Home

The smaller shore birds, like the northern phalaropes, stilt sandpipers, red-backed sandpipers, and dowitchers, usually flew from their eggs 40 or 50 feet ahead of us. But even when the approximate spot was noted, it was often difficult to locate their nests, so protectively colored are their eggs.

A Dive Bomber Lands in a Treetop

Bonaparte's gull frequently "dive-bombed" the author from behind, though it rarely struck with its bill. This bird is a great destroyer of insects, which it gathers in the air and on the marshes and prairies. It ranges from Alaska to the Bahamas, around the Gulf coast to Texas and Yucatán, and winters from Washington to central Mexico. It is small for a gull, and in the air it flies lightly with the grace of a tern. Its marine diet consists principally of crustaceans and marine worms (page 124).

Ptarmigan, on the other hand, would let one almost step on them before leaving, and, since the females are invisible at five or six paces (pages 195 and 196), their nests were exceedingly hard to find.

To one familiar with wild geese only as the conspicuous wedge of migrating birds during spring and fall, their behavior on their nesting grounds may be a surprise.

If you take no notice of the old gander standing in the shallow water at the edge of a pond, he will honk wildly to attract your attention.

Then you may walk within twenty feet of his mate, flattened on her island nest with her long neck and head pressed to the ground, and not ever see her, though the short brown sedges offer little concealment. Indeed, she can sneak off the eggs without being observed and then noisily take wing a hundred yards away as if she were just leaving her nest.

The pintail duck sometimes performed the same trick, but most of the waterfowl, of which the old-squaws and red-breasted mergansers were most numerous, merely flopped from their nests at our approach and thus made them easy to find.

Nest of Wary Harris's Sparrow

Nest hunting among the dense dwarf spruces at timberline was really difficult, and we considered ourselves fortunate in finding four nests of Harris's sparrow and one of the northern shrike.

As mentioned above, the eggs of Harris's sparrow had never been described prior to the building of the railroad, and once its completion made it possible to get to timberline during June, a race ensued among rival ornithologists to be the first to find them.

The Harris's sparrow is a fairly common bird in the central United States during winter, and the naturalist Ernest Thompson Seton in 1907 found the nest and young in Last Woods on an expedition from Great Slave Lake to the Barren Grounds. It remained for Dr. George M. Sutton, formerly curator of birds at Cornell, to find the first set of eggs on June 16, 1931, near Churchill.

Since then a number of nests have been found, but the bird is so wary that photography is extremely difficult; our single picture of the bird on its nest gave us more trouble than any other. We spent nearly a week getting the bird accustomed to a blind, and then at the first click of the shutter she left and did not return until I gave up after two hours of waiting (opposite page).

The young shrikes left the nest the middle of June, indicating that nest building must have started in early May, when the ground was still covered with many feet of snow and

Nest-building Gannets Take Time Out to "Neck"

Resembling a mirrored image, they rub bills after tucking some seaweed into the nest. Courtship antics continue even after the birds have become parents.

Hatched nearly bare, gannets develop a thick white or yellowish down. Later, their dark juvenile feathers push out the down, and by the time they are 12 or 13 weeks old they are heavier than adults.

At this age they are abandoned by their parents and, like young petrels, they starve and lose weight for ten days or more before finding their way to the sea, where for a time they lead an exclusively swimming life.

Gannets plunge for fish like animated javelins; nets have trapped them at 14-fathom depths (pages 132-136).

Robert C. Hermes

A Sight Few Human Eyes Have Seen—a Nesting Harris's Sparrow

Although fairly common in central States in the winter when it frequents hedgerows and borders of woods, this secretive bird breeds far in the North, and not until 1931 did a scientist succeed in finding its eggs. Immediately after this photograph was taken, the startled bird fled and did not return, although the author waited two hours (opposite page). Once the bird was known as the mourning sparrow, probably because of the black markings about its head and its plaintive song. Audubon named it Harris's sparrow in honor of his "excellent and constant friend Edward Harris, Esq.," who sent Audubon his first bird specimens. Its nest, eggs, and general behavior resemble that of the white-crowned sparrow (page 105).

the temperature was still far below freezing. Indeed, there were still many snowdrifts among the spruces when the young birds left home, and we had a few snow flurries as late as June 27.

The shrikes disliked our close approach to their nest, which was located in the top of one of the taller spruces about 15 feet from the ground (page 54). When David climbed to the nest, they attacked him furiously, striking his head and neck with bill, wing, and claw. It was just as well for David that the bird was the size of a robin and not that of a hawk.

The arctic terns and Bonaparte's gulls likewise were not timid in protecting their nests, and the latter bird in particular had a disconcerting habit of dive-bombing an intruder from behind, even at considerable distances from its nest. Though it seldom struck with its bill, the accuracy of its bombs was extremely disagreeable (page 122).

Most gulls nest on the ground on rocky islands or in marshes, but the Bonaparte's gull nests on horizontal branches of spruces, usually 15 or 20 feet from the ground. We were fortunate in finding one in a dead spruce only five feet up. This made the building of a blind much simpler, except that it stood in a pond where the water was knee-deep and ice-cold.

Grebes Build Floating Nest

Churchill is rather far north for horned grebes, but this same pond, which had been formed by the damming effect of the new road leading to the airport, gave shelter to two pairs.

With great anticipation we watched one pair building its floating home, and when, after a week, I could discern the female flattened on the nest, I waded out to see if it was time to set up a blind.

To my sorrow I discovered that the female was dead. Her oviduct was clogged with the first egg, perhaps the first she had ever tried to lay. There was no mark of violence on her body and her plumage was unruffled; so I assumed that Nature had gone awry and that the bird had made the supreme sacrifice in trying to reproduce her kind.

The other pair was found shortly afterward, and when they finally accepted our blind, which was unavoidably conspicuous, we were successful in preserving their home life in Kodachrome (page 128).

A few species at Churchill eluded us, and we never found their nests, notably the Hudsonian godwit and the Bohemian waxwing. The latter may not have started nesting until after we left, but we had several pairs of the former under observation and spent many hours watching them from concealment to no avail whatever.

Though seemingly attached to a definite area and behaving as if they were about to give up their secret, they invariably flew clear out of sight—only to return to the same spot later, for we repeatedly found them there the next day.

Fickle Arctic Weather's Whims

No account of Churchill and Hudson Bay would be complete without some mention of its weather. To say that of the 21 days spent there it stormed all day on nine days, was clear all day on six, and clear half of the time on the other six, while the wind seldom stopped blowing, may give some idea of its fickleness.

"Nice day, Mr. Reid," I said to the hotel proprietor, one of the older residents who knew his Churchill weather.

"Yes, fine," he replied, "so far."

It was then 8 o'clock in the morning, and the sun was bright; there was not a cloud in the sky and the wind was only moderate from the northwest.

We started in his car for the reservoir, three miles away over the new highway. Before we reached it the wind was howling out of the north, the sky was completely clouded, the temperature had dropped 10 degrees, and a spurt of cold rain greeted us as we stepped from the car.

"Never mind," he said. "It may clear." And sure enough, with no change in the wind, it was all clear by noon and the temperature was up 20 degrees.

Cold pockets of air could drop down in the middle of the day or the middle of the night. If the evening was quiet and warm, as sometimes happened, and one left the window open, it was pretty sure to blow up a gale and drop almost to freezing by morning.

But in spite of the small percentage of sunshine and the high winds that made the use of blinds so difficult, we were able, because of the long days, to accomplish most of our objectives. In fact, many of our photographs were made at 8 or 9 o'clock at night after the wind had stopped (page 206).

These quiet evenings on the moss-covered rocks overlooking the deep-blue waters of Hudson Bay and its shining icebergs were most restful.

The long tramps over the tundra hunting the nests of rare birds; the hours spent in blinds with the intimate observations of strange denizens of the Arctic at close range; the delicate flowers peeping through the moss; the friendly people; the howling dogs; the bronzed Indians and trappers, all combined to make a memorable experience where the North begins.

125

↑ A Crazy Bird on a Crazy Nest,
the Loon Occupies a Minute Island

All loons have a reputation for insanity because of their wild, fiendish cries. This **Pacific Loon's** madhouse is a tiny artificial island built up with mud pellets to support the two dark-olive eggs.

↓ Flipping an Egg into the "Incubator"
Is a Delicate Operation for a Loon

When eggs threaten to roll off the nest, they must be tucked into the small brood spot between the bird's legs or they will never get warm. The rest of the **Pacific Loon's** breast is covered with dense insulating feathers.

"Hey, Dad, Wait for Me; I'm Tired."
Baby Loon Aims to Hitch a Ride

Ever vigilant, the **Common Loon** is difficult to approach. The bird dines on fish 7 days a week. Its cry suggests demoniacal laughter; hence the expression, "crazy as a loon." This youngster, swimming in an Adirondack lake, soon will clamber aboard for a pickaback cruise.

Expert Swimmer Becomes
Clumsy Waddler on Land

Red-throated Loons, like the female at right, summer across the entire Arctic. Florida sees some in winter; then the red throat mark disappears. Weird and harsh, the loon's cries have been mistaken for the yells of attacking Eskimos.

Eared Grebe's Nest—
A Soggy Houseboat
Moored to Rushes in
North Dakota Marsh

Grebes build floating nests of decayed vegetation and usually bind them to aquatic plants. When disturbed, they cover eggs with strands from the nest and dive into the water. Though strong flyers, they seldom take wing. Lobed toes aid swimming; Nature waterproofs plumage.

As divers, grebes compete for the championship of the bird world, earning the nicknames "hell diver" and "water witch." Clumsy on land, they move on their bellies like seals or sit up like penguins.

Eared Grebes, nesting in scattered colonies, range over wide areas of western North America. Usually they are found on inland fresh waters, but migrations may take them to sea. They feed chiefly on fish, larvae, crayfish, and other crustacea. Sometimes feathers are fed to the young.

Grebes' eggs, bluish white when laid, soon are stained a yellowish brown by the wet nest. Eggs sometimes are hatched when partly covered by water. This raft dweller shared its marsh with a colony of Franklin's gulls.

© National Geographic Society

Photographed in Lower Souris
Refuge, North Dakota

Photographed near Churchill, Manitoba

"What's That Noise?" A Startled Hell Diver on Its Houseboat Anchored Among the Reeds in a Pond near Churchill

Horned Grebes get their nickname from marvelous proficiency in swimming and diving, but their legs are set so far back that they are almost helpless on land. Their floating nest makes them independent of changes in water level. In fall, when they move south to the Gulf of Mexico, they lose their bright colors.

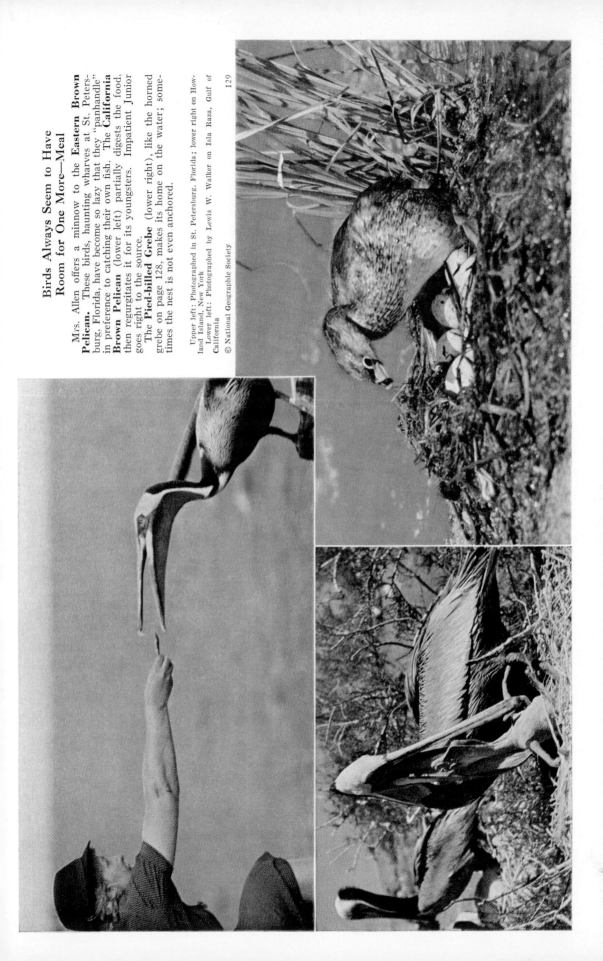

Birds Always Seem to Have Room for One More—Meal

Mrs. Allen offers a minnow to the **Eastern Brown Pelican.** These birds, haunting wharves at St. Petersburg, Florida, have become so lazy that they "panhandle" in preference to catching their own fish. The **California Brown Pelican** (lower left) partially digests the food, then regurgitates it for its youngsters. Impatient Junior goes right to the source.

The **Pied-billed Grebe** (lower right), like the horned grebe on page 128, makes its home on the water; sometimes the nest is not even anchored.

Upper left: Photographed in St. Petersburg, Florida; lower right on Howland Island, New York
Lower left: Photographed by Lewis W. Walker on Isla Raza, Gulf of California

© National Geographic Society

129

130

Parenthood Means a Series of Strenuous Ordeals for Pelicans

The ravenous **White Pelican** fledgling above, seemingly headless, has rushed his returning parent. Now he plunges into her gullet. Muffled whinnying and violent wrestling attend regurgitation. Soon the young bird, fed to giddiness, will be shaken loose. The mother bird in the lower picture shades her brood from 120° temperatures on Salton Sea islands, California; evaporation from drying breast feathers sets up a natural air-conditioning system.

131

Photographed by Luis Marden in the Gulf of Mexico

Going Fishing, Father Pelican Takes Off over the Stormy Gulf of Mexico

The **Eastern Brown Pelican** is a familiar sight along the south Atlantic and Gulf coasts of the United States. The brown pelican is especially fearless of people (page 129); the white pelican (opposite page) is much more wary. Louisiana, the Pelican State, uses the bird as a symbol on its State seal and flag. During the Civil War when the State had two Governors, both used pelican seals. The Federal choice turned the bird's head right; the Confederate to the left, where it still is today.

132

18,000 Loving Couples Nest on Bonaventure, the Sea Birds' Skyscraper City

Once fishermen slaughtered **Gannets** for bait; now Canada protects them. Powerful flyers, they cruise 100 miles a day or more for food. *Gannet* has the same origin as *gander;* solan goose is another name.

Photographed on Bonaventure Island off Gaspé Peninsula, Canada

Gannets Bleach Penthouse Ledges; Gulls Stake Claims on the Ground Floor

Gannets spear fish with 100-foot dives from the air, splashing water 10 feet. Their skin's pneumatic cells cushion the blow. Fish nets 14 fathoms deep have trapped diving gannets.

134 Photographed on Bonaventure Island, Canada

Like Marble Statues, Bonaventure's Gannets Stand in Cold, Motionless Dignity

An overstuffed young **Gannet** looks like a black-tipped powder puff. Born nearly as bare as a human, he now wears down. At 13 weeks he'll outweigh his parents, so he must starve and reduce before flying.

Wings Stretched, Head Wagging Side to Side, a Gannet (Left) Avows His Love

Three birds (right) remain aloof. Another grooms its tail. The remaining one, bestowing a benevolent look, admits she's touched. **Gannets** thus perform before their young, as if to teach courtship ritual.

Girl Cuddles Baby Gannet. Adult Birds (Right) Are Natty Dressers

Born black and bare, it took "Fluffy" a couple of weeks to develop his downy coat. A long adolescence with dark feathers ends about the third year with the handsome adult **Gannet** plumage at the right.

136

Gannets and Their Young Blanket the Ground Like Snow

There's "No Vacancy" on Bonaventure Island, sanctuary for **Gannets**, off the tip of the Gaspé Peninsula.

Disturbed, Least Bittern Freezes; American Bittern Angrily Fluffs Feathers

When an intruder approaches, bitterns may strike a statuesque pose, relying upon protective coloration to escape detection. Here the **Eastern Least Bittern** simulates a broken reed. The **American Bittern** also depends upon color and freezing for defense; when these methods fail, the bird, as in the picture at the right, spreads its wings in eloquent defiance. Wounded, it is a dangerous enemy, striking for the face of its foe. Its call, a liquid "Oblee-oob, ooblee-oob," sounds like water gurgling from a jug. Clapping of the bill helps give the bird its alias, "stake-driver."

© National Geographic Society

Photographed near Ithaca, New York

137

138

↑ Startled, "Thunder Pumper" Freezes

The **American Bittern** received its nickname because of its booming call. Sneaking back to his nest, this one came so close that the camera caught only his head and shoulders. Standing like a statue is this marsh dweller's best defense; but if wounded he may deal a wicked blow with that javelinlike bill.

↓ "Let's Sell Our Lives Dearly, Mates!"

These young **Eastern Least Bitterns** were not much larger than sparrows, but they stuck their little bayonets into the air and tried to appear as formidable as possible. Their down, like hair standing on end, rather belies their courageous attitude, as it makes them look scared to death.

139 Photographed on Avery Island, Louisiana

Ladies' Hat Fashions Nearly Exterminated the Snowy Egret in the Gay Nineties

So great was the demand for the filmy aigrettes that adorn this heron's back in spring and summer that it became extremely rare. Protection, inspired and directed by the National Audubon Society, has made the **Snowy Egret** familiar again along southern lakes and shores. Florida visitors may see flocks of thousands as they drive along the Tamiami Trail between Miami and Fort Myers.

140

Reversed Question Marks on a Texas Island Are American Egrets in Nuptial Plumage

These graceful birds, like their snowy cousins (page 139), have prospered under humane laws. **American Egrets** nest in southern swamps, wandering north in late summer. They are much larger than the snowy egrets.

141

Black-crowned Night Heron, Dusk's Fearsome Fisher, Spends the Day Hatching Quadruplets

Nesting in colonies, **Black-crowned Night Herons** usually build homes in trees or marshes. Pity the frog or fish in spearing distance of this mother's javelin bill! Three white plumes form a tiara worn for the mating season.

142

Perch if You Will on a Pincushion, Reddish Egret—but Don't Sit Down!

This unbarbered fellow stands watch from a cactus bush. The **Reddish Egret** is found from the Gulf coasts of
Florida and Texas south to Guatemala and the West Indies. It seldom ventures inland.

143

A Vicious Bill, Swung with Trip Hammer Force, Is the Heron's Hunting Weapon

Herons make lightning-fast stabs with rapier beaks to disable, then swallow, their prey. **Ward's Heron,** southern variety of the great blue heron species, has a wingspread of more than six feet, greater than an eagle's.

← This Architect Prefers a Ramshackle Home

Nesting time finds the **Eastern Green Heron** piling sticks to make a crude platform. Where marshland alders and willows are not available, the quaking structure may be found in trees some distance from water. Unlike most of its kin, the hermitlike green heron usually does not nest in colonies. It enjoys a wide distribution in North America, seeking areas where the fishing is good.

Photographed near Ithaca, New York

144

↓ Ibis Builds a Nest Among Cattails

This proud **White-faced Glossy Ibis** stoops to household chores in Utah's Bear River marshes. There he feeds on frogs, crayfish, and aquatic insects. Irrigated fields he combs for worms.

© National Geographic Society

Photographed in Bear River marshes, Utah

145

Roseate Spoonbills Are Back with Gorgeous Plumage and Faces Only a Spoonbill Could Love

After virtually disappearing for nearly 50 years, **Roseate Spoonbills** have returned to the Gulf coast. Hundreds of them now congregate each spring and summer in nesting colonies on oyster-shell islands off the Texas shore.

Photographed by Paul A. Zahl on Andros Island, Bahamas

146

Pink Flamingos, Their Outstretched Necks and Legs in Perfect Balance, Sail Through an Azure Sky

Once abundant in Florida, the **Flamingo** appears now only as a storm-tossed straggler or as a pet in Hialeah Park (page 148).

Fragile Heads Snap Up Like Jack-in-the-Boxes. Flightless Youngsters Herd Together at Sign of Peril

Pale-pink five-month-olds, roaming a lake in the Bahamas, lack maturity's bright coloration. A moment after this picture was taken, the entire flock of 1,000 **Flamingos** stampeded, knocking Doctor Zahl into the water and almost ruining his camera.

147

Photographed by Paul A. Zahl on Great Inagua Island, Bahamas

148

First Families of Flamingos Turn Their Hialeah Park Lagoon into a Nursery

The late Joseph E. Widener brought these **Flamingos** from Cuba to the enclosure near Miami, Florida. During the first seven years of their stay, they raised no young. When park attendants provided the birds with loose soil, sticks, and dry grass on an island in the lake, they erected turret nests and produced 115 fledglings in two years. The colony now numbers some 500 birds.

Duck Hunting with a Color Camera

DUCK hunting is a sport so contagious that millions of people the world over have become infected and plan their lives so that they can be in a certain place at a certain time when they expect a flock of ducks to fly by.

Duck hunting is big business that employs thousands of workers, directs millions of dollars into unusual channels, and has caused both State and Federal Governments to step in and offset the threat of "duck trusts" to control all duck hunting for the enjoyment of relatively few.

Thousands of legislative hours and much acrid debate have been devoted to setting up regulations designed to provide good hunting without extermination. Millions of dollars are being spent annually by the Federal Government, State, and Canadian conservation departments and by private agencies to provide better habitat for the ducks and make our wet lands more productive.

The new science of wildlife management, which has swept over the country and given rise to training courses for students in many of our State universities, had its beginning in the waterfowl shortage that threatened the country. Some of the most spectacular discoveries in the cause and prevention of wildlife catastrophes have been made with the waterfowl.

The literature on waterfowl is enormous, and every year sees some new and beautifully illustrated volume devoted to ducks and geese to delight the web-footed nimrods. It seems that everything that can be said about ducks has already been printed and every approach to the subject thoroughly documented.

But talk to a group of dyed-in-the-wool duck hunters and the subject becomes as fresh as if it had just been discovered. Ideas for killing more ducks or for preventing their extinction are as numerous as the duck hunters themselves.

This little essay, therefore, will not enter the controversy of killing or saving ducks. It will mention only incidentally the 196 Federal refuges designed to save them and other migratory waterfowl and the multiplicity of regulations controlling their hunting.

Taking Trophies That Never Die

The man with a camera knows neither season nor bag limit. He is restrained only by the limitations of his equipment, the weather, the thickness of his skin, and his ingenuity in getting close enough to his quarry to make his trophies worth while.

Those of us who have shifted from gun to camera now get greater satisfaction from the string of Kodachromes we can show to our friends than we ever did from the string of ducks hung up in the woodshed or concealed in the home freezer.

The trophies are much more durable and have more points to be judged in competition with those of others; and they leave us with the satisfaction of knowing there are just as many ducks when we are through with our hunting as when we started—ducks in better physical condition because of having been filled with corn instead of lead pellets.

Lest someone think there is no uncertainty to the sport of hunting with a camera, however, I mention the fact that one spring I used up two tons of cracked corn in front of three blinds to secure only 7 of the color illustrations which follow this chapter. The "trophies" offered there are selected from more than 2,000 camera shots, the results of five seasons' expeditions from Florida to Quebec Province and from Mexico to Alaska.

Most of the misses in Kodachrome duck photography come from the slowness of the film, with resulting motion of the subject, or from imperfect lighting, owing to clouds or improper angle of the sun when the ducks are before the camera.

Feeding Time Best for Photography

When ducks are feeding, there is a great deal of activity, and even when the lighting conditions are ideal, one has to use the lens wide open and speed up the shutter.

This results in little depth of focus; therefore, if there are several ducks in the picture, at least one is sure to be fuzzy (pages 173 and 176). It is much more simple to take motion pictures than satisfactory stills.

When ducks are not feeding, they seldom come close to blinds; they are, moreover, very allergic to having lenses pointed at them. Even in parks or refuges, where they have become accustomed to people, they resent cameras and turn their backs on photographers. A flash gun has nearly as frightening an effect as a shotgun.

Many of the brighter colors on waterfowl are not due to pigment but to iridescence, and even the slightest turn of the head may change a brilliant green to dead black.

One can frequently make a dozen exposures of a pintail or a mallard or a wood duck (page 177) standing in the same spot and have no two of them turn out exactly the same. If the sun is a little too low, there will

"Step Lively, Please!" Mrs. Mallard Takes Her Fluffy Brood for a Stroll

This family was found in the garden of a home in London's East Dulwich and transferred to pleasanter surroundings in St. James's Park. Here, to the delight of onlookers, a bobby stops traffic while the mother and 13 ducklings march briskly across a walk.

be an unnatural redness to all of the pictures; if it is too high, the black shadows under the head and breast will ruin their perfection.

Bad Shots Cripple Only the Wallet

So the hunter with a lens comes to expect a very low average from his camera shooting, though he has the satisfaction of knowing that his misses cripple nothing but his wallet.

On some of the refuges, and especially on private sanctuaries where an effort is made to maintain a breeding stock of hand-reared birds, some of the waterfowl lose their fear of man and become pets.

Recently I visited the Severn Wildfowl Trust, in England, where Peter Scott, the illustrious waterfowl artist, has built up a collection of more than 100 species of ducks and geese from all over the world.

Many of these, including the Ross's goose, for which he endured the hardships of an expedition to the Perry River country of northern Canada in 1949, and the nene, the nearly extinct goose of the Hawaiian Islands,

are as tame as barnyard fowls and cluster about anyone with a feed bucket.

If one desires merely photographs of the various species, such a spot is an answer to the photographer's prayer. It is, likewise, yielding facts and observations of much scientific interest. Most of the hand-reared species perform their courtships and other behavior patterns in a normal manner, and since they are more easily and more continuously observed than is possible with their wild brethren, new facts in their behavior or life histories are often discovered.

The difference between wild-trapped and hand-reared birds in this particular is very marked, since it is unusual for wild-trapped birds to breed in captivity, even after they have lost their fear of man and seem perfectly contented on the ponds with others of their kind.

When armed with a camera, a duck hunter prays for quiet weather and sunshine, so that there will be minimum motion and the ducks will be looking their best. Winds and low temperatures freeze up his shutter and make photography impossible, even if the sun continues to shine.

The camera hunter naturally hopes to photograph his birds in their best plumage. He is restricted, therefore, largely to the winter and early spring, when the weather is normally at its worst and sunny skies are at a premium. One cannot wait for summer, for by that time the brightly colored males will be assuming dull feathers, like those of the females.

"Winter Plumage" in Spring and Summer

It is a curious fact that most waterfowl are different from other bright-colored birds in that during the summer they acquire what corresponds to the dull winter plumage of other birds (pages 168 and 172). Indeed, old-squaws get their "winter plumage" in April, while they are still migrating and a long way from their nesting ground. By early June many mallards, wood ducks, and gadwalls have dark-brown feathers scattered throughout their bright plumage.

Waterfowl are also different from most birds in that they lose all their flight feathers at once and for several weeks are unable to fly (page 172). This happens as soon as they have acquired all their dull winter plumage in July or August. As soon as they have replaced these flight feathers, they start coming back into their bright breeding plumage.

By late September wood ducks and mallards are once again in full regalia, when most birds have just donned their dull winter attire. Some species, like the blue-winged teal, which frequently winters as far south as Colombia and Venezuela, delay getting their breeding plumage until January or February, and the ruddy duck waits until March or April; but they are exceptional.

Differences in the feeding habits of the various species add to the photographer's troubles. Baldpates, shovellers, and ruddy ducks are difficult to bait up, because they do not care for grain; and I have yet to find a suitable bait for fish-eating mergansers. Shovellers and cinnamon teal, when feeding, put their heads beneath the water and steam along as if they had plankton nets attached to their bills. They must strain a great deal of water to get any food.

Canvas-backs, redheads, and scaups are members of the subfamily of diving ducks, which feed in deep water by diving. Frequently, after they have discovered the bait in front of a blind, if they are at all suspicious they will dive far out and swim under water to the grain, so that the photographer never gets a chance for a close-up.

Real diving ducks, like canvas-backs and redheads, use only their large feet under water and seldom splash when diving. A good push from their great webbed feet throws the body clear of the water (page 176), but at the same instant the bill enters and the body follows with little disturbance to the water, save for the "boiling" set up by the broad-webbed toes.

When mallards, black ducks, or other dabbling ducks find that their ordinary tipping fails to reach the food and start diving, they use their wings under the water like flippers, and the splashing, as they start down, is in great contrast (page 173).

In either case, the motion is difficult to stop with a camera loaded with Kodachrome.

Then there are a thousand and one little interruptions from well-intentioned but curious people who approach the blind at inopportune moments. They frighten the ducks away or prevent them from coming within camera range. Often the cause of the interruption is not evident to the photographer until he leaves the blind and finds some near-by cottager hanging up the week's washing, or some young lady taking a sun bath, in plain view of the ducks.

Sometimes the best-laid plans are foiled by the weather, when the sun does not shine for a week and the ducks just will not delay their migrations.

Dust Bowl Refuge Full of Ducks

In 1949 Dr. Paul Kellogg, associate professor of ornithology at Cornell University, and I drove our sound truck to the Lower Souris National Wildlife Refuge in North Dakota, hoping to add to our album of duck portraits as well as to our library of bird songs.*

The refuge area was part of the Great Plains Dust Bowl from 1927 to 1935, but in the wet and muddy spring of 1949 the bowl was full of soup—duck soup, in more ways than one.

There were ducks everywhere, even sitting in the middle of the road like sparrows. The air was full of them: flocks bound for the low spots in the grainfields, which were still full of water and grain scattered from last fall's harvest; trios whizzing by in their nuptial flights; and singles flushed by passing cars from trysting posts in the roadside ditches, where they had been awaiting the coming of their sweethearts from their nests so well concealed in the prairie sedges.

The males were still resplendent in their breeding plumage, but the females were demure in their various shades of brown and looked much alike.

* See "Hunting with a Microphone the Voices of Vanishing Birds," by Arthur A. Allen, NATIONAL GEOGRAPHIC MAGAZINE, June, 1937.

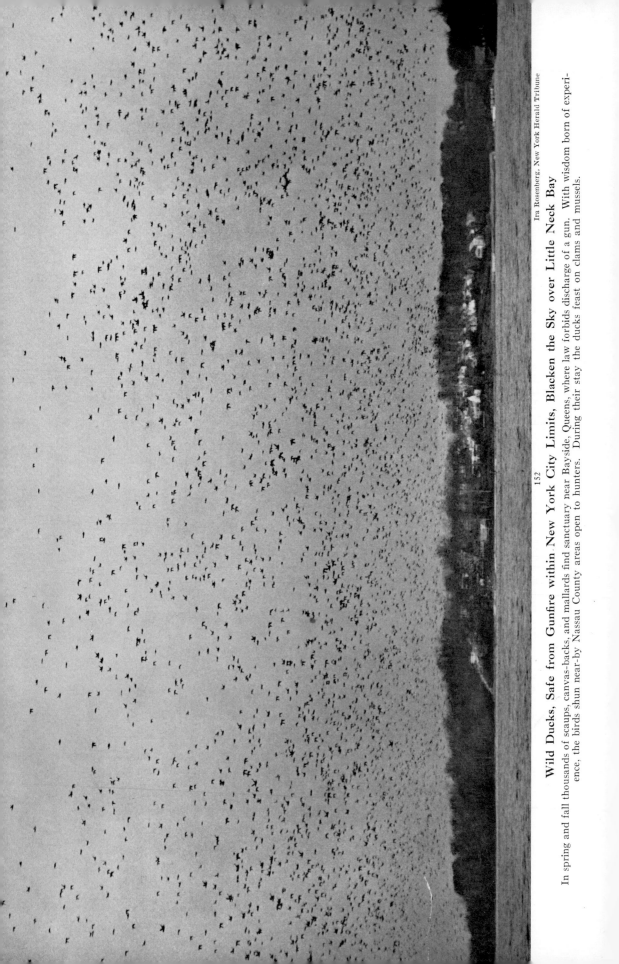

152

Wild Ducks, Safe from Gunfire within New York City Limits, Blacken the Sky over Little Neck Bay

In spring and fall thousands of scaups, canvas-backs, and mallards find sanctuary near Bayside, Queens, where law forbids discharge of a gun. With wisdom born of experience, the birds shun near-by Nassau County areas open to hunters. During their stay the ducks feast on clams and mussels.

A Bird's-eye View of Bird Watchers: Audubon Society Members Scan the Sky from a Long Island Dune

With more than 360,000 members, the National Audubon Society and its affiliates interest an estimated 2,000,000 people in their programs to conserve wildlife. As part of the organization's 1950 convention in New York City, about 200 ornithologists, amateur and professional, swarmed across beach and marsh in a record-breaking expedition. These enthusiasts combined lunch with watching near Westhampton Beach. They observed gannets, mute swans, ducks, geese, cormorants, gulls, and others.

Nat Fein, New York Herald Tribune

153

Black-tipped Wings Beat Furiously as Lesser Snow Geese Leave Their Feeding Ground
Acres of rice stubble lure the shining white birds. In the San Francisco Bay region and the lower reaches of
Sonoma Creek they also feed in the wheat fields and grasslands.

Paul J. Fair

A Deafening Gabble of Harsh Cries Resounds Across the Hills in the Sacramento Valley
Lesser snow geese come south from their northern breeding grounds in October and remain until May. The
most abundant goose in western North America, it is often called "white brant."

National Geographic Photographer Robert F. Sisson

Handsome Pintails Bump Chests as if to Say, "Wanta Start Something?"

These handsome males measure one another in a 62-acre waterfowl sanctuary at Roaches Run, Virginia, across the Potomac from Washington, D. C. Here as many as 5,200 birds at a time, permanent residents and migrants, enjoy food handouts, undisturbed by the noise of near-by National Airport, cars whizzing along Mount Vernon Memorial Highway, and trains crossing a railroad bridge.

Blue-winged teal (page 173) were most abundant, gadwalls next (page 169); but mallards, pintails, shovellers, and redheads were nearly as common, and there was a good scattering of other species.

Here we had hoped to complete our survey of the waterfowl, which had started in the Finger Lakes of New York State and had taken us to the wintering grounds on Currituck Sound and Mattamuskeet Lake in North Carolina; Bull Island, South Carolina; Florida, Louisiana, Texas, Mexico, California; the Bear River marshes of Utah; Alaska, Hudson Bay, and Quebec Province.

At the North Dakota refuge there were certainly enough ducks to fill the eyes of the most ardent ornithologist or to tantalize the most devoted duck hunter. There was little indication of the ravages of drought, disease, and overshooting that had brought the duck population, especially that of the eastern United States, to such a low ebb.

But it is one thing to see ducks or to shoot ducks, and quite another to get close enough to photograph them; it is still another to get them to sit still long enough for portraits in color. One can pass in a car within 20 feet and take motion pictures of them as they jump the moment the car stops. One can set up blinds by their nests and get pictures of the plain-colored females sitting on their eggs. But to catch the brightly plumaged males napping is quite another matter.

We were faced with the problem of getting these shy birds accustomed to some sort of blind, where we could hide with our cameras without arousing their suspicions. We decided on two procedures:

First, for those like the ruddies and shovellers which do not care for grain but return to trysting places not far from their nests, we set up blinds of grass cloth or burlap on the shore, hoping that sooner or later they would come back.

For others, like the canvas-backs, redheads, and baldpates, which sun themselves on the mud flats, we found an island in the lake. There we sank an inconspicuous blind into the gumbo at the base of a point—at least, it was inconspicuous until a big storm carried away most of the dead weeds that blended it into the general contour of the island.

That storm, incidentally, carried away all our other blinds and flattened the cattails and sweet clover as if they had been cut by a mower.

In North Dakota the radio talks about the weather almost continuously and makes hourly predictions of what is likely to happen during the following 60 minutes. I had not been listening to the radio when I changed my mind about paddling out to my island duck blind a half mile offshore. But a dark line of clouds along the horizon told me it would probably be cloudy before the ducks would come back; so it might be better to spend the time locating another likely spot for a "trysting blind."

Hailstorm Kills Birds, Breaks Eggs

Fifteen minutes later a cloud of black dust enveloped us as Merrill C. Hammond, the refuge biologist, and I drove north along the gravel highway. We could not see the edges of the road, and a moment later came the rain on a 70-mile-an-hour wind. We turned about and headed for home, but before we got there the rain had changed to hail, which pelted us like shrapnel.

Some of the hailstones were the size of pigeons' eggs, and they smashed windows and killed birds. Roofs were torn from houses, barns were flattened, trees were uprooted, and outhouses rolled across the prairie.

It was all over in 30 minutes, but about an inch of rain had fallen and there were scenes of devastation all about. What chance had my frail blinds? I shouldn't be surprised if they landed in Minnesota or even Michigan.

The next day we visited a colony of Franklin's gulls (page 251) and found many of the eggs broken and small young killed. Tough duck eggs were dented by the hail, and the floating nest of a Holboell's grebe, near which I had placed a blind, had disappeared entirely, along with the tent.

Curiously enough, a colony of some 500 common terns, on a low, unprotected island in one of the lakes, in some miraculous fashion escaped entirely the force of the storm and remained unscathed. Also unharmed were several fragile mourning dove nests near the headquarters, where 26 windows were broken in one building.

This storm set us back about a week in our operations. It was followed by a couple of bright days, but four cloudy days in a row brought us to the verge of discouragement.

It was not only the cloudy weather that impeded us. When the rain ceased, we attempted to drive down the south side of the refuge. A thin coating of gravel covered the black gumbo beneath, and the weight of our car was sufficient to press the slippery black ooze to the surface. We skidded on the slightest grade and almost slid into the ditch at every turn.

The black soil of this region has a curious consistency, for it seems almost impervious to water except for a thin, slippery film.

When Hammond and I dug a pit on the island, we found it easy to sink the shovel its full depth into the gumbo. It was not too difficult to lift out, but to get the sticky mass off the shovel was a different matter. Thereafter it was part and parcel of the shovel and would not shake off.

The first shovelful I scraped off with my boot, to which it remained attached with the same grim force, so that I could not walk and certainly could not scrape off the second shovelful. We were finally forced to break the black clay into lumps with a pickax and lift it out of the depression with our hands.

Quickly I changed my plan. Instead of a comfortable 2-foot pit, I settled for a mere scrape, with a higher superstructure. After the storm the deeper portion of the blind, designed for my feet, closely resembled a hog wallow.

To the average person a duck is a duck, and even informed duck hunters may speak of ducks as if they were all alike except for size, color, and taste. As a matter of fact, the different species of ducks are just as different as the various species of sparrows or thrushes or blackbirds.

All ducks belong to the same family, but no two species have exactly the same distribution, migration, breeding habits, calls, food and feeding habits, and environmental requirements. Conservation practices that are highly beneficial to some species might even be detrimental to others; and, similarly, hunting practices which are successful for some bring no results with others.

World's Most Widely Distributed Duck

The most widely distributed duck the world over is the mallard (pages 166-168). It is the ancestor of all our domestic breeds except the Muscovy.* The curly upper tail coverts of the males of the white Pekins and pied Indian runners give evidence of their mallard ancestry, even though they have changed so drastically in size, shape, and color.

Mallards are found throughout the Northern Hemisphere, but are by no means evenly distributed. In North America the main breeding ground is in the prairie Provinces of Canada, and the principal migratory highway is the Mississippi Valley. But there is scarcely any place in the United States or Canada where a few mallards never drop in at the proper season.

In eastern North America the mallard is largely replaced by the black duck (page 173), a closely related but somewhat less adaptable species that is scarce west of the Mississippi.

From September to June the male mallard wears the bright-green head feathers and red-

* See "Fowls of Forest and Stream Tamed by Man," by Morley A. Jull, NATIONAL GEOGRAPHIC MAGAZINE, March, 1930.

dish breast of the breeding plumage and is very different from his streaked brown mate. But in July he assumes his "eclipse plumage" (page 168) and for two months is scarcely distinguishable from her or from the juvenile birds, except by the trained eye.

How Mallards Make Love

The courtship antics of mallards may start in the fall, shortly after the males have come back into their breeding plumage, though active love-making does not start until the winter or early spring. At this time the female urges him on by swimming close, turning her head to one side, and giving little cackling notes.

To this coquetry he responds by standing straight up on the water and throwing his head down on his breast, at the same time giving a single curious peeping note. As he settles back into a horizontal position, he raises his tail, displaying his shiny black under tail coverts, which are bordered by white. At the same time he may throw up a little jet of water with his bright-orange feet for the entertainment of the girl friend.

Each species of dabbling duck has a somewhat similar performance and a characteristic call, which in no way resembles a "quack."

The diving ducks, on the other hand, have a different courtship.

Canvas-backs, for example, indulge in a sort of communal love-making. The females huddle together, breasts touching, necks stiff and straight. The males then circle about them, each one in turn throwing his head backward until it strikes his back, at the same time emitting his love call—a very unducklike "Ick-ick-cooo."

Under similar circumstances redheads call "Caar" and golden-eyes, "Beard."

A courting group can be heard for half a mile on a quiet day.

Nor is this the end of the love-making, for a courtship flight seems essential to the course of true love. The female mallard leaves the pond, pursued by several males, but the competition soon settles down to two chief competitors for her favor. Round and round they go, the males trying to interfere with each other's flying and even with hers, so as to force her down to the water; but she leads them a merry chase.

On the water again, the competing males may go at each other with bills and wings and thrash it out in a shower of spray.

Not so with the dignified canvas-backs. The competing males approach each other, breast to breast, turning their heads so that their long bills will not interfere, and then each swims just as hard as he can push with his great webbed feet. When one feels himself going

backward, he is licked and must turn and dive before his opponent gets him by the back of the neck.

In some such manner with each species of wild duck the annual competition for mates is settled. Then the females search out satisfactory places for their nests.

Some, like the wood ducks, golden-eyes, and buffle-heads, search out hollow trees and have been known to lose their lives on lake shores when investigating the chimneys of cabins from which they could not escape. Most species, however, nest on the ground under some sort of cover from the eyes of marauding crows, magpies, skunks, and other egg-loving enemies.

The actual number of eggs varies from the 4 or 5 of the eiders to 15 or 20 with mallards, but incubation does not start until all are laid, because it is important that all should hatch at about the same time.

At first, the eggs themselves are not covered. As their numbers increase, however, one being laid each day, and as the time for incubation approaches, the mother duck starts pulling the down from her breast to cover them.

Ducks Lack Brood Spot

Plucking the down serves a double purpose, because ducks do not have the bare area, or brood spot, in the middle of the breast, so familiar in most birds, and the eggs must touch the bare skin to receive the heat from the mother's body.

The length of time required for the eggs to hatch varies with the different species, from only 21 days for the pintail to 30 days for the wood duck; the mallard normally requires 27 days.

At the time of hatching, the soft bill of the duckling develops, near the tip of the upper mandible, a sharp, hard, calcareous tubercle called the egg tooth. With this the duckling cuts through the shell and rolls out, all wet and stringy.

Within an hour, however, the down has dried and fluffed out; and as soon as all the eggs have hatched, the youngsters are ready to follow their mother to water. This may be nearly a mile away, although it is usually much closer and, in the case of diving ducks, often within one jump.

Wood ducks and others that nest in holes in trees have been reported to carry their ducklings to the water on their backs, but plenty of observers have seen the little ducks jump from the hole, even when it is 30 feet up and over hard ground, and then follow their mother to the water.

When the eggs are being laid and for a short time after incubation starts, the male usually dozes at some trysting place on near-by water.

There he is joined by the female whenever she gets hungry or bored, but the male himself never sits on the eggs.

Even among the geese, which enjoy a model family life, the male merely accompanies the female to the nest and stands guard near by; he never sits on the eggs.

Swans, Geese Are Models of Fidelity

Swans and geese retain the same mates from year to year, but if ducks do, it is mere chance, for they may be widely separated during the winter. However, the same duck tends to return to the same spot to nest year after year, and, if her mate does the same, they may well remate. This often happens with semi-domesticated mallards that do not migrate.

One mallard returned to nest on the identical spot at the base of a hemlock above my pond for 12 years, even though there was no water in the pond for much of that time. For many years she had the same mate, a friendly drake

Butzko and Susott

Banding a Hen Mallard on Nesting Grounds

If the aluminum band with number on it is recovered and sent to U. S. Fish and Wildlife Service, it will help reveal how long a duck lives, its migratory routes, the hunting toll, sex ratio, and other facts. This mallard, illegally trapped on Virginia's Chesconessex marsh, was rescued, banded and released. Over 1,241,555 waterfowl—ducks, geese, and swans—have been banded. Mallards are swift travelers. One banded in Green Bay, Wisconsin, was shot five days later at Georgetown, South Carolina, 900 miles away.

we called Jack. He disappeared long before Mary, the female, met some untimely end and failed to return in the spring.

It is sometimes reported that if one of a pair of swans or geese is killed, the survivor will not remate. I know from experience that this is not true, although if a mated pair in captivity is separated, neither one will take a new mate so long as it can hear its former mate calling.

During the nesting season the various species of waterfowl in North America are widely scattered through suitable habitats from Florida to Alaska. A few species, like the eiders or even the gadwalls, may seem almost colonial when nesting on small islands. Usually, however, nests are placed far apart,

and broods of young are so scattered that their paths do not cross.

Occasionally with geese and regularly with eiders, broods may be pooled, and some of the less domestic females may desert the nursery for the company of the males. Normally only one brood is raised each season, but if a nest is broken up during the early stages of incubation, the female will usually nest again, laying somewhat fewer eggs the second time.

As soon as the ducklings are able to fly, or even before, they sometimes assemble in large flocks and get ready for the fall migration. Long before this, however, and even as early as mid-June, the males have assembled in huge flocks to complete their molting. The dabbling ducks head for the large marshes, so that, by July first, flocks of a thousand or more male pintails are frequently seen on the extensive Bear River marshes in Utah.

The male diving ducks, on the other hand, like the canvas-backs and the redheads, head for the deep water of lakes, where they raft out over submerged weed beds that supply their food. Out there they are not inconvenienced by their lack of flight, either in feeding or in escaping enemies.

Then comes the completion of the molt and the fall migration to the winter quarters.

Thousands Die When Botulism Strikes

Unfortunately, in the warm days of early fall waterfowl sometimes concentrate on some of the shallow alkaline lakes and marshes of the West. Here decaying aquatic vegetation has set up a culture of *Clostridium botulinum*, which makes conditions ideal for the death-dealing disease called botulism (page 316). Thousands of ducks are overcome by its paralysis; their heads fall into the water and they drown.

As many as 50,000 have died in a single week at some of the concentration points before help could be brought to them.

Nowadays an effort is made to deepen and freshen the water in these areas or to drive the ducks from them. If the ducks do become infected and can be rescued in time, they still can be saved by an abundance of fresh water.

But it is not botulism alone that has caused this country's recent duck shortages.

When northern nesting grounds freeze over, waterfowl funnel southward into an ever-decreasing area suitable to their feeding habits and concentrate by thousands in the coastal marshes of the southern United States. As these areas have decreased in recent years through drainage and contamination, the unfortunate ducks have had to undergo still greater concentration; consequently, the toll that is taken by hunters and commercial interests has been out of proportion to their real number.

At times careless ship captains pump out their oily bilges within a few miles of the coast, and these oil slicks seem to have a fascination for the waterfowl wintering or migrating near by. The oil glues together the feathers and down, destroying the insulating effect and permitting the water to penetrate to the skin. If the water is cold, it soon chills and stiffens the birds, so that they can neither fly nor dive.

If they do not drown, they frequently die of pneumonia.

In October, 1948, an oil barge ran aground in the St. Lawrence River near Quebec, and thousands of migrating greater scaup ducks, as well as black ducks, became coated with oil. The duck population that normally winters on the Finger Lakes of New York State has not yet recovered from this disaster, which decimated its ranks on the way south.

Lead Pellets a Hazard to Ducks Even When Taken Internally

Lead poisoning is another hazard for which man is responsible. Ducks and other waterfowl feeding in shot-over areas swallow lead pellets from shotgun shells and quickly sicken and die. Chief offenders are "sky-busting" hunters with more shells than good aim.

Occasionally numbers of waterfowl are reported to have frozen into ponds after sleet storms and sudden drops in temperature. Usually, however, waterfowl in good physical condition develop sufficient body heat to melt any ice that forms about them, and those that actually freeze to the ice are ones already in poor physical condition.

Some species, like the buffle-heads and ruddies, unable to adapt themselves to changing conditions, have suffered more than others, but Canada geese and mallards, leaving the marshes to feed on winter wheat and cornfields, have more nearly maintained their numbers. Indeed, the mallards have learned to feed on the waste grains largely by night and thus escape the gunners.

If drainage projects continue, however, we may be faced with the near extinction of many of our interesting species. This danger is double, threatening the birds both on the wintering grounds and on the breeding grounds of the prairie Provinces, where periodic summer droughts prevent the rearing of young.

When nothing but the breeding stock returns in the fall to face the 2,000,000 gunners who take out Federal licenses entitling them to hunt migratory waterfowl, the result is as might be expected; and two or three dry summers in succession periodically bring the birds to the verge of extinction.

Fortunately, today, the United States Fish and Wildlife Service has been given the power to set the regulations controlling the annual harvest of waterfowl. With a host of trained observers it makes every effort in late winter to census the breeding stock left after the hunting season and, in summer, to judge the size of the broods reared, before formulating the regulations for the following hunting season.

With the full cooperation of the sportsmen and all the commercial interests involved, such measures should go far toward perpetuating the sport of wildfowling and preserving for Nature lovers plenty of these most interesting subjects for their color cameras.

161

⋏ June Finds a Whistling Swan Incubating Eggs on an Alaskan Hillside

Unlike the vanishing trumpeter, the **Whistling Swan** is a hardy, prolific species. When migrating, its call is often heard from aloft on moonlit nights. Whistlers nest in Arctic areas and winter chiefly on the east and west coasts of the United States.

⋎ Tail Erect, Air Sacs Inflated, a Ruddy Duck Courts His Ladylove

A persistent wooer, the **Ruddy Duck** may continue such antics throughout the nesting season. Though other male ducks are poor parents (page 165), this little bird escorts and protects his young. Both male and female are pugnacious and fearless.

Photographed by S. A. Grimes near Jacksonville, Florida

162

Canada Geese Mate "Until Death Do Us Part"

Both parents cooperate in raising the family, braving all dangers in defense of their young. Wintering in southern States and nesting mostly in Canada, migrating flocks of **Common Canada Geese** flying in V formation herald spring or the approach of winter. Many a heart thrills at their wild honking.

Great and Small of Goose World; Big Fellow at Left May Be Triple the Weight of His Cousin

Canoeing down the Hamilton River of Labrador, Andrew H. Brown and Ralph Gray of the Geographic Staff encountered a **Common Canada Goose.** Usually a wary creature, this one had shed its flight feathers and was unable to do anything except waddle ashore. Smallest of the seven races of Canada geese is the **Cackling Goose** (right), photographed on the "curlew expedition," sponsored by the National Geographic Society (page 217). It has a relatively short neck and stubby bill.

Photographed by Andrew H. Brown at Ossokmanuan Lake, Labrador   © National Geographic Society   Photographed by the author in Yukon Delta, Alaska

163

164

Photographed near Igiak Bay, Alaska

Emperor Goose, Dweller in Alaska's Yukon Delta, Plucks Down from Her Breast for Nest Lining

Unlike most waterfowl, the **Emperor Goose** is not an inveterate traveler, generally limiting its range to Bering Sea regions. A few flocks sometimes migrate as far as California. The down, helpful in retaining heat, is also used to hide the eggs from marauders when mother "empress" leaves the nest.

A Nesting White-fronted Goose Raises Her Periscope Neck to Scan Alaska's Tundra for Signs of Danger

Geese, models of fidelity like the swans, retain the same mates year after year. Though the male never sits on the eggs, he stands guard near the female and helps to raise the young. Ducks usually take different mates each nesting season, the male abandoning the female soon after incubation begins.

White-fronted Goose enjoys a wide distribution. It breeds in northern climes in both Old and New Worlds and migrates far to the south. At times this alert female was partially hidden from the camera by swarms of midges. Her white front (forehead) is discolored by impurities in water.

The young **Cackling Goose** (upper) will develop into a shrill-voiced chatterbox. Far less noisy is the **Emperor Goose** (lower) whose adult cry is an infrequent "Kla-ha, kla-ha."

165

Photographed in Yukon Delta, Alaska

Photographed on Cayuga Lake, New York

166

Mallards Loaf in a Sheltered Cove, Waiting for Rough Water To Subside

To photograph **Common Mallards** in their best plumage, the color cameraman must brave winter's icy winds. Hours of patient waiting may be spoiled by foul weather, inadequate light, or the birds' quick movements. A slight turn of the head may change iridescent plumage colors.

Proud Mallard Convoys Her Downy Flotilla on a Shakedown Cruise Across the Author's Pond

Devoted and courageous, the **Common Mallard** drives away small enemies; big ones she lures off while her ducklings hide. This mallard returned to the pond each spring for 12 years, always nesting at the base of the same hemlock. When the young were a few days old, she would disappear with them toward Cayuga Lake.

Photographed in Ithaca, New York

168

Photographed near Ithaca, New York

↑   Mallard Drake in Breeding Plumage
Stands on the Ice

All breeds of domestic ducks, except the Muscovy, are descendants of the wild **Common Mallard,** found throughout the Northern Hemisphere.   This drake wears gay dress from September to June.   In summer molting season he resembles his drab mate.

↓   Molting Male, Brilliant Colors Gone,
Gazes at His Dull Reflection

Flight feathers are lost during the July "eclipse," or molt season; for a month the drake **Common Mallard** cannot fly.   He hides in marshes until again airworthy.   Inexplicably, Southern Hemisphere ducks have no eclipse, even when living in cold climates.

169

Photographed at Roaches Run, Virginia

ʌ **Male Baldpate, Inviting Battle, Hurls
Raucous Insults at a Rival**

Stealing wild celery from other ducks is a favorite
pastime of the **Baldpate,** or American widgeon. It is
extremely wary and often acts as flock sentinel, whistling an alarm when danger looms. Baldpates seem
equally at home in sunbaked climes or Arctic chill.

ᐯ **Gadwalls Will Never Win the Title
of "Best-dressed Duck"**

Dark-colored, with few distinctive markings, the
Gadwall is often difficult to identify when feeding with
other species. Mid-June finds the male (left) losing his
breeding plumage. His egg-heavy mate, grubbing for
food, resembles the female mallard.

Photographed in Lower Souris Refuge, North Dakota

170

Cayuga Lake's Expert Divers Chart an Underwater Bonanza

These ducks have been attracted by beds of wild celery and musk grass. Group feeding, or "rafting," made
many waterfowl easy prey in the days of market hunting and no bag limits.

171

Photographed on Cayuga Lake, New York

Redheads, Canvas-backs, and Greater Scaups Share in the Strike

Feeding beds here are 8 to 10 feet below the surface. Much greater depths are easily reached by the diving
ducks; **Redheads,** for instance, may submerge 40 feet or more.

Pintails, Like Robins, Are Sure Heralds of Spring

↑ Farmers in northern States, hearing the musical whistle of the **American Pin-tail**, know winter's end is near. Flocks arrive when open water appears on lakes.
→ **European Widgeon**, a frequent east-coast visitor, displays his breeding plumage (lower) and eclipse plumage (upper). While molting primaries, males cannot fly.

Splashes Betray Black and Mallard Ducks as Amateur Divers

Black Ducks and **Common Mallards**, surface feeders, usually tip to reach their food. Occasionally they dive, raising a shower of spray. A bag of corn, tossed into Cayuga Lake, led this group to forage in deep water. True diving ducks submerge with scarcely a splash. They are aided by their much larger feet and legs set farther to the rear.

Blue-winged Teal, a surface feeder, acquires its bright plumage after December, later than most ducks.

Left: photographed in Lower Souris Refuge, North Dakota   Photographed on Cayuga Lake, New York

© National Geographic Society

173

174

↑   Pintails, Arrow-swift in Flight, Are
the "Greyhounds of Waterfowl"

Hunters need steady nerves when an **American Pintail** rockets overhead. The species, though widely dispersed, is more common in the West, nesting from Nebraska and California to the Arctic. This male made a migratory stop near Washington, D. C.

↓ While Father Goes His Carefree Way,
Mother Pintail Tends the Nest

Drakes soon lose interest in their nesting mates. Forming huge flocks, they revert to bachelor habits. Offspring never see their fathers unless by chance at the fall migratory assembly. This **American Pintail** chose Utah's Bear River marshland for a homesite.

175

Photographed near St. Petersburg, Florida

↑ **Lesser Scaups, Enjoying Florida's Sun, Paddle Lazily in Crystal Waters**

Commonly known as blackheads and little bluebills, **Lesser Scaup Ducks** closely resemble their larger relatives, the greater scaups. Identification anklets, visible on two of the birds (left), help game authorities in studying duck migratory habits and age expectancy.

↓ **A Cinnamon Teal Looks for a Spouse; Ringnecks Prospect for Corn**

Mating season finds the male **Cinnamon Teal** (left), a western bird, at his favorite trysting place in a Utah swamp. The **Ring-necked Ducks,** feeding near a baited blind, have just bobbed to the surface of Cayuga Lake. Another common name is ringbill.

Photographed in Bear River marshes, Utah

Photographed near Ithaca, New York

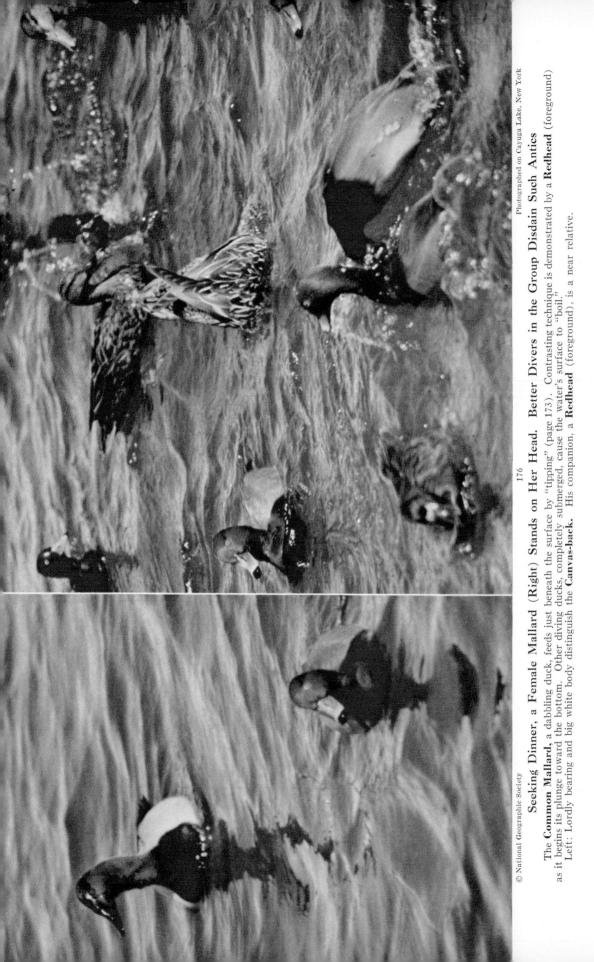

Photographed on Cayuga Lake, New York

Seeking Dinner, a Female Mallard (Right) Stands on Her Head. Better Divers in the Group Disdain Such Antics

The **Common Mallard,** a dabbling duck, feeds just beneath the surface by "tipping" (page 173). Contrasting technique is demonstrated by a **Redhead** (foreground) as it begins its plunge toward the bottom. Other diving ducks, completely submerged, cause the water's surface to "boil."

Left: Lordly bearing and big white body distinguish the **Canvas-back.** His companion, a **Redhead** (foreground), is a near relative.

Nature Paints the Male Wood Duck with Bold Lines and Rich Hues. His Mate's Subdued Plumage Is Drab in Contrast

Wood Ducks once were classed as a vanishing species; hunting them was forbidden until flocks increased. Now one may be included in a day's bag. Fishermen use the male's barred flank feathers to tie the popular Cahill trout fly. These birds, lured in front of the author's blind by a food handout, were suspicious and ready for instant flight. They nest in hollow trees. Acorns, a favorite food, they swallow whole.

© National Geographic Society

Photographed near Ithaca, New York

177

178

↑ A Noisy, Gabbling Call Won This Duck Its Name: Old-squaw

Northern portions of both hemispheres know the garrulous **Old-squaw.** New Englanders believe the male's cry sounds like "South-south-southerly." This female, whose nest contains seven eggs, was photographed in Alaska.

↓ Mama Eider's Downy Nest Has a Modern Touch—Radiant Heat!

This **American Eider** nests off Quebec, where surplus down is gathered to make soft, warm quilts. Once the ducklings have hatched and dried, they run for water. Mothers often pool broods into flocks containing as many as 50 birds.

179

↗ **It's Easy to See Why This Handsome Bird Is Named Spectacled Eider**

Velvety white feathers surround each eye of the male. Females wear darker, less pronounced eye patches. The **Spectacled Eider,** very limited in range, breeds only in Bering Sea coastal areas of Alaska and Siberia. Eskimos make caps of its skins.

↘ **Her Long Vigil Will End with the Arrival of Quadruplets**

A severe summer molt denudes the **Spectacled Eider** of flight feathers. While the birds are helpless, Alaskan natives slaughter them with clubs and stones. This female nests on open tundra not far from water. Winter may find her on an Aleutian island.

180

Our National Emblem, the Bald Eagle, Scans Florida's Air Lanes from a Lofty Snag

Federal law has protected the majestic bird's dwindling numbers in 48 States since 1940 and in Alaska since statehood, 1959. From 1917 to 1952, Alaska paid a bounty for killing it. One of the few remaining places where **Southern Bald Eagle** nests in numbers is Florida's Everglades National Park.

The Bird's World

MY PET crow, Jim, has given up the world of crows and prefers to live with me. Although he is free to fly off with his wild neighbors, they seem to hold no allure for him.

"Hello, Jim," I say to him. He bows very politely, spreads his wings, wags his tail rapidly from side to side, and makes a rattling noise in his throat, a greeting I have never seen a wild crow give another (page 186).

I did not teach Jim to do this; and since he was brought to me as a very young bird when his eyes were scarcely opened, I doubt that he learned it from his parents. I prefer to think of it as a spontaneous reaction developed through crow ages, like a human smile.

At the approach of my pointer or a stray cat, Jim stands high on his legs and hurls invectives with wide-open mouth and vigorous shakes of his head. He sometimes scolds the wild crows that come into the trees near the house, though more often he pays no attention to them.

The Same World Different to Man and Crow

Jim's physical world and mine are fairly similar, but our reactions to parts of it are so different that I wonder whether he sees the same things I do, hears the same sounds, smells the same odors, and feels the same heat and cold. Surely, if things tasted the same to him he would not go after worms, grubs, and spiders with such avidity. He pays no attention when I talk to him in low tones, but if I whistle or squeak he shows instant alarm. Is he deaf to certain sounds and overresponsive to others?

How much of our world goes undetected by birds and how much of their world is beyond our ken? Some questions we may never answer, but others lend themselves readily to study and experimentation.

Today it is comparatively simple to record accurately on film all the sounds made by birds and then to analyze the visible sound-track record and compute the exact changes in pitch of a bird's song. Indeed, the late Albert R. Brand, who started the bird-song recording project at Cornell, did exactly this for more than a hundred of our common birds (footnote, page 307).

From his studies we know that the highest note of the black-poll warbler is about 10,225 vibrations a second, and the lowest note of the horned owl only 150. The average for some 60 songbirds is 4,280, or a quarter note higher than the highest note on the piano.

An ingenious method of testing the hearing of birds, similar to that of the conditioned reflex developed by Ivan Petrovich Pavlov in his classical experiments on animals, was devised by Mr. Brand and Paul Kellogg of the Cornell Laboratory of Ornithology. Giving some unexpected results, it helps to show how the bird's world differs from ours in at least one particular.

Captive starlings, sparrows, and pigeons were trained to feed from a tray so wired that a slight shock could be given to their feet and at the same instant a note of known frequency sounded from an oscillator directly overhead. After a few repetitions of the sound-shock stimulus the birds would jump from the tray when the sound was given without the shock. When the birds were thus conditioned, the note from the oscillator could be raised or lowered until no response was forthcoming.

What Birds Hear

Through many repetitions of this experiment it was learned that the range of hearing in starlings is from 700 to 15,000, that of the English sparrow from 675 to 11,500, and that of the pigeon from 200 to 7,500 cycles a second. A man can hear about four octaves lower than the pigeon, or down to about 20 cycles a second, and most of us can hear the highest note detected by a starling.

The sounds we hear extremely well, such as middle C on the piano, having a frequency of 259, would pass entirely unnoticed by sparrows and starlings, but are just within the hearing range of pigeons. When you talk to your canary, he may seem to be listening as he watches your lips move, but he does not hear a word you say.

When I talk to Jim Crow in a low voice, it is little wonder he turns a deaf ear to my crooning. If I speak loudly, even at the same pitch, I doubtless set up overtones that become audible to him, and he pays attention. What a lot of noise he is spared! His world is different from mine in this respect, although he surely hears more of the world's uproar than does the canary or the starling.

In our laboratory at Cornell, Ernest Edwards, a graduate student, made tests of the hearing of horned owls and determined that, in spite of the comparatively low frequency of the call (150), the owl's range of hearing extends downward only to about 70 cycles a second. This explains why the ruffed grouse can drum with impunity even at night in woods inhabited by horned owls, for the vibration frequency of the grouse drum is only 40 a sec-

Ospreys Are Like Bombs with Built-in Sights

As they plunge at their prey, their hawk eyes enable them to correct their aim with every movement of the target. Here a pair are hovering over their nest—a mass of sticks on top of a dead tree. These huge nests are familiar sights along the Atlantic seaboard from Florida to New England (page 184).

National Geographic Photographer Edwin L. Wisherd

"Mr. Ramshaw," Performing Eagle, Gives an Audience an Extra Thrill

Capt. C. W. R. Knight, British falconry expert, climaxed a National Geographic Society lecture in Constitution Hall, Washington, D. C., by releasing Mr. Ramshaw over the spectators' heads. The 22-year-old Scotch golden eagle, apparently blinded by the photographer's flash bulb, alighted on a lady's red hat. Then he stepped down on her shoulder and waited patiently for Captain Knight to pick him up. The 11-pound bird appeared with his master in the British film, "I Know Where I'm Going."

ond and therefore below the hearing range of the owl (page 51).

Most species of birds utter distinctive call notes—chips, chirps, or squeaks quite apart from their songs. Is it too farfetched to suppose that their ears are especially attuned to these notes, which sound much alike to man, and that they are thus able to exchange with their own kind a considerable range of feeling and experience? On the other hand, man's wide range of hearing enables him to detect many sounds inaudible to birds.

When I place some unfamiliar object before my crow, he usually scrutinizes it carefully, turning his head first on one side and then on the other, as if listening to see if it could make a noise. He is not listening any more than the robin cocking his head to one side as he seeks worms on the lawn. Birds, having their eyes on the sides of their heads, do not see near objects straight ahead so easily as those at the side. They turn their heads in order

to center the vision of one eye on the object.

On the retinas of such birds as the robin and the crow there are two spots of keenest vision, one for monocular vision of things close up and one for binocular vision of more distant objects (pages 184, 185). Owls, whose eyes are directed forward, see more as we do and turn their heads in the direction they wish to see most clearly.

How Owls See at Night

When the light fails and we begin to see poorly, the owl starts to waken, and the iris in its eye opens up to let in a maximum of light. In the horned owl photograph on page 278 the distended iris proves that the picture was taken by flashlight in the dark. In bright sunlight the pupil might be the size of a pinhead (page 277).

In still another way do owls have an advantage over man: their retinas, like those of cats, are more sensitive to the blue end of

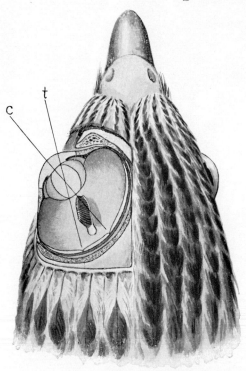

Drawn by Walter A. Weber

The Way a Bird Sees

The head of this red-shouldered hawk is dissected on the left side to show the extraordinary size of the eye. The retina has two depressions, or foveae, for sharpest sight. The line of binocular vision (t) is that for both eyes together; that of monocular vision (c) is for each eye independently. These are adjusted by the large lens in front, while below lies the dark-colored pecten, behind which is the light-colored end of the optic nerve. The eye is not symmetrical (page 183).

the spectrum, which dominates at night. The retina contains two types of light-sensitive cells, the rods and the cones. The cone cells, which contain a drop of oil, are apparently more sensitive to the red end of the spectrum, while the rods are more sensitive to the blue. In the retina of the owl and other night-roaming creatures, the rods predominate.

Is it not possible that the periods of activity of the many kinds of birds are determined even more by the proportion of rods and cones in their retinas than by the size of their eyes or the activity of the pigment cells?

Cardinals Sing Early and Late

Certain species start their May morning concert much earlier than others. For example, a pair of cardinals are the first dawn visitors to the feeding station near my window and the last to leave at night. Chickadees (page 29) and woodpeckers (pages 9-14) often do not show up for an hour after dawn, and retire long before the cardinals.

When winter shadows lengthen on Cayuga Lake, the canvas-backs and bluebills (pages 170-171 and 176) cease diving near shore and swim farther out to sleep. While sleeping, they paddle occasionally with one foot to keep traveling in circles and not drift ashore. They obviously do not like the dark.

On the other hand, the black ducks and mallards (pages 166 and 173) that have been dozing out the day in the middle of the lake now become active. Like the woodcock (page 232), they go in search of food just when the diving ducks cease their activities.

Differences in responses to sunlight control all birds' selection of habitat and time their daily activities.

To a barn owl (page 276), the world viewed by the light of the moon and stars must be a cold, colorless place, but to the swallows (pages 30-32), which dart about in full sunlight, it takes on a riot of color.

The oven-bird and mourning warbler (page 66) choose the dense shade of the woodlands for their abode; the orioles (pages 77-80), cuckoos (pages 274-5), and kingbirds (page 18) like the light shade of gardens; the sandpiper (pages 210-213) and the terns (pages 256, 257, 260) prefer the bright sun of the open shores. And each species may be unhappy in the preferred habitat of the others.

The Arctic tern probably enjoys more daylight than any other bird, for it nests in the Arctic region during the period of almost perpetual daylight and winters in the Antarctic during a similar period. On the 22,000 miles of its migrations it enjoys the periods of longest days and shortest nights. Is there a material difference in its eye structure that stimulates such a tremendous urge for migration? So far as I know, no scientist has yet worked this out.

Birds' Eyes Adjust Themselves Instantly

I have often watched an osprey (page 182) or a kingfisher (page 290), hovering 50 to 75 feet over a lake, suddenly half close its wings and drop headfirst toward a fish it has spied in the water.

Despite the rapidly increasing speed of its plunge, it apparently keeps its eyes focused on its prey, for it sometimes swerves when only three or four feet from the water to transfix a moving target!

Human eyes require a fraction of a second to adjust from the distant road to the speedometer of a fast-moving automobile, but with birds adjustment seems to be instantaneous.

In the back of a bird's eye a little black vascular comb called the pecten projects from the region of the optic nerve into the vitreous humor behind the lens. One of the supposed functions of this pecten is to throw its shadow on the retina, so that the slightest motion of the object under scrutiny is perceived and tele-

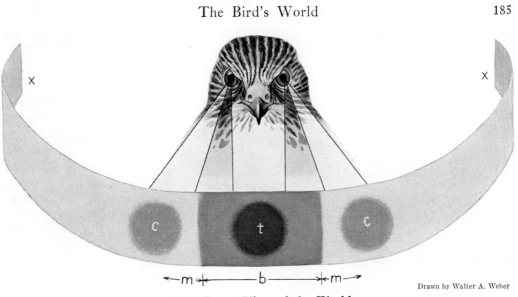

Drawn by Walter A. Weber

A Bird's-eye View of the World

This red-shouldered hawk looks straight ahead with both eyes together; this binocular vision covers the dark central band with the central spot (t) of sharpest sight. Two circles (c) at either side designate the acute field of monocular vision for each eye alone; the gray band from x to x marks a segment of total arc of vision in this bird. This drawing was adapted from a sketch by Gordon Lynn Walls in *The Vertebrate Eye*, published by the Cranbrook Institute of Science.

graphed to the brain. Mammals do not have this structure.

The tiniest mite on the bird's nest is immediately picked up if it moves, but even large enemies escape detection if they are quiet.

A wounded grouse I once held in my hands at the edge of a wood was obviously frightened at being caught; yet, despite its predicament, it suddenly turned its head to watch the sky. After several moments I made out the tiniest black speck of a hawk flying so far above the earth that it was nearly out of range of human vision.

A hawk or an owl, however, that does not move often escapes detection even when close at hand. Bird-eating hawks like the Cooper's (pages 189, 190) and sharp-shinned take advantage of small birds by perching motionless until their prey has become oblivious of their presence.

Once while banding canvas-backs on Cayuga Lake I sat in a blind on a bag of grain from which I had baited the trap, a small enclosure of wire netting in the shallow water. I had inadvertently spilled a trail of corn along the shore. Before I realized what had happened, several black ducks had guzzled their way around and behind my little hideout and were nosing the grain from right under my coat-tails.

So long as I kept still, I was just a part of the landscape to them; but the instant I moved they sprang away in such alarm that one boxed my ear with his wing as he passed over my head.

Hunters consider the black duck the wariest and most sagacious of all our waterfowl. For this reason friends have remarked rudely that the ducks' failure to distinguish between me and the sack of corn was no compliment!

Do Birds Have a Sense of Smell?

Some duck hunters aver that the black duck is the only duck that has a sense of smell and that consequently it is as difficult to sneak up on as a deer. This opinion brings up the question of the importance of odors in the bird's world.

A few years ago one of our graduate students, Victor Coles, attempted to settle the age-old question of whether turkey buzzards find their food by sight or smell.

John James Audubon thought he had settled it when buzzards were unaware of a carcass he had concealed under a canvas but were attracted by his painting of a dead sheep. Later observers, however, discovered that buzzards often found carcasses concealed in woodchuck holes or under boxes.

After watching the buzzards of Barro Colorado Island, Canal Zone, discover the hiding place of some dead fish concealed under a thatched roof, Frank M. Chapman, until his death curator of ornithology for the American Museum of Natural History, became convinced that they must have a keen sense of smell.

For two years we housed Victor Coles's three buzzards while he carried on a series of experiments testing their olfactory sense. He has not yet published his thesis, but before he received his degree he had convinced even the

When the Author Says, "Hello, Jim," His Pet Crow Bows Very Politely

At stray cats the bird unleashes a torrent of invective, opening his mouth wide and shaking his head vigorously. He never wanders far from his master's home (page 181).

most skeptical that his captive buzzards' sense of smell was so poor as to be of little more use to them than their sense of taste in locating food.

The olfactory lobe of the brain is very small in buzzards, as in all other birds, and the turbinal bones of the nose over which are spread the olfactory membrane and nerves are only partially covered with the sensory tissue.

The buzzard's vision, on the other hand, is exceedingly keen. Doubtless the bird has learned to associate buzzing flies and crawling beetles with its type of repast, even when the carrion itself is not visible from the air.

Its poor sense of smell spares it a discomfort that might become unbearable even to a scavenger.

One of the favorite foods of the horned owl is the common skunk. Probably the skunk's unique method of defense, so effective as far as man and dog are concerned, is scant protection against the night marauder with no sense of smell.

Psychologists tell us that there are only four tastes—sweet, sour, bitter, and salt—and that all the rest of those delectable sensations a good chef invokes are really smells. If that be so, the birds' poorly developed sense of smell may account for their strange choice of foods. If worms were only sweet or sour and all bugs tasted the same, we could close our eyes and never starve in the jungle.

Some birds are guided by sight, touch, and experience in their selection of food. Only recently rodent exterminators have learned that poisoned grain stained blue or red will not be touched by birds but will be devoured, despite its coloring, by such creatures as rats and mice that find their food to a great extent by smell.

Why Birds Eat Few Japanese Beetles

The Japanese beetle looked different from the beetles our birds had customarily fed upon. For that reason it was virtually overlooked by them for several years.

William R. Van Dersal, biologist and botanist, lists 16 species of birds as having been observed eating the persimmon in the South, where it is native; yet in 25 years I have never seen a bird touch one of the fruits of a persimmon tree in my garden. My tree is, so far as I know, the only fruiting persimmon in this part of New York State, and consequently, though many of the birds Van Dersal lists pass through my grounds every fall and spring, it stands inviolate.

Similarly the high-bush cranberry, relished by birds in New England, where it is native, is recommended by landscape gardeners elsewhere because "it holds its bright-red berries all winter and the birds don't bother it."

I once fed a lot of cabbage worms to a young cedar waxwing I had rescued when it fell out of its nest. Apparently these caterpillars taken in large quantity are toxic to birds. They made the waxwing sick. After that experience he would not eat any kind of green caterpillar, though he readily took brown ones.

Birds Use Touch in Choosing Food

When I swept a hayfield with an insect net and dumped the contents before him, he at first sailed into the squirming, buzzing, crawling, jumping mess of bugs and devoured them indiscriminately. He soon learned, however, to avoid the little bees and other stinging species, and to pass up all Hymenoptera and even the little tree hoppers with spines on their backs. Touch as well as taste and sight seems to enter into a bird's selection of food.

Both scientists and laymen are still debating the problem of bird migration and the guiding principle that carries the travelers safely to their appointed summer and winter homes through clouds and storms, fog and darkness, without chart or compass. Is it possible, as many have suggested, that birds have a mysterious sense of direction which enables them to utilize the magnetic lines of force on their long journeys?*

Prof. Henry L. Yeagley of Pennsylvania State College has performed experiments which lead him to believe birds do have this magnetic sense. Prof. Donald R. Griffin of Cornell, on the other hand, after following carrier pigeons, gulls, and gannets with a light plane, feels that they depend entirely on landmarks to guide them.

Are birds mere automatons which receive stimuli and react mechanically, or are some of these stimuli cogitated and some of their actions controlled by an inner force?

Grosbeak and Thrasher React Differently

An albino rose-breasted grosbeak (page 90) occupied a cage in my kitchen. Pursued by a hawk eight years before, it flew into a window and stunned itself. It was at that time probably only a few months old, for conspicuous albinos usually do not last long in the wild.

Though it lived in our kitchen for eight years, it was still a wild bird. It learned by long association not to fear us; yet it attacked my hand viciously when I cleaned the cage or offered it food. Through the window it watched the sky for hawks and the shrubbery for cats, and it was a veritable watchdog for notifying us in its own way when a predator was in sight.

It learned to get along without insects and became overfat on a vegetarian diet, but it still behaved as a normal grosbeak. The Allen family became a part of its habitat, to be accepted guardedly, but it bore toward us no affection or gratitude for solicitous care.

Why should its behavior have been so different from that of Jim Crow?

A few years ago we were presented with a brown thrasher reared by Miss Edna Becker, one of my graduate students. A great pet, this bird had the run of the house. When we gave it entire freedom of the out-of-doors, it stayed in the shrubbery about the lawn and greeted all comers with friendliness, if a severe peck on the ankle or a tweak of the ear can be called friendly. Even our pointer received attention, a yank of the tail or the hair on his back. Quick as the dog was, he never quite caught Rufus.

There was never any question that we were as much an integral part of the thrasher's life as we were of Jim Crow's; yet when fall came, Rufus started wandering farther afield and then suddenly disappeared. Perhaps his friendliness toward human beings or his lack of fear of dogs got him into trouble, but I prefer to believe that the instinct to migrate, inherent in thrashers, stimulated him to take off south without understanding what was happening.

Effects of Early Training

But why the difference in the behavior of the thrasher and the grosbeak—a difference that anyone who has ever kept wild birds in captivity has experienced? The grosbeak had passed at least the first month of its life in the wild, where the only part man played was that of an enemy. The thrasher, on the other hand, had been conditioned to man as a companion during this formative period.

Two barred owls (page 279) were brought to us 12 and 16 years ago, respectively. One was a tiny downy youngster when he was found and the other nearly grown, though still with down on his plumage. For nearly 10 years they lived together, but their responses to us were entirely different. The one we received very young flew to us; the other flew away. Throughout life birds retain the perspective pattern of their early life.

In a report on her studies of the common song sparrow, Mrs. Margaret Nice, a painstaking observer, lists 59 activities which she was able to recognize and record as they first appeared or matured in some young birds she was rearing by hand.

Such things as preening, yawning, standing on the tarsus, standing on the feet, scratching, fluttering, stretching, hopping, jumping, pecking, drinking, bathing, etc., were done for the first time at definite ages. Thus while the birds started preening when they were six days old, they did not scratch until they were

* See "Bird Banding, the Telltale of Migratory Flight," by E. W. Nelson, NATIONAL GEOGRAPHIC MAGAZINE, January, 1928.

seven, and did not start bathing until they were thirteen.

These were all activities in which the young bird would engage for the rest of its life, and the order of their appearance is much the same, as she points out, in many of the common birds.

What Mrs. Nice was unable to record, but which likewise will be preserved for the rest of the bird's life, was the influence of the young birds' immediate environment and companions in imprinting a mental habitat picture that will affect all later behavior. That of the hand-reared bird is entirely different from that of the young bird reared by its parents, and one can expect that its later responses to man and to its environment will be somewhat different.

Our thrasher, one barred owl, and Jim Crow passed their early days in man's world; the grosbeak and the other owl grew up in the wild, and after eight and ten years they still retained the picture of that habitat in which man was a disturbing element.

Effect of Captivity on Nesting Habits

When the nesting season rolls around, the song sparrow that was reared in the wild will search out a nesting site that conforms to the important features of the one in which it was raised. The hand-reared bird, on the other hand, while it may instinctively build a typical song sparrow nest, if it be given the right material, will be just as happy to build it in a box as in a bush.

For years I raised ruffed grouse in captivity under highly artificial conditions (page 71), on wire netting so that their feet never touched the ground. Their behavior was in most ways normal for grouse, except that they were absolutely devoid of fear of me or anyone else. At nesting time they were satisfied to lay their eggs in boxes prepared for them, although they still went through the gestures of tossing leaves upon their backs during the egg-laying period, even as do the wild birds. At best they had only shavings or sawdust to toss.

For another decade I attempted to get wild-trapped canvas-backs and redheads (page 176) to nest in captivity by keeping them on an enclosed spring-fed pond of several acres, with plenty of good nesting cover where they never had to be handled and where they could have seclusion if they wished it. They became quite tame; but though they went through all the behavior of courting and mating, females never built nests or laid eggs.

After four years an occasional black duck and a green-winged teal, captive on the same pond, laid eggs and reared young, but the canvas-backs and redheads maintained their egglessness.

Next I secured from Alberta some stock which had been hatched from wild eggs set under hens. When these birds were put on the pond, they nested and laid eggs the first year. So resistant to breeding in captivity are wild-trapped waterfowl that even artificial lighting and injections with gonadotropic hormones, which stimulate pheasants, grouse, and hand-reared ducks to lay two months early, did not cause them to lay an egg.

Why should there be such a difference between wild-trapped and captive-raised waterfowl? Is the mosaic of their juvenile habitat so deeply impressed upon the wild birds that they cannot form eggs until they duplicate the conditions of their youth?

Birds Take Time to Get Used to Camera

When any new feature is introduced into the natural habitat of a bird, it is scrutinized with the greatest caution. If the change is at all fundamental to that species, the bird may move to another locality where there has been no change rather than try to adapt its life.

A pair of catbirds or thrashers nesting in the bushes in the garden will probably move to another yard if a garage replaces the shrubbery. Such a change may make little difference to the robins, but the catbirds and thrashers will seek new bushes which have grown to just the requisite density.

When preparing to photograph a bird at its nest, I do not immediately place the camera or the blind where I want to use it. I have learned by experience to set it some distance away until the birds have grown used to it and accepted it as part of their mental picture (page 226).

The longer I leave it, the more quickly will they accept it when I move it up to the required four or five feet from the nest.

The birds' parental instinct will overcome to some extent fear or objection to change, the reaction varying with the individual and with the particular stage of the nesting cycle. All birds, however, are resistant to change, and an understanding of their reactions is essential to a bird photographer.

In the world of his choice, the bird passes through a cycle of behavior which is repeated each year with the greatest precision. Migration in the spring, selection of territory, mating, nest building, egg laying, incubation, care of the young, fall flocking and wandering, fall migration, and choice of wintering grounds—these are major activities over which the bird as an individual has as little control as it has over growth and feather change.

The account of the bird's year, however, is another story.*

* See "The Bird's Year," page 69.

Maternal Duties Keep the Female Marsh Hawk Quiet and Contented

Brooding her young in a nest of giant fireweed, this **Marsh Hawk** is well concealed. Owllike ruff of short feathers around the face indicates large external ears and keen hearing, helpful in following rodent prey as the hawk beats back and forth over hayfield, pasture, or plain.

Downy Hawks Will Soon Grow Up to Be Killers

Preying upon other birds as well as on small mammals and reptiles, chicken hawks flit through the forest like deadly shadows. **Cooper's Hawks** even raid poultry yards in the face of irate owners' attempts to frighten them away.

This is one of the few really destructive birds; some hawks perform services highly useful to man.

Photographed by A. M. Bailey and R. J. Niedrach in Colorado High Country

189

Speed Lighting "Mounts" Hawks More Faithfully than Taxidermy

Cooper's Hawk, commonly called chicken hawk, and not without reason, regularly feeds on small birds.

This fierce but doting parent, acting according to instinct, has decapitated its prey, a starling, and plucked most of the feathers. An orange-colored eye is a sign of the bird's immaturity; in time it will be red. The youngsters have bluish eyes. They are very hungry, having waited for three hours (as did the author!).

To obtain the picture, the author and one of his students spotted the birds lodging high in a tree. They rigged this dummy nest below it and transferred the fledglings. Their deception succeeding, they lowered the nest 10 feet a day until it was at camera level. Then they photographed the blissful home-coming from the privacy of a blind (page 21).

Photographed near Ithaca, New York

Red-tailed Hawk Pounces on Master's Gauntlet for a Meaty Reward

Falconry, like archery, goes far back into antiquity. Chinese appear to have practiced hawking 2,000 years ago. Ancient sculptures attest the sport's favor in Egypt and Persia. Greeks and Romans left written accounts. In medieval Europe falconry became a favorite pastime of the nobility.

Though gunpowder brought about its decay, the sport never died out. Today it is gaining favor among young Americans. Central Asians still train the golden eagle to hunt foxes.

Usually the hawker obtains his birds by taking nestlings or trapping adults. With hoods, lures, whistles, and gentleness he trains them until they become accustomed to man and his dogs. Many show affection toward their owners.

Though it makes an interesting pet, the **Eastern Red-tailed Hawk** is too clumsy in the air to be an accomplished hunter like the peregrine falcon (page 192). Owing to an undeserved reputation as a chicken thief, it has been relentlessly persecuted. Actually, it deserves protection as the assassin of mice, rats, gophers, snakes, and other vermin.

Leather thongs, known as jesses, are worn by this bird for tethering to its perch.

Photographed near Ithaca, New York

192

Bold and Ruthless Is the Peregrine of Taughannock

This falcon makes its home and rears its young in central New York near 215-foot Taughannock Falls (background). Magnificent pirate of the air, the bird knows neither fear nor pity. **Duck Hawks,** sometimes known as peregrines, are found in several forms throughout the world and in many places are used for hunting feathered game. The duck hawk nests from Alaska and the west coast of central Greenland to Baja California, Kansas and Maryland. In winter it ranges south to Panama (page 48).

⋏ Eaglelike Ospreys Build Huge Nests

The wild-eyed, fierce-looking hawks are almost exclusively fish eaters, catching their prey in lightning dives. They defend their stick and weed nests with utmost courage. Nearly full-grown **Ospreys** (left) have tested their wings and are about to leave their parents (right). The osprey ranges all over North America and south to Peru, Chile and Paraguay.

Sparrow Hawk Lives → in Flicker's Dugout

Smallest of the native hawks, the **Eastern Sparrow Hawk** sometimes occupies back-yard bird boxes. So obviously harmless, this bird has escaped the extermination campaigns aimed at its larger relatives.

193

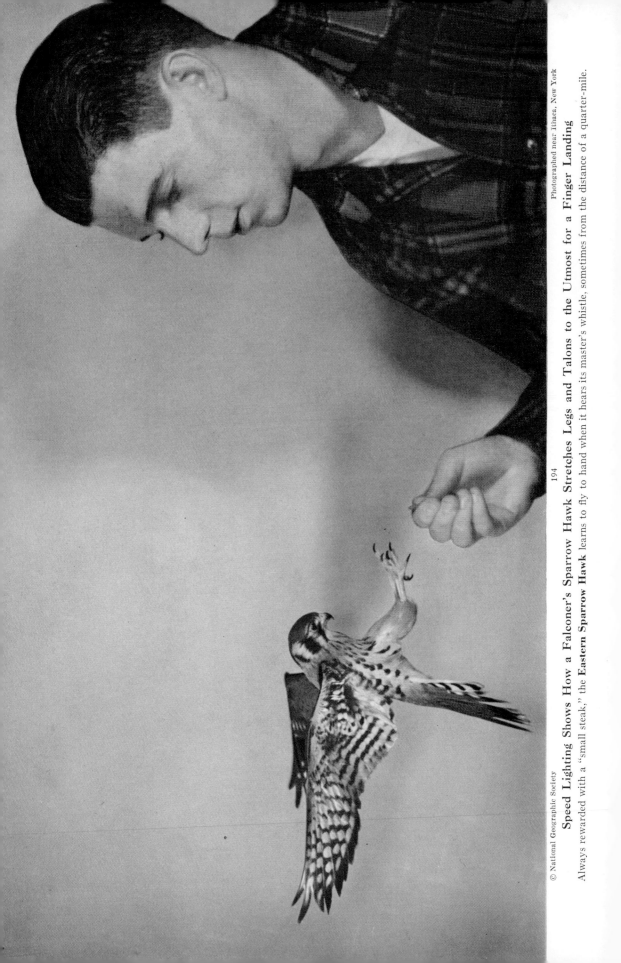

Photographed near Ithaca, New York

194

Speed Lighting Shows How a Falconer's Sparrow Hawk Stretches Legs and Talons to the Utmost for a Finger Landing

Always rewarded with a "small steak," the **Eastern Sparrow Hawk** learns to fly to hand when it hears its master's whistle, sometimes from the distance of a quarter-mile.

Visibility Zero when Viewed from Above! A Female Willow Ptarmigan Almost Matches the Reindeer Moss

So protectively colored is the **Willow Ptarmigan** that one can pass within three feet of an incubating bird without seeing her. To overcome this camouflage, the photographer lowered the camera to ground level and caught her in silhouette. In winter this Arctic dweller lives on birch and willow buds projecting above the snow.

Photographed near Churchill, Manitoba

195

Photographed by Alfred M. Bailey in Colorado High Country

Bird World's
Beau Brummell

The **Southern White-tailed Ptarmigan** of the Rockies molts almost continuously. Pure white in winter and heather brown in summer, with intermediate plumages for spring and fall, it enjoys year-round camouflage. The female in top picture is attempting to decoy the human intruders from her brood. At left, a close-up.

Photographed by Alfred M. Bailey and F. G. Brandenburg in Colorado High Country

197

↑ Curious Stiff-legged Dance
Attracts Ladylove

The **Prairie Sharp-tailed Grouse** makes a less musical and more abrupt call than the prairie chicken (below). The mating dance tramples the ground, leaving it hard and bare. Sharptails range from Wisconsin and Colorado to Alaska.

↓ Mating Calls Ring Out
Across Pairing Grounds

Male **Greater Prairie Chickens** inflate their neck sacs as sounding boards and send their "Oom-boom-boom" often two miles across the prairie. The birds range from Indiana to Colorado and into Canada, but are scarce.

198

⋏   Here Is a Real Ruff-neck

Eastern Ruffed Grouse, or "partridge" of northern United States and Canada ("pheasant" in the southern Appalachians), shows off for courtship or challenge. He shakes his head until the ruffs seem to rotate. A difficult bird to shoot, the grouse is tame when unmolested. Female builds nest on ground.

⋎   Drummer Beats Tattoo, Then Rests

With his fan tail touching the log, the **Eastern Ruffed Grouse** whips the air with forward and upward strokes of his wings to produce a thumping sound which ends in a roll like thunder. During the unexplained fall "crazy season," many birds kill themselves by flying into obstacles (pages 51 and 52).

A Plump Californian Poses at Her Doorway

Though no longer so numerous as in earlier years, the **California Quail** is still a familiar game bird in many upland areas of the Golden State. During most of the year it frequents chaparral-covered hillsides and brushy draws. If unmolested, it may take up residence in suburban gardens or city parks. The nest usually is hidden beneath undergrowth or other shelter.

Conservation authorities successfully introduced California quail into Utah, Hawaiian Islands, and Chile. Similar efforts failed in eastern United States, although the birds are raised there in captivity.

This female was photographed at Berkeley. The male wears a high crest and a black throat like Gambel's quail (below), but lacks the chestnut flanks.

Photographed at Berkeley, California

Like Other Desert Creatures, Gambel's Quail Can Go Weeks Without Water

Yet when offered a pan of water in an Arizona garden, this family drank copiously. **Gambel's Quail** inhabits semiarid areas of southwestern United States and northern Mexico. Male and young right; female left.

199 Photographed near Tucson, Arizona

⋏ **Relatives of This Wild Gobbler
Journeyed to Spain in 1519**

Rio Grande Turkey is the New World's principal
contribution to man's kept birds. Conquistadors, exploring Mexico, found captive turkeys and shipped them
home. Europe misidentified the bird with the turkey
cock, a guinea fowl imported into Turkey from Africa.

⋎ **About Face! Three Indian War Bonnets
Flash Copper in a Texas Sunrise**

In spring the tom turkey would rather strut than eat.
Nature sustains him with a heavy pad of reserve fat
over the breast. These chummy gobblers drove other
males away from their 20 hens. They are **Rio Grande
Turkeys,** one of five wild races.

Sandhill Crane Struts Beside a →
Favorite Marsh

He promenades in stately manner here, but
when courting he performs in the best square-
dance fashion. In early spring, **Florida Sandhill Cranes** assemble in groups of four to forty
to perform an old-fashioned "minuet"—bowing,
pirouetting, and high-stepping.

↓ Seeking Snails, a Noisy Limpkin
Wades the Shallows

Its nickname, "crying bird," stems from an
eerie, penetrating call, "Aow, aow, aow, aow,
oooooooow!" **Limpkins** dwell in southern
swamps and cypress-lined streams where they
feed almost exclusively upon a large nocturnal
snail *(Pomacea)*. This photograph was made at
Wakulla Springs, Florida, famous for its wonderfully clear water and banshee-voiced residents,
the limpkins.

202 Photographed near Igiak Bay, Yukon Delta, Alaska

A Crane with a Stain Guards Two Large Eggs on an Alaskan Hillock

This northern representative of the sandhill crane is called the **Little Brown Crane** because of its smaller size and apparently brown coloration. The brown, however, is merely a stain that varies considerably with individuals of many of the northern waterfowl and is probably acquired from the ponds which they frequent. This is the female; the male is whiter about the face. So wary is this bird that it usually spots visitors a quarter of a mile away and leaves its nest. Thus the eggs often fall prey to parasitic jaegers (page 236). Newly hatched young have brighter coloring, about the hue of a red fox. In fall these cranes fly off to California, Texas, and Mexico.

203

↑ **Expression "Thin as a Rail"
Might Refer to This Bird**

Compressed for slipping through the dense vegetation, the **Virginia Rail** lives in the fresh or brackish water sedge and cattail marshes throughout the United States and southern Canada. Female lays 5 to 12 eggs of cream buff color with spots of reddish brown (p. 50).

↓ **From the Salt Marshes
Comes a Noise Like Applause**

The call of this **Northern Clapper Rail,** however, sounds more like a rattle than hand clapping. Known as the "marsh hen" in Sidney Lanier's *Marshes of Glynn,* it is found in coastal salt-water marshes from Connecticut southward.

204

The Purple Gallinule Is Up-to-the-minute in Attire, but Likes Its Feet Wet

Flat little blue hat perched cockily, and with bright-red beak and yellow legs, this flashy bird could serve as a fashion plate. Here a male rearranges the nest in a Louisiana marsh. The northernmost breeding range of the **Purple Gallinule** is the Gulf States, but it occasionally surprises bird lovers in New England and Canada.

205 Photographed on Howland Island, New York

↑ Water Chicken Returns to Its Nest

Often called "mud hen," it is properly named the **Florida Gallinule.** Close relative of the European moor hen, it dwells in large fresh-water marshes from Ontario to the Galapagos Islands.

↓ Orange Feathers Top Coot Chicks

But their bodies are covered with black down. "Half duck, half chicken" describes the **American Coot.** In nesting season adults explode with cackles, clucks, and wails; they splash, wave wings, and chase one another.

Photographed in Bear River marshes, Utah

A Vanishing Species—the California Clapper Rail

Its salt-marsh home in the San Francisco and Monterey Bay regions is being transformed rapidly into building lots or wharves. The **California Clapper Rail's** brown color more nearly resembles that of the king rail than the familiar clapper rail of the eastern coast of the United States.

Semipalmated Plovers Choose Gravelly Sites, Sometimes Between Railroad Tracks

Common at Churchill was this **Semipalmated Plover,** sometimes called the ring-necked plover. It looks like a small killdeer (page 209), but has only one band across its breast. This photograph was made between 8 and 9 p. m., thanks to the long Arctic evening.

No Soft Nest →
for the
Snowy Plover!

Its eggs, protectively colored, are laid in sand or pebbles. This nesting female, a **Western Snowy Plover,** deposited her speckled treasures on a gravel road in Utah. Only six inches away was a wheel rut made by passing cars. An eastern form of the same bird is called Cuban snowy plover (page 316).

Photographed near Brigham, Utah

207   Photographed near Churchill, Manitoba

A Globe-trotter Rests at Journey's End

American Golden Plovers nest in Arctic areas and winter on Argentina's pampas. During fall migration, strong gales over Atlantic often force them to make unscheduled stops in east-coast States. Pacific golden plovers nesting in Alaska find Hawaii, mid-Pacific isles, Australia, and New Zealand with the accuracy of a B-36 navigator.

208 Photographed near Igiak Bay, Yukon Delta, Alaska

↑ **Breeding Season Finds This Plover Wearing Snowflake Plumage**

Black-bellied Plover is one of the few birds found over almost the entire world. It summers in Arctic climes and winters as far south as Africa, India, Australia, and South America. Showy plumage is molted in August and September, when the adults resemble their adolescent offspring. Black-bellies perform their courtship antics in the air while flying at great speeds.

∨ **To Make a Living, He Leaves No Stone Unturned**

Trotting along a beach, the **Ruddy Turnstone** flips over shells, pebbles, and seaweed in search of beetles and worms. In August it quits Arctic breeding grounds in favor of South America. Old World turnstones are a little larger and darker than the American birds. This male is incubating four large eggs. As with other shore birds, parental instinct sometimes is stronger in males.

209

Photographed near Ithaca, New York

ʌ **Killdeer Wear Identical Costumes
Winter and Summer**

Male, female, and immature **Killdeer** look exactly alike throughout the year. Even the downy young closely resemble their elders. This baby bird has not yet lost its egg tooth, a calcified deposit at the tip of the bill, which enables the youngster to break from its shell. Newly hatched killdeer find their own food. Adults devour many kinds of harmful insects.

ᵛ **A Beachcomber Takes Time Out
for Parental Duties**

The **Black Turnstone** prospects for food in the same manner as its cousin, the ruddy turnstone (opposite page). They are often found together in migration, although the black species is more restricted in range. It nests along Alaska's Bering Sea coast and may winter as far south as Baja California. White markings on head and shoulders are worn only in summer.

Photographed near Igiak Bay, Yukon Delta, Alaska

210

↑ **When Fall Paints Forest,**
Sandpipers Turn Leaden Gray

Gayer than most is the **Red-backed Sandpiper,** nesting on a grassy ridge in a pond. It showed more fear of parasitic jaegers skimming the tundra in search of eggs than of the camera or blind. The male's flight song has been compared to the call of a toad.

↓ **The Gentle Dowitcher Was Once**
Nearly Wiped Out by Hunters

Tangled tundra grasses screened the incubating bird, but the author pressed them down to reveal her and to obtain probably the first photograph of this species on its nest. In the fall, the **Eastern Dowitcher** drops its bright colors. Its name comes from its call.

211

Little "Sandpeep" at Home: It Looks to the Surf for Supper

Following the receding waves, the **Semipalmated Sandpiper** seizes tiny crustaceans while avoiding wet feet. Common on beaches east of the Rockies, it migrates to the Gulf, West Indies, and even Patagonia. Its mating cry is a buzz rather than a song.

When Standing, He Towers on Stilts above His Cousins

Long spindly legs of the **Stilt Sandpiper** are folded up as he takes his turn on four beautifully spotted eggs. The nest is a sparsely lined depression on a grassy bit of tundra near Hudson Bay. He likes to feed along the margins of shallow ponds.

Photographed near Churchill, Manitoba

"Keep-a-going, Keep-a-going," Whistles the Lesser Yellow-legs, Self-appointed Sentinel of the North

The keen eyes of this sandpiper spy the trespasser a long way off. The call of the **Lesser Yellow-legs** alarms other birds and makes observation and nest finding difficult. A fairly common visitor on shores and mud flats during spring and fall migrations, it sometimes winters in Louisiana and Florida, but usually travels to Argentina and Chile.

← This Sandpiper's Nickname, "Teeter-tail," Describes a Nervous Mannerism

"Tip-up" is another name often applied to the **Spotted Sandpiper,** a fidgety bird which never tires of tilting its body up and down. No other shore bird is more widely and intimately known in the United States. In summer it is found over most of North America, surpassing even the familiar robin in breeding range. In winter its residence extends from the Gulf coast as far south as Argentina. Breast spots indicate summer plumage.

Photographed near Ithaca, New York

Her Mate Is a Chesty Fellow; Hence → the Name "Pectoral Sandpiper"

In spring the male inflates his breast until he is as misshapen as a pouter pigeon; then he flies in circles over the tundra, calling "Wood-wood-wood" to prospective mates or antagonists. **Pectoral Sandpipers** breed in Arctic areas and winter in South America. During semiannual migrations they seem to avoid the Pacific coast; they are common on the east coast in fall but not in spring. Most flocks prefer the Mississippi Valley flyway.

Photographed near Churchill, Manitoba

214

Worn Wing Feathers Are Eloquent of the Long Distance Flown by This Hudsonian Curlew

An inter-American traveler, the **Hudsonian Curlew** spends the winter in South America and nests only on Arctic coasts. Here the long-billed bird is settling on its eggs in the reindeer moss. The breast feathers are being lowered to expose double brood spots of bare skin which will make contact with the eggs.

Saberlike Bills Distinguish the "Big Curlews" . . . Canada-bound Greater Yellow-legs Stops in Texas for Refueling

Long-billed Curlews might truthfully claim that their bills are their fortune. The odd-looking beaks are efficient instruments for digging fiddler crabs and crayfish from muddy burrows. These birds, once hunted to the point of extinction, are staging a comeback under protective laws. Very few visit eastern States, where they formerly were plentiful. March finds this hungry **Greater Yellow-legs** (right) already wearing summer plumage, evidenced by barred flanks.

Photographed near Brigham, Utah

Photographed near Austwell, Texas

© National Geographic Society

215

216

A Bird of Mystery No Longer—the Bristle-thighed Curlew at Its Alaska Home

Although known to science for 163 years, this member of the sandpiper family was the last of all North American birds to give up the secret of its nesting place. On June 12, 1948, north of Mountain Village, Alaska, its nest and eggs were found at last by an expedition sponsored by the National Geographic Society, Cornell University, and the Arctic Institute of North America. A migrant between northern wilds and South Sea islands, the **Bristle-thighed Curlew** was observed and collected on Tahiti in 1769 and was first described in 1785. Bristles on feathers of flanks and belly show clearly as the female perches on a boulder near the long-sought nest.

The Curlew's Secret Revealed at Last

UP TO June 12, 1948, one bird—and one only—of all the 815 species of North American birds had successfully hidden the secret of its nesting place and summer home from the eyes of man.

This bird of mystery was the bristle-thighed curlew, so named because of dubious adornments sprouting from its flanks and even its belly (opposite page).

No bigger than a pullet, but strong of wing, this great little traveler was known to winter on Tahiti and other South Sea islands and in spring to fly 5,500 miles, often by way of the Hawaiian Islands, to the coast of Alaska (map, page 220). But there it seemed to vanish into the thin air of the north.

The story of the curlew's secret begins before the American Revolution, with the famous round-the-world voyage of the British navigator, Capt. James Cook, during the years 1768 to 1771. It ends with a 1948 expedition sponsored by the National Geographic Society, Cornell University, and the Arctic Institute of North America, organized in 1944 by distinguished Canadians and Americans.

First Specimen Found in 1769

Captain Cook had already demonstrated his appreciation of science, his knowledge of navigation, and his administrative ability when he was selected by the Lords of the Admiralty to sail the *Endeavour* on a voyage of exploration around the world.*

The main objective from the standpoint of the Royal Society was to make observations on the transit of Venus across the sun, which might give information of value to astronomy and navigation. This happens about once in a hundred years, and the Society, desiring data from widely separate points, wished the transit of June 3, 1769, observed from an island in the South Pacific.

Tahiti, then called Otaheite, had been visited by Capt. Samuel Wallis, R.N., the year before and was selected as the most likely spot. Thither Captain Cook directed his course, leaving Plymouth, England, late in August, 1768. Sir Joseph Banks, an ardent naturalist, was chosen by the Royal Society to accompany the expedition.

After an unusually well-ordered voyage, the expedition anchored at Tahiti on April 13, 1769, and stayed until July 13. It established friendly relations with the natives and recorded successfully the transit of Venus.

Three months on the island gave Banks and his helpers plenty of time to harvest a representative natural-history collection, which was made available to other scientists upon the return to England.

Examining the expedition's bird collection, and those of Cook's two later voyages, John Latham, a leading ornithologist of the day, recognized a curlew from Tahiti as different from the European whimbrel. When he published his *General Synopsis of Birds* in 1785, he listed the new bird as the Otaheite curlew. Its present scientific name is *Numenius tahitiensis*.

Bristles Noted by Titian Peale

After Captain Cook had shown the way, practically every naturalist who visited any of the South Sea islands between September and April found Otaheite curlews and sent specimens back to museums in Europe.

From 1838 to 1842 Titian Peale, son of the artist Charles Willson Peale, accompanied the United States Exploring Expedition to the South Seas under Lt. Charles Wilkes and found a curlew, in the Low (Tuamotu) Archipelago, which he thought to be a new species. Because he noted curious bristlelike feathers on the flanks and belly, he called it *Numenius femoralis,* and the common name, "bristle-thighed curlew," has stuck to this day.

The bird proved to be the same as the one in Sir Joseph Banks's collection. The characteristic bristles, more conspicuous in some individuals than in others, appear to have gone unnoticed by Latham.

For a hundred years after the discovery of the bird, naturalists believed it to be a resident of the South Seas and thought it must nest on some other island than the one they were studying. Then on May 18, 1869, Ferdinand Bischoff collected a bristle-thighed curlew at Kenai, Alaska, across the Kenai Peninsula from Seward.

On May 24, 1880, Dr. E. W. Nelson, who later became Chief of the United States Biological Survey, found two curlews on the west coast of Alaska near St. Michael.

Five years later, on August 26, Dr. C. H. Townsend found one still farther north on the Kowak (Kobuk) River, and it began to be suspected that possibly the summer home of the mystery bird might be Alaska.

Nevertheless, as late as 1896, when R. Bowdler Sharpe published the 24th volume of *Catalogue of Birds in the British Museum,* covering the shore birds of the world, he still gave as the range of the bristle-thighed curlew

---

* See "Columbus of the Pacific," by J. R. Hildebrand, NATIONAL GEOGRAPHIC MAGAZINE, January, 1927.

Curlew's nest
discovered
June 12, 1948

Drawn by Harry S. Oliver and Irvin E. Alleman

Vast Alaska Was the Haystack, a 6¾-inch Nest the Needle

Air transportation and a combination of good weather, good judgment, and good luck enabled the National Geographic Society-Cornell University-Arctic Institute of North America expedition to find the first known nest and eggs of the bristle-thighed curlew. This ornithological hide-and-seek ended in one of the loneliest spots on the continent, a stretch of tundra above what the expedition named Curlew Lake.

"Northwestern North America (rarely), visiting most of the islands of the Pacific Ocean, in some of which it is supposed to breed."

Early in the 20th century an increasing number of observations on this interesting bird were made without dispelling the mystery.

Homer R. Dill and William A. Bryan, returning from Laysan Island in the Hawaiian group in 1911, reported about 250 bristle-thighed curlews using the island and even roosting on the roofs of old buildings in a manner very unorthodox for shore birds.

In 1922 Dr. Paul Bartsch, Curator of the Division of Mollusks at the United States National Museum, writing of a trip to the Midway Islands, reported these curlews abundant

and tame there during November. They were feeding on Scaevola berries.

Curlews on Laysan Steal Eggs

The following year Dr. Alexander Wetmore, now Secretary of the Smithsonian Institution and a Trustee of the National Geographic Society, visited Laysan Island and found the curlews numerous. He reported them behaving in a still less orthodox manner—eating the eggs of terns, frigate birds, and boobies.

The curlews were undisturbed by the presence of the observers, and Dr. Wetmore's companion, the late Donald R. Dickey, made motion pictures of them stealing the eggs of a frigate bird. Two of these pictures were

"Better Take Rations for Two or Three Weeks in Case I'm Grounded by Weather"

With a National Geographic map in hand, Nat Browne, veteran bush pilot, checks plans with expedition members at Mountain Village, Alaska, and warns that fog and storm may prevent him from picking them up on schedule. Ready to load supplies are Warren Petersen (left), David Allen, and Henry Kyllingstad (right). Beyond, Nat's red single-engined Bellanca bobs at anchor on the Yukon beside native fishing craft.

published in the NATIONAL GEOGRAPHIC MAGAZINE for July, 1925, accompanying an article by Dr. Wetmore, "Bird Life Among Lava Rock and Coral Sand."

Sometimes the curlews impaled the eggs, but more often they carried them away in their bills to break them on the sand.

So far as I know, this is the only time that anyone has ever seen any shore bird eating the eggs of other birds, and we are at a loss to explain how the habit may have developed.

The curlews were often accompanied by ruddy turnstones, which also departed from all shore-bird tradition by plunging their bills through the eggs of terns.

Meanwhile, these curlews continued to turn up in Alaska. In August, 1911, Rollo H. Beck collected a series of the birds about Nome, although farther to the northwest, around Wales, Alfred M. Bailey, Director of the Colorado Museum of Natural History, got but a single bird in some 20 years of collecting.

In 1924 Herbert W. Brandt, of Cleveland, and Henry B. Conover, research associate at the Chicago Museum of Natural History, made an 850-mile trip by dog team from Fairbanks to Igiak Bay and Hooper Bay on the Bering Sea, by way of Mountain Village on the Yukon. Their explorations gave us the clues that finally led us to the nesting ground.

On May 22 Conover collected one curlew at Hooper Bay, but saw no more until the

From South Sea Isles the Curlew Flies
5,500 Miles to Bleak Alaskan Tundra

last day of July and the first week of August. Then, about 20 miles from the head of Hooper Bay, he found the curlews in abundance, already started on their fall migration. Several hundred were seen scattered over the tundra, feeding on blueberries. All were adults without young, as is usual with shore birds starting their southern migration.

This discovery led Brandt to surmise that the nesting ground might be "at the eastern end of the Askinuk Mountains, or on Kusilvak Mountain, and perhaps the mountains to the northward of Mountain Village on the Yukon River" (map, page 218).

In 1929, however, Arthur C. Bent, in his monumental work, *Life Histories of North American Shore Birds,* summarized what was known at the time:

"The above facts would seem to indicate that the main breeding grounds are somewhere in the interior of extreme northern Alaska, probably on the barren grounds."

Added weight was given to this belief when David Brower collected an immature bird on the Meade River in northern Alaska in August, 1943. E. L. Jaques had found adults near Teller, northwest of Nome, in July, 1928.

On the other hand, Ira N. Gabrielson, while Director of the Fish and Wildlife Service, visited Alaska in 1940 and reported flocks of curlews around Naknek and the Kvichak River the last of July.

This was the status of our knowledge in the fall of 1947. The nest and eggs of all other North American birds had been found; this curlew alone defied the ornithologists.

About this time I received a friendly letter from Warren M. Petersen, an Alaska Native Service schoolteacher at Kalskag, on the Kuskokwim River. He wrote me of his in-

terest in birds and of efforts that he and Henry Kyllingstad, teacher at Mountain Village, had made to find bristle-thighed curlews.

In the summers of 1946 and 1947, following the suggestions of Brandt and Conover, these two men had searched in vain the eastern edge of the Askinuk Mountains. Earlier, Kyllingstad, with his small son, had climbed to the top of Kusilvak Mountain without getting a clue to the whereabouts of the curlews.

Expedition by Plane Proposed

Petersen suggested the possibility of employing local bush pilots for transportation from one lake to another after the ice melted in June. He sent photographs he had made the previous year and convinced me that even a one-month trip might yield results of interest and value.

Alaska was one of the objectives listed in the general plan of bird study which the National Geographic Society's Research Committee had tentatively approved, and the quest of the unknown had occupied the Cornell Laboratory of Ornithology for years.

I immediately wrote Dr. Gilbert Grosvenor, President of the National Geographic Society, suggesting a cooperative expedition with Petersen, Kyllingstad, and the Arctic Institute of North America to find the bristle-thighed curlew's nest. By return mail this proposal received Dr. Grosvenor's cordial approval.

Then ensued weeks of correspondence with Petersen and Kyllingstad, made simpler by the air-mail service and by the fact that they could talk to one another by radio, although they were more than 100 miles apart.

One factor worried us more than any other —the weather. Fogs often roll in from Bering Sea and last a fortnight. Flying is then impossible, and even tramping over the mountains or tundra may become precarious.

To get color films of the bird life under bad weather conditions, we knew we should have to be prepared with some sort of artificial sunshine, as well as with waterproof protection for our equipment. Since all transportation in Alaska would be by air, equipment would have to be light and reduced to a minimum.

Weeks of planning, testing, and packing followed. One gadget after another was tried and discarded; but the total of essential equipment made us decide that it would be best to have my son David start two weeks ahead with the heavy luggage. I would follow by plane as soon as University duties permitted.

Ithaca to Anchorage in a Day

David left Ithaca, New York, by train on May 18, bound for Seattle and thence by ship to Seward and train to Anchorage. There he arrived on May 29.

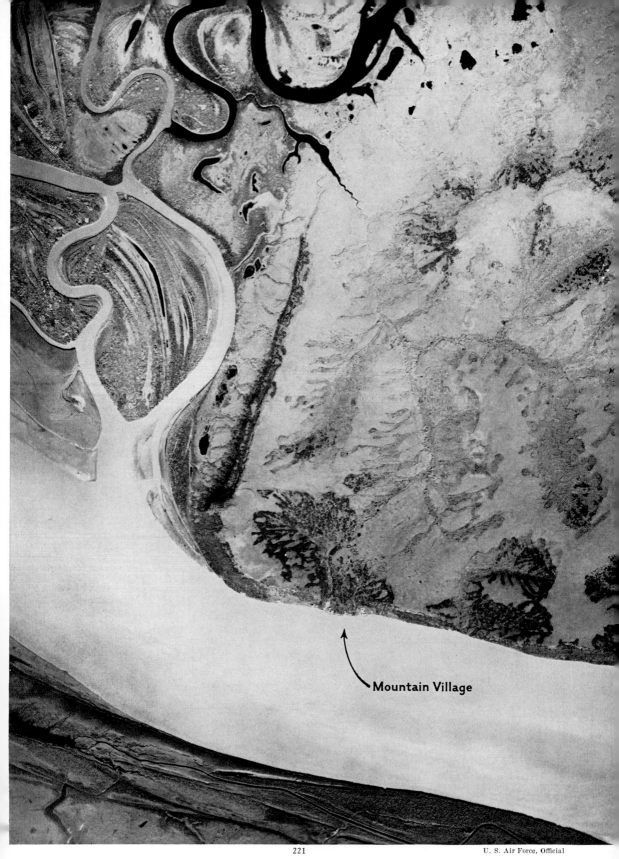

Mountain Village

Jumping-off Place for the Curlew Quest Was Mountain Village, on the Yukon

So full of sediment is the river—here nearly a mile wide—that its channels photographed white. Black stream and ponds at top (north) were clear and absorbed light. The nest was found 20 miles north of this Eskimo town.

Leaving Ithaca on May 28, I arrived at Anchorage on the same day as David, but some six hours earlier, after 18 hours of flying.

Beyond Edmonton, Alberta, the plane followed, more or less, the Alaska Highway. We watched the flat, carpetlike wheatlands gradually change to rolling hills covered with light-green cottonwoods and birches, then to black spruces for miles on end.

Innumerable ponds and lakes dotted the landscape, and I imagined them teeming with waterfowl, although we were flying too high to see individual birds. The streams were all running full and brown, with more loops and bends than a snake.

Snow-capped mountains began to appear, and we could see the highway winding its tiny thread up valleys and ridges toward a pass. Soon we were looking down on snow-covered ridges through drifting clouds and snow squalls like fine horizontal lines of white.

Swinging southwesterly over the pass, we followed the Glenn Highway down the famed Matanuska Valley to the bustling little town of Anchorage, where we arrived at Elmendorf airport shortly after noon.

I like to say that the whole town turned out upon our arrival, and so it did. The demonstration, however, was not for our benefit, but just the response to a fire on the main street. This volunteer fire department quickly subdued with modern equipment.

Streets were crowded with cars, store windows were full of equipment, building was going on everywhere, and all prices were high.

Birds abounded in the near-by spruce forest, and we heard our first varied thrush's song— a long-drawn-out, buzzy policeman's whistle of one note, quite disappointing when coming from so distinguished a bird.

Next morning we shipped all our baggage by air and boarded the Alaska Airlines' two-motored plane bound for Bethel, with stops at Homer and Naknek.

Moose and Grizzlies Sighted from Plane

The pilot flew low along the Kenai Peninsula, which is largely a game reserve. Perhaps he enjoyed seeing moose and grizzlies as much as we did. Several moose had calves and one had twins; and once we saw five bears within a stone's throw of one another.

On our way from Homer to Naknek we passed over beautiful Lake Grosvenor, long and narrow and blue, like the Finger Lakes at home, and Mount La Gorce, snow-capped and enshrouded in clouds.

From Naknek we followed the low-lying coast, then climbed once more to cross the snow-covered Kilbuck Mountains before we broke out over the tundra marking the delta of the Kuskokwim River, on which Bethel

is located. Green trees fringe the river, but elsewhere there is only the brown tundra with its thousands of lakes, ponds, and tidal channels, like a giant jigsaw puzzle.

At Bethel we met Nat Browne, the bush pilot to whom we were to entrust our lives for the next month (page 219). His muscular frame, kindly smile, and matter-of-fact manner gave us confidence as he showed us the red Bellanca we were to use, anchored in the river in front of his home.

Warren Petersen, who had flown down from Kalskag two days before with his wife and daughter, joined us and showed us the "sights" —a group of houses and other buildings set along the streets at odd angles indicative of their temporary nature. The river changes its channel frequently, and the whole town stands ready to move on short notice.

Because the ice never goes out of the ground, cellars and stable foundations are not practicable for even the largest buildings, including a modern hospital. A good jack is part of the necessary equipment of any home.

At 7:30 in the evening Nat Browne flew us to Mountain Village, on the Yukon (page 221), a 70-minute flight, and landed us at the front door of Henry Kyllingstad. Henry was not only the Native Service schoolteacher for this area but weather observer and radio operator as well.

Schoolteachers Are Jacks-of-All-Trades

So far as I could see, this whole country revolves around the schoolteachers, who are supposed to know everything and do anything, from mending motors to bringing babies into the world and looking after the health of the whole community. Of course they cannot prescribe medicine without first locating the hospital physician and describing to him over the radio all the symptoms of the patient.

In the Kyllingstad home we were entertained for two days, while Nat Browne carried a planeload of natives to one of the canneries on the coast and returned to fly up the river with the local guardian of the peace. On this trip they brought out a native who had gone berserk and attempted to decoy his companion within range of his gun by honking like a goose!

The delay afforded us opportunity to complete our plans for the curlew hunt, as well as to scour the hills for 10 miles around.

Each May since 1944 Henry had seen a few bristle-thighed curlews passing over Mountain Village, calling as they flew, and so low that when he answered their clear whistle he had been able to make them circle back. Our search yielded us little, however, except a pair of Hudsonian curlews that David located about five miles inland, the nest of a golden plover, and that of a Wilson's snipe, in addition to many nests of hoary redpolls and varied thrushes in the alders.

We planned to make our first trip to Igiak Bay and the foothills of the Askinuk Mountains, a little farther west than the region which had been explored by Henry and Warren in 1947. This was not because we really expected to find the curlews there, but because I wanted to get color plates of the other shore birds and waterfowl for the NATIONAL GEOGRAPHIC; and this region had the reputation of being a wildfowl metropolis.

Furthermore, I thought it might be unwise to find the curlews until they were surely nesting, lest we be distracted by migrating birds and waste our time on an unproductive area. It never occurred to me that they would start nesting, as apparently they did, shortly after the middle of May.

Our plan was to work near Igiak Bay for a week or 10 days, then to start hopping northward. Avoiding the coastal area that had been combed unsuccessfully by our predecessors, we would concentrate on the foothills of the coast range about 70 miles inland, if we could find a lake on which to land within walking distance of the mountains.

Two or three days at each stop, we hoped, would be enough to determine whether curlews existed in the area.

As soon as Nat returned from transporting the Eskimo prisoner, we loaded part of our supplies into the plane and started for Igiak Bay, 80 miles to the southwest. Warren, David, and I were to pitch camp, while Nat returned for Henry and the rest of the supplies.

The trip across the Yukon and over the tundra had an air of quiet excitement. The

Discovered, the Curlew Abandons Attempts at Camouflage

A quick dash that flushed the sitting bird first revealed the actual nest of the bristle-thighed curlew. The male soon returned to incubate, and this time David Allen approached more quietly. When he was almost within arm's length, the bird, flattened out and motionless, realized it had been found. Suddenly a bit of tundra sprouted an eye and a bill! After the second day the birds became so accustomed to observers that one could practically touch them on the nest.

fringing thicket of cottonwoods and alders along the Yukon passed below us; then numerous old flood channels and winding estuaries; and finally thousands of ponds, lakes, and channels of most irregular shapes and sizes. Occasionally we could see flocks of ducks and geese, and especially white whistling swans, tiny specks on the water.

Engulfed in Cloud amid Mountains

The plane droned past Kusilvak Mountain, a 2,449-foot cone rising from the flat tundra. Foothills of the Askinuks appeared, rounded ridges with projecting castlelike rocks.

Finally Igiak Bay hove into sight, and we began to look for a landing place that gave

David Allen

Dr. Allen Serves as "Midwife to a Curlew"

The author aids the chick's debut to keep the shell as intact as possible for the National Museum, Washington, D. C. Taken from the first set of eggs of the bristle-thighed curlew ever found, the egg was hatched by Dr. Allen in a crude incubator and the warmth of his sleeping bag. Six hours after this photograph was made, the chick had emerged, dried off, and was indistinguishable when placed with its brothers and sisters (page 228).

the mountains were towering on either side.

Fortunately, we passed out of the cloud, and there was our lake below us. Gliding down and banking abruptly, we found ourselves in a flurry of swans that had risen at our approach. On terrified wings they were escaping in all directions. For a moment the air was filled with geese, ducks, and cranes. We had come to the right spot!

The pontoons struck the water and we skittered along for half a mile; then we came back to a quiet mooring on what we now called Igiak Lake, since it had no name on the map. Two feet of snow still lay in the alders, and the lake was fringed with ice.

For the first nine days we camped on an open spot in the alders with snow all about us and a rivulet running through the cook tent. We had found a drier knoll for our sleeping tents a couple of hundred feet up the side of the mountain.

A fascinating week of activity followed. Up early for a good breakfast, we shouldered cameras, tripods, and blinds and were off for the day in four different directions, carrying bars of chocolate for lunch. We explored the dry ridges of the mountains for curlews and the castlelike outcroppings for rough-legged hawks and gyrfalcons.

Henry made one 20-mile hike to the top of the highest peak, looking for surf-birds, but the only birds he found that were not nesting in the valley were snow buntings and Baird's sandpipers.

One after another the birds gave up their secrets, until we had marked the nests of 44 of the species that dwelt in the valley.

Birds such as the western sandpiper, northern phalarope, Alaska longspur, hoary redpoll, tree and savannah sparrows were so common

promise of birds and a modicum of comfort.

We flashed by a valley that showed a sizable lake hugging the foot of the hills. By shouting and pointing we let Nat know that we wanted to look it over.

All this time the sky had been beautifully clear, although we could see clouds along the horizon, hanging over the tops of the Askinuks.

Nameless Lake Alive with Wings

We came to another pass through the mountains, and Nat banked to circle back to our first valley. All went well until we rounded the first mountain, when suddenly we were engulfed in clouds. It was like jumping into bed and pulling the sheet over your head. We could see absolutely nothing, but we knew that we scarcely bothered to look for their nests when the birds fluttered out before us.

Nests of white-fronted, emperor, and cackling geese (pages 163–165) were plentiful; we found 15 nests of the little brown crane and 5 of the whistling swan.

Upon finding a nest we wished to photograph, we first marked the spot with high-visibility orange cloth.

To get the birds used to a blind, we usually set up a dummy blind, a tripod of three sticks and a shelter half, about 20 feet from the nest. We left it for a day or two, or until the weather cleared sufficiently for photography, then replaced it with a more commodious blind set 6 to 15 feet from the nest, depending on the size of the bird (page 226). Soon we had eight dummy blinds and three full-sized blinds and were moving from one nest to the next, as occasion demanded.

David shared my pack and served as "go-awayster" by tucking me into the blinds and conspicuously leaving the vicinity so that the birds would think the coast clear.

On one of the brighter days I started the morning in a blind by the nest of a little brown crane, about two miles from camp. Two hours later, having obtained stills and motion pictures of this bird, I jumped to the blind by the nest of an emperor goose and then to one by a black-bellied plover. I finished the day with a western sandpiper, Sabine's gull, old-squaw, and spectacled eider (page 179), the last two not requiring blinds.

It was all very exciting to an ornithologist. Fortunately, the days were long; sometimes we did not get back to camp until 7 or 8 in the evening, tired and hungry.

Watery Labyrinth—and No Detour Signs

A real difficulty was the endless labyrinth of irregular ponds that always barred the direct route back to camp after a long day on the tundra (page 227). With my binoculars I could spot the white tent from afar, but as soon as I directed my course toward it, I would come to a pond too deep to ford.

There were no detour signs, and I had to learn from sad experience which side of the lake led into another and worse detour. What should have been two or three miles as the crane flew ended up as four or five as the ornithologist plodded.

By the end of the week I had punched two more holes in my belt. I was feeling fine and could tramp two miles without puffing, but then it was time for Nat Browne to return. We had satisfied ourselves that there were no bristle-thighed curlews in this area.

Nat arrived at 4 p. m. on Friday, June 11, as arranged. We were scarcely expecting him, because clouds hung low on the mountains.

In the first planeload went Henry and David, with half the equipment, bound for Mountain Village to pick up supplies and then to fly to a lake 20 miles to the north. Camping there for two days, David and Henry could explore for curlews until Warren and I arrived Monday on Nat's second trip.

When the pilot returned for us, he lifted his plane over the Askinuks, followed the shore of Scammon Bay, with its high cliffs, then flew over the pond-filled tundra, across the coffee-colored Yukon, and finally to what we christened Curlew Lake at the base of a low range of mountains.

As we glided down, we spotted the white tent and the two boys on the shore.

Behind the tent the mountain rose at a 60-degree angle, but from a height of 2,000 feet we had seen a whole series of barren, desolate ridges beyond. The lower face of the mountain was a tangle of alders, but toward the top it was typical tundra with patches of snow still defying the sun.

163-year-old Mystery Solved

"What news?" I called as the red Bellanca taxied up to the shore. We were planning merely to take on supplies and head for the next lake.

"Seen any curlews?" I queried, half facetiously, as neither Dave nor Henry replied.

I saw them exchange peculiar glances, and I expected one of Henry's Swedish stories or some joke from David. They apparently had a story, and perhaps they had rehearsed it. Something misfired, however, as it often does in times of excitement, and out it came—*"We have found the curlew's nest!"*

Who said it? I looked from one to the other in amazement. There was such a degree of sincerity and pent-up feeling in the simple little statement that I didn't for a moment doubt its truth. There was no question; the 163-year-old mystery had been solved. They had found the summer home of the bristle-thighed curlew; they had seen the actual nest!

I can't remember getting out of the plane. I can't remember any incidents of the landing, but that story of the discovery, as it unfolded in the next few minutes, is as clear to me now as if I had been there myself.

Nat Browne had delivered the two boys at the lake at 11 p. m. on Friday, June 11, and they had pitched camp in the afterglow of a sun that had just passed below the horizon. From the air they had seen the ridges behind the mountain and had decided to explore them the following day.

Next morning they were up early and climbed to the top of the ridge behind camp. David started south and Henry north, along the plateau behind the mountain, skirting the

David Allen

An Empress Sits for Her Portrait

Inside the blind crouches the author and trains his lens of 200-millimeter focal length on a female emperor goose. Technique calls for placing blind near the nest several days before making pictures so that birds may become accustomed to it (page 188). Color picture of emperor goose on page 164 was made in this manner.

alders and scrutinizing all of the open areas.

Two hours from camp, when they were perhaps a mile apart, they heard, at about the same time, a peculiar whistle, somewhat like that of a black-bellied plover—"Piu-wit" —and spotted a curlew flying toward David.

Henry had heard the bristle-thighed curlew in previous years as it flew over Mountain Village; David was familiar with the Hudsonian curlew from Churchill on Hudson Bay. Neither one doubted they had found the long-sought bird. They froze in their tracks.

The curlew circled and set its wings for a plateaulike area a mile away. This area differed from most of the tundra in that it had some broken rock protruding and had numerous clumps of black lichen spotting its surface.

Hours of Watching, Then a Dash!

A couple of hours of intense watching with binoculars ensued. Meanwhile, the watchers kept out of sight, but drew steadily closer.

The curlew was plainly more interested in this one piece of several acres of tundra than in any other. Even after long sorties he kept coming back to it.

Occasionally a parasitic jaeger (page 236) would skim over the tundra. The curlew paid little attention to it until it approached a certain place. Then he would call excitedly and fly at the jaeger and drive him away.

There was now little question in the boys' minds that they had found the curlew's nesting ground. Somewhere before them the female bird was sitting on her long-sought eggs.

After spending years hunting birds' nests, one develops an understanding of bird behavior. Gradually, as he watched the guardian curlew, David eliminated one spot after another until he felt he knew just about where the nest should be.

Even so, it is not always easy to find the actual nest. Sometimes when a bird sees an enemy approaching, it will sneak off its nest and flush ostentatiously from a different spot. Again, the bird will freeze and rely upon its

227

Tents of the Expedition (Left) Lie amid a Maze of Lakes and Ponds

David Allen surveys Igiak Valley, between foothill ranges of the Askinuk Mountains, where the expedition found scores of nesting birds but no bristle-thighed curlews. Such a labyrinth of lakes is a paradise to waterfowl and shore birds, but a headache to men on foot (page 225).

protective color to escape detection (page 223).

David had no way of knowing how bristle-thighed curlews would react. There is one technique, however, that is often effective when nothing else works—surprise. If a bird can be faced with an unusual situation suddenly, its reaction is likely to be less favorable to itself than if it has a moment's time.

David removed his rubber boots lest they impede his actions, beckoned to Henry, who had now moved up to the same side of the promised land, and sprinted the 100 yards that intervened between him and the chosen spot.

The reaction of the bird was as he had hoped, and the result is now history. She flushed 20 feet in front of him, and he found the curlew's nest!

In the nest were four eggs nearly as large as those of a domestic hen. Dull greenish with spots of gray and dark brown, they blended well with the tundra (page 230).

The nest itself was a mere depression be-

side one of the clumps of black lichen and a mat of Alpine azalea *(Loiseleuria procumbens)*. It measured 6¾ inches across and 2½ inches deep, and was very smooth on the inside, though made of the surrounding reindeer moss and grasses which ordinarily present a rough appearance.

Birds So Tame No Blind Was Needed

After finding the nest, the boys hurried back to camp, fearful lest the jaegers should steal the eggs, and returned with blinds and cameras. They did not realize that no blind would be necessary for a bird that perhaps had never seen a human being at close range.

Since many of the South Sea islands, where these birds winter, are uninhabited, and since not even an Eskimo would visit this forlorn bit of tundra, we were doubtless as unusual to the curlews as the curlews were to us. We set up a mutual-admiration society, the birds scrutinizing us as closely as we watched them.

We soon discovered that the eggs were

already pecked and the young birds could be heard peeping inside the shells. This perhaps helped to tame the curlews because birds' attachment to the nest is strongest at the time the eggs are ready to hatch.

Since we needed a specimen to deposit in the United States National Museum, to serve as the type, it was necessary to take one of the eggs immediately and remove the chick through a door in one side.

In the meantime, we located another nest. After seeing this second pair of curlews on the tundra, we spent hours dragging the area with a rope and scrutinizing every depression before Warren Petersen finally spotted the incubating bird. Flattened on her nest three feet in front of him, she matched the moss and grasses so well that at first he wasn't sure whether he was looking at a bird or just another piece of tundra (opposite page).

In the second nest the jaegers had stolen two eggs and a third had a large hole in it. The fourth was pecked and ready to hatch, like those in the first nest. What worried us now was the danger that the jaegers might get the remaining egg, or even all those in the first nest, before we could see and record the downy young.

An Ornithologist "Mothers" a Curlew

We were on the point of setting up camp next to the nest, where we could take turns guarding it, when it occurred to me that it would be easier to carry one of the eggs back to camp and hatch it in an incubator.

I had in mind my experience in Quebec, where I successfully mothered a baby red-throated loon in my sleeping bag (page 242).

Returning to camp, I heated stones over our gasoline stove, wrapped them in a towel, and placed them in one of our spare water buckets. I made a nest for the egg out of cotton and an old sock.

At night, instead of getting up every few hours to heat stones, I placed the nest in an empty tin can and took it to bed with me in my sleeping bag.

All the next day I heated stones, and as the little bird squirmed inside the egg and its tiny egg tooth gradually cut through the shell, I helped it along with judicious use of forceps. I wanted it to emerge without ruining the shell for scientific purposes.

The youngster was not yet out of the shell when bedtime came, so once more I took the egg into my sleeping bag. The following day I had the satisfaction of making the final delivery and claiming for myself the distinction of being the first and only midwife to a bristle-thighed curlew (page 224).

In the meantime, providence watched over the nests, the jaegers did not get the eggs,

and they hatched normally. The parent birds by this time paid no attention whatsoever to Henry and Warren, who obtained some truly remarkable photographs of the birds with their young and of themselves less than a foot away (opposite page).

During this time David covered many ridges, and, though he found no more nests, he saw a total of about 20 bristle-thighed curlews. This indicates that the area we discovered is undoubtedly a part of the main summer range of the species, which may extend northward for several hundred miles and even into the foothills of the Brooks Range.

Why these curlews should want to leave the warm, luxurious shores of Tahiti and the other South Sea islands, fly 5,500 miles over the open sea, and arrive at one of the most forlorn stretches of tundra in North America, deserted by all other birds and still largely covered with snow, just to lay four eggs, is hard to understand.

The rest of our trip would have been anticlimactic had it not been that we were working with such exciting birds as whistling swans, Pacific godwits, and an emperor goose that became as tame as the curlews (page 226).

Since there was no need of continuing northward up the range, Nat Browne flew us back to Igiak Lake, where we had left so much unfinished business. The next day it rained, and it kept on raining for a week, with hardly a break in the clouds.

Back to Civilization Just in Time

The following Sunday it cleared, and we had a full day with our cameras before the plane came for us at 6 p. m.

On the first trip Nat took Warren and Henry and most of the baggage back to Mountain Village.

"Hope you kept out your sleeping bags," he called as he left.

It had an ominous sound. But the sun was still shining brightly, although we did notice a few clouds peering over the Askinuks.

At 8 o'clock Nat was back and obviously in a hurry. We dumped the gear into the plane, roared across the lake and up over the mountains, then discovered the reason. A great sea of fog concealed everything.

Overhead the sun shone as brightly as ever, but, had we been 30 minutes later, our valley would have been filled with clouds and we would have been stormbound without provisions or sleeping bags.

How serious it might have been we did not learn until after we had returned to the States. Then a letter from Warren Petersen told us that we were the last people to move and that for two weeks thereafter all planes had been grounded.

229

↑ Protectively Colored, the Motionless Bird Was Invisible Three Feet Away

Warren M. Petersen, Alaska Native Service schoolteacher and member of the National Geographic Society expedition, found a second nest of the **Bristle-thighed Curlew** only after scrutinizing for several hours every square foot of an acre of tundra (opposite page).

↓ First Nestling of Its Kind to Be Seen by Man

A venturesome "first-born" **Bristle-thighed Curlew** crawls from beneath his father's wing to get his initial view of the big world. Idly he picks at the dwarf azalea that grows beside his Alaskan home, a mere depression in the tundra moss.

230

⋏ From the Newly Discovered Eggs Emerged This Downy "Four of a Kind"

The eggs in both nests were "pecked" and emitting peeps when found. To ensure a safe debut, one of these youngsters was hatched in an improvised incubator and the author's sleeping bag. He claims to be the first and only "midwife to a **Bristle-thighed Curlew**" (228).

⋎ End of a Long Quest Came with Finding of These Four Eggs

The discovery of **Bristle-thighed Curlew** eggs by David Allen and Henry Kyllingstad, members of the National Geographic expedition, completes the record for all the 815 species of North American birds, as the eggs of the others were already known.

Photographed near Mountain Village, Alaska

← In the Alaskan Tundra
the Author Discovered
This Elusive Bird's Nest

When the author came upon the hitherto unknown nesting place of the **Bristle-thighed Curlew** in June, 1948, his find made front-page headlines in the Nation's newspapers. The Associated Press credited the National Geographic Society-Cornell University-Arctic Institute Alaskan Expedition with solving a "major mystery of the bird world."

Shown here in full profile at its nest, the bristle-thighed curlew derives its name from the lengthened shafts of some of its flank feathers. Without barbs, and projecting like bristles or stiff hairs from its sides, they are visible in the picture at left. Protective coloration of the eggs at the bird's feet causes them to blend with the brownish-green tundra.

Photographed near Rome, New York

Humane Laws Saved →
the Upland Plover

In former years the **Upland Plover** was a familiar summer resident in eastern States. Little by little, through excessive hunting and destruction of nests in cultivated areas, this graceful bird became rare. In 1916 it was placed on the protected game list and now is fairly common in some northern States (page 49).

The upland plover's haunts are dry, grassy fields, where it dines on locusts, grasshoppers, and other insect pests. Flying in great circles, it utters an eerie whistle—"Whip-whip-whee-ee-ee-ou-u."

On her nest the female resembles a clump of dead grass and is very difficult to detect. She will remain with her four eggs until almost stepped upon. In July, when the young are able to fly, the family begins its southern migration to the pampas of Brazil and Argentina.

© National Geographic Society

232

Photographed near Ithaca, New York

Natural Camouflage Takes Care of Danger from All Save the Keenest-eyed Searchers

Incubating **American Woodcock** so relies on protective coloration, where line and pattern are similar to dead leaves, that it will sit without winking until nearly stepped on. It is found in summer from southern Canada to Florida and Louisiana east of the Rockies; in winter from New Jersey southward wherever it can get earthworms.

Beanpole Legs Straddle a Nest

The **Avocet** inhabits States west of the Mississippi, migrating as far south as Guatemala. Gawky limbs enable shore birds to wade the shallows.

Photographed near Bear River marshes, Utah

Black-necked Stilt Rolls an Egg

Its toothpick bill is useful in spearing aquatic insects. **Black-necked Stilts** nest from South America to our western and Gulf Coast States.

234

↑   **This Sandpiper Nests in Alaska**   ↓   **He Spends His Summer in the Red**

Western Sandpipers lose their rusty markings in winter, when they resemble semipalmated sandpipers.

Red Phalarope wears bright plumage in summer; in winter the upper parts are gray, the lower white.

235

↑ Male Phalarope's Place Is in the Home   ↓ Camera-shy Model Debates Retreat

A **Northern Phalarope** sits on the nest, deserted by his spouse who lets him do the incubation work.

Wilson's Phalarope nests farther south than kindred species. It winters in South America (page 76).

236

Photographed near Igiak Bay, Alaska

ʌ   Long-tailed Jaeger, a Predatory
Gull, Makes Crime Pay

Most of the **Long-tailed Jaeger's** food is obtained
by robbing terns of their fish and by stealing eggs and
young from nesting birds. This feathered freebooter is
found in summer on Arctic coasts.

ᵥ   What's in a Name? In This Case,
a Clue to Social Standing

Parasitic Jaegers, like their smaller relatives, the
long-tails, live by piracy. Victims are bullied until they
disgorge their food, which the jaeger seizes in midair.
Eskimos believe this bird once killed and ate men.

Photographed near Churchill, Manitoba

Sea Bird Cities Off Audubon's Labrador

FROM vast reaches of the sea, bizarre birds congregate to breed on islands in the Gulf of St. Lawrence south of the lonely Labrador Peninsula, which John James Audubon more than a century ago called "wonderfully grand, wild—aye, and terrific."

Those adjectives still apply, as we discovered on a trip for the National Geographic Society to photograph in color the sea birds the great naturalist painstakingly drew and painted. Often he worked 17 hours a day to draw details of color and form that cameras now catch in split seconds.

All traffic to the north shore of the Gulf is by boat in summer and dog sledge in winter, or by plane, since no roads reach into this wild region. Though actually a part of Quebec, it is still often called Labrador, as it was in Audubon's day (map, page 241).

Kittiwake Homes on Sheer Cliffs

Leaving our station wagon at Rimouski, Quebec, on the broad estuary of the St. Lawrence River, Mrs. Allen and I boarded the steamship *Matane I* and arrived next morning at Seven Islands (Sept Iles), on this coast of storms. There we were met by game warden Ben Bijoud, who had instructions from Ottawa to take us to the bird sanctuary on Carrousel Island near by. Like everyone else on the coast, he went out of his way to be helpful.

It was June and a new generation of birds was just emerging. On two of the vertical cliffs facing the sea we found 300 nesting kittiwake gulls (page 253).

Kittiwakes derive their name from their three-syllable call. About the fishing banks they are among the most familiar birds, especially in winter. Then they often assemble in thousands and are known as "winter birds." They never venture inland, however, and are rare even about the harbors, where they are called "offshore gulls."

Unlike most other species of gulls, the kittiwakes always select narrow shelves on sheer cliffs for their homes and build substantial nests of seaweed which will not blow off in the storms that so often batter the rocks below.

Landing at the foot of the cliff in the lighthouse keeper's boat, we rigged up a blind on a ledge about 20 feet from the nests.

Luckily, the birds paid little attention to the blind. Soon after the boat disappeared they came back, and I was able to observe them at close range. Their dark eyes gave them a much gentler expression than the pale-yellow eyes of other gulls on this coast, and their small black feet were likewise distinctive.

Day-old youngsters, visible in some of the nests, were covered with fluffy pale-gray down without the dark spots that are so conspicuous on most young gulls.

My contemplation of the home life of these interesting visitors from the high seas was suddenly interrupted by a gust of wind that caused the blind to careen. In my efforts to hold it in place, I felt one foot slip from the ledge and had a momentary vision of camera, blind, and photographer plunging into the sea 30 feet below.

It proved fortunate that we made photographs the first day, because thereafter we had high winds or fog which would have made the approach to the cliffs most dangerous.

On Carrousel Island there was also a colony of some 1,100 herring gulls (page 258). A few great black-backed gulls (page 254), or "saddlebacks," and a couple of hundred razor-billed auks and black guillemots (page 261) were incubating their eggs in the numerous fissures in the rocks. About 150 eider ducks were breeding on the island, and more than 300 double-crested cormorants (page 306) could be seen nesting in the tops of the dead spruces on the highest part of the island.

Miss the Boat and You Wait a Week

From this lonely rock of whirring wings and raucous, haunting cries, we returned to Seven Islands to catch the steamship *Sable Isle,* scheduled to dock the next morning at 6 on its way to Harrington Harbour.

Because of the wind we saw few birds in the spruce woods behind the village. But ruby-crowned kinglets, fox sparrows (page 109), redstarts (page 67), and yellow-bellied flycatchers were not uncommon; and along a sandy ridge covered with spruce and scattered jack pines we found a pair of yellow palm warblers, as Dr. Harrison F. Lewis had promised us we should.

It was Dr. Lewis who first introduced me to this coast in 1928. Then Chief Federal Migratory Bird Officer for Ontario and Quebec, he had explored the north coast for sites for sea bird sanctuaries in 1925, as provided for by the treaty of 1916 between Canada and the United States for protection of migratory birds. His successor, Dr. Oliver H. Hewitt, was awaiting us at Harrington Harbour.

Not at 6 but at 4 in the morning, Mr. Bijoud rushed to the inn with the news that the *Sable Isle* had already docked and probably would stay only 15 minutes. We were dressed and had moved our 12 pieces of luggage to the pier in 14 minutes and 55 seconds.

This was our first taste of the advertised "vagabond cruises" along the north shore. Because of whims of wind, fog, and tide, no definite schedule of arrival and departure can be maintained, and the passenger who isn't ready will wait a week for the next boat.

Once aboard, he gets a cabin, if he is lucky, but if there are many passengers—and there often are—he may have to be content with the dining salon upholstery.

Decks are crowded with oil drums which, though empty, permeate the air with the odor of seal or cod. At his destination the vagabond is as likely to be cast ashore in the middle of the night as at noon, and he may walk down a gangplank in a dignified manner or climb down a ladder into a bobbing dory.

After braving the chill blasts that whipped off the icebergs to the east, we found a warmish spot in the lee of the pilothouse where friendly fumes from the kitchen poured out of a ventilator.

Montagnais Indians Crowd the Wharves

Most of our fellow passengers were fishermen and small businessmen traveling from town to town. But some were sportsmen heading for clubs on the Moisie, the Godbout, or other famous salmon streams, still dreaming about the big ones that got away last year.

Others were young men taking summer jobs with construction companies. A few were girls returning from school or employment in Quebec and Montreal and looking forward to the simple pleasures of their rugged homes.

On the boat was an interesting group of Anglican ministers and Catholic priests. Their flocks included many Montagnais Indians, who crowded about the wharves to shake a clergyman's hand and hear his words of encouragement. The men were white-jacketed and gaunt, the women bulky and ungraceful in their voluminous multicolored petticoats and tight bodices.

Invariably the Indian women dressed their black hair as of old, rolled into buns over their ears. Atop this coiffure they perched their time-honored but unbecoming liberty-bell hats, broadly striped with red and blue.

Despite their uncomfortable costumes, their bowlegs and swinging hips, the women are remarkably hardy. Women and children travel with the men up the rocky streams for hundreds of miles in late summer to trap all winter in the interior.

Cold Breath of the Labrador Current

They all come out in the spring to trade their furs at the Hudson's Bay post for the next year's provisions, but during the summer they loiter about the posts, do a little fishing, repair their canoes, and rest up for the next trek into the interior.

To the eastbound traveler along the coast the effect of a branch of the cold Labrador Current, which flows through the Strait of Belle Isle, becomes more and more apparent. Trees become stunted and disappear; rocks, with a deep covering of reindeer moss, curlewberry, and other creeping or sprawling vegetation, take their place.

The shore for hundreds of miles is broken up into innumerable islands surrounded by waters studded with rocks and reefs which plague the mariner.

Trees, sometimes of fair size, grow along the sheltered stream valleys on the mainland. Elsewhere, however, for every acre of trees there are a thousand acres of moss stretching far inland, until the effect of the Labrador Current is finally lost.

The interior is heavily forested, but adjacent to the cold water Arctic conditions prevail; deep snowdrifts lurk behind the sheltering cliffs, and icebergs float with the current in mid-July.

We reached Harrington Harbour in two days. There we were met by Dr. Hewitt and his boatman, Samuel Robertson V, in the patrol boat *Alca of Ottawa*, 38-foot cruiser built on the coast.

The Robertsons have lived at La Tabatière since before Audubon's time. Audubon tells of meeting with Samuel Robertson I at the same spot in 1833. So little has been the change of blood in the population of this coast that our Sam had an uncle or cousin in nearly every port we visited. He himself was as familiar with all the rocks and reefs from Harrington to Blanc Sablon as with his own dooryard, for at the age of 11 he had started carrying the mail with his father, by boat in summer and by dog team in winter.

Seeking Birds in Wind and Fog

It was now June 25, and for the next five weeks the four of us were to live snugly on the *Alca* with all of our luggage and equipment—especially snugly for the last two weeks when we had two more passengers. Fortunately, no one suffered from claustrophobia, although our heads became almost calloused bumping the cabin roof, and we suffered miscellaneous bruises when the sea got rough.

Our first official inspection was of the St. Mary Islands Sanctuary, about 13 miles from Harrington, in the open gulf. Here wind and fog have full sway and often isolate Fred Osborne, the lighthouse keeper and caretaker of the sanctuary, for days at a time.

We had good weather the day of our arrival, but during the following week fog, rain, and high wind were almost continuous. At

Elsa G. Allen

As if a Feather Mattress Had Burst, Gannets Cover Bonaventure Cliffs with White

On these ledges the birds have nested uncounted centuries. Accustomed to sanctuary, they treated the author (above) with indifference. As they soared past on black-tipped wings with a six foot spread, "they gave an impression of abstract power perfectly at home in storm or fog" (pages 132-136 and 248).

black guillemots, scatter more widely, and, although they are often seen in flocks, they nest in isolated pairs.

The guillemots choose narrow crevices in the rocks, the eiders more open spots on the tundra. Never does more than one pair of red-throated loons occupy each of the small fresh-water lakes, and seldom does more than one pair of great black-backed gulls (page 254) nest in a colony of herring gulls or on a rocky headland. In all, there were 16,000 to 17,000 birds nesting in this sanctuary.

Murre Returns Yearly to Same Spot

Year after year the murres, returning from the open sea, show up on their nesting ledges on the same date. Each bird apparently occupies exactly the same spot it used the previous year.

For 10 years now, a single Brünnich's murre has claimed foothold on a narrow shelf of Cliff Island facing the sea. Here he stands in the middle of a flock of common murres—the tenth bird from the right and the

Dr. Oliver Hewitt

"Comparisons Are Odious," Says the Author's Wife

For two hours Elsa Allen twitted her husband for failure to match her four-pound brook trout, caught in the Blanc Sablon River. Then he landed his four-and-three-quarter pounder. On the next day he hooked a monster, "a yard long if he was an inch"; but his tackle snapped and he "quit fishing because the fish were too big!" (Page 245.)

times we could scarcely see the shore from our mooring in the narrow, well-protected harbor, and again we could see waves dashing 40 feet into the air as they hit the outer rocks.

Working fast to seize the few hours of sunshine, we explored most of the sanctuary. We took the bird census and made studies of the common cormorants and murres (pages 261, 262, and opposite) of Cliff Island, the red-throated loons (page 126) and black guillemots (page 261) of Harbour Island and the eiders (pages 178 and 179), auks, and puffins (page 260) of Middle Island.

Some species, like the murres and cormorants, breed in compact little groups on cliffs which they have occupied since long before records began. Others, like the eiders and

fifteenth from the left. Storms may rage, but nothing budges him from this particular spot. Of course he leaves it to go fishing, but he returns soon to the same few square inches.

Ten years before, Dr. Robert Johnson, at that time a graduate student at Cornell, banded a black guillemot that was incubating its two eggs in a deep crevice near the mooring in the harbor. When we inspected the crack in 1947, there was the bird again, for we could see a thin, very worn band on its little red leg (page 261).

We had an interesting time on Cliff Island with the European, or "common" cormorants. These are not common in the usual sense, since there are only three or four colonies of

Theodora Price and Irvin E. Alleman

↑ Thousands of Sea Birds Call Quebec's Rock-bound, Fog-ridden Shores "Home"

From Rimouski to Blanc Sablon the author took a summer's leisurely voyage. Clear days, he and his companions spent in blinds observing and photographing birds; foggy days they tried their luck with fish, and as the picture on the opposite page attests, their luck was good. On the jagged cliffs of island sanctuaries they counted 99,000 nesting birds (page 248). For gannets observed off Bonaventure cliffs, turn to page 239.

↓ Young Cormorants Ram Their Heads Far Down Their Parents' Throats for Food

Into the gaping lunch basket this Cliff Island youngster thrusts a probing beak and fastens onto the pièce de résistance. Like a dentist pulling an obdurate tooth, he yanks his elder's head from side to side until a fish pops out. Often, when the fish is too big for him to swallow, a watchful herring gull darts down and gobbles it up. These are European cormorants (opposite page). Double-crested cormorants are shown on page 306.

them on this continent. The really common cormorant of North America is the smaller, double-crested species, which occurs in one or another of its races from the Arctic to the Tropics and from the Atlantic to the Pacific (pages 241 and 306).

The larger bird, with white bordering its pouch and with a blue-black neck and breast, was originally called the common cormorant because it was found also in Europe and Asia. Some of them were still incubating eggs, but the majority had black, woolly young, a few nearly as large as their parents.

After I was safely hidden in a blind and my accomplices had disappeared over the ridge, the old birds returned to their nests all about me. Youngsters were clamoring for food, but no meals were served during the next half-hour. I began to fear that I might miss the amazing spectacle, for the fog, which already concealed the sea below me, began to rise and obscure the birds.

Cormorant Cafeteria

At last, however, one little brood that had been stretching up their necks with quivering pouches began to get results. What a party it was, as both father and mother opened their blue-lined mouths and let the children dive down their throats for dinner (page 241).

During this grotesque performance the herring gulls hovered low overhead or darted into the melee whenever one of the youngsters brought out a fish too large for it to swallow.

Absorbed in the antics of the cormorants, I tarried until we had to start back to Harbour Island in fog so dense that we had to depend on the foghorn for general direction and trust to luck to avoid two dangerous shoals. Our thoughtful host became alarmed about us, however, and we had covered scarcely a mile before the chugging of Fred's motor told us he was on his way to guide us among the dangerous rocks. By the time we were back in our harbor, it was dark.

Elsa (Mrs. Allen) had rescued a newly hatched red-throated loon from a black-backed gull, intending to give it for adoption to the pair nesting on Harbour Island. Since it was now too late an hour to disturb the loons, and since someone would have to keep it warm during the night, we matched pennies. Thus it fell to my lot to sleep with a baby loon.

Foster Mother to a Baby Loon

I fashioned a little box that would fit into my sleeping bag—large enough to give me some warning if I turned over on it, yet small enough not to dissipate the heat. The next morning the baby loon was alive and wheezing for a fish. Our next problem was to introduce him to the Harbour Island loons.

By some strange quirk in loon psychology, the youngster now regarded me as his mother. He followed me around the pond and tried to get into the blind with me. We finally had to tie him in the loon's nest until he felt acquainted with his new mother.

Fortunately, red-throated loons (page 126) brood their young for some time in the nest where they are hatched, returning to it from their swims on the pond whenever the youngsters get cold. Either loons cannot count or they have that same friendly spirit toward travelers in distress that we noted in the human inhabitants of this area, because I soon observed that the little orphan was definitely adopted.

Returning to Harrington after a stormy week, we visited the Grenfell Mission and hospital, the westernmost of a chain of institutions founded along the coast by Dr. Wilfred Grenfell. He felt the lure and poverty of Labrador so keenly that he devoted his life to these fisherfolk and brought them what they most need in times of distress: doctor's care and hospitals.

More recently, the missions have invited teachers to help in developing new home industries, thus adding to the meager income of the families. Now many of the people devote the long winters to wood carving and making hooked rugs, for which the mission finds a ready market.

Most of the doctors and teachers volunteer their services, and many a college student has passed a soul-satisfying summer at one of the Grenfell missions.

La Tabatière, Six-family Town

Our next stop was planned for the mainland at the six-family community of La Tabatière, home of the Robertsons, in an area of stunted Hudsonian forest surrounded by Arctic tundra. Theoretically, such a sheltered area, with its innumerable "edges" of woods, should have supported an abundance of wildlife, but actually birds were scarce.

Fox sparrows and white-crowned sparrows were the most numerous; Lincoln's sparrows and gray-cheeked thrushes could be heard occasionally; Wilson's and black-poll warblers were not uncommon. There were scattered Tennessee warblers, mourning warblers, and yellow-bellied flycatchers, which we know as transient visitors in the States in their passage to and from their winter homes in South and Central America.

There were, of course, some robins and juncos, a few red-breasted nuthatches, winter wrens, ruby-crowned kinglets, white-throated sparrows, and yellow warblers, so common much farther south, and a few flocks of crossbills and pine siskins, already finished nesting.

243   National Geographic Photographer John E. Fletcher

Fish-cleaning Time Means Chow Call for Herring Gulls

Always hungry, these "appetites with wings" swarm to the feast when Gaspé Peninsula fishermen return from the nets to dress their catch on shore. Although able to catch their own fish, gulls prefer to have it done for them. Background: Rocher Percé (Pierced Rock) gives the Quebec village of Percé its name.

The birds were so scattered, however, and the tangled spruces made observation so difficult that we were lucky if we were able to find one or two nests in a morning's hunt of several hours' duration.

Although offered rewards, the few children living about the harbor could give us little help. Their eyes evidently were trained for the sea, and the only land birds they knew at all were the dooryard "stripities" (white-crowned sparrows), "brown bobbers" (gray-cheeked thrushes), and "brown diggers" (fox sparrows). We had to content ourselves with studies of the fox sparrow (page 109), gray-cheeked thrush (page 41), and Wilson's warbler (page 65).

Before leaving La Tabatière we enjoyed a fine dinner at the comfortable home of our boatman's parents, Mr. and Mrs. Sam Robertson IV. Although isolated from centers of culture and industry, they keep in touch with affairs of the world by radio, and the mail-order houses enable them and their scattered neighbors to enjoy many modern conveniences.

The mail boat, piloted by Sam's brother, arrived while we were there, piled high with bags of parcel post but with only half a bag of first-class mail for the whole coast from Harrington to Blanc Sablon.

From La Tabatière a few hours' run took us to Gull Island in St. Augustin Sanctuary and a fine colony of ring-billed, herring, and great black-backed gulls, as well as eider ducks. A little flock of green-winged teal and a few black ducks were frequenting one of the ponds; also a couple of least sandpipers and a greater yellow-legs. But none of these were nesting.

I was surprised to find eider ducks nesting within 15 feet of black-backed gulls' nests, since the birds apparently are ancestral ene-mies (pages 178 and 254). The gulls never miss an opportunity to steal an egg or carry off a young eider. Indeed, the saddleback is the most unpopular bird on the coast because of these depredations.

Even among the fishermen, who, formerly at least, were accustomed to taking the eiders' eggs for their own use, the sight of a saddle-back doing the same thing arouses anger; when they see one pounce on a young eider, they become quite vindictive. Often it is their own approach that gives the gull his opportunity, for the sight and noise of the boat frightens the mother away and leaves ducklings unprotected.

The great black-backed gulls have learned to watch for just such eventualities. Many times we ourselves, after passing a family of eiders and scaring away the mother, looked back to see a pair of blackbacks harrying the little flock.

If the mother did not return promptly, the youngsters would keep diving until exhausted and then were easy prey.

Eider Routs a Black-backed Gull

I set up a blind one morning near a black-back's nest and some 10 feet from an eider's nest, and awaited the arrival of either bird.

The eider came first, flying to a small pond about 100 feet from the nest and walking the rest of the way. Evidently she did not like the blind. She sat down on the rocks about 15 feet from her nest. Because of the location of the gull's nest on the end of a little ridge, her enemy's natural approach was past this rock, unless he flew directly to his nest.

Finally the gull circled about, landed be-yond the duck, and started to walk past the rock where the duck was contentedly resting.

Never have I seen greater fury than the bristling rage that greeted this gull when he started to enter the eider's territory. All her feathers stood on end, her bill opened, she made jabbing motions in his direction, and then she flew at him with such force that she bowled him over.

Picking himself up, the gull grabbed a small stick in his bill and advanced toward the eider; but once again she ruffled her feathers and pointed her bill, bringing him to a dead stop. Wanting nothing more to do with such a vixen, he turned tail, walked away 25 feet, and nonchalantly sat down. There he sat for an hour.

I was obviously threatened with a stalemate. At last, however, the gull took wing, circled about, and dropped beside his eggs in an evi-dently unaccustomed position. He kept twist-ing and turning, but could not decide how to approach the eggs from that side.

What was the final outcome of the placing of the two nests in such close proximity I never learned; but I left with a feeling that, when man does not interfere, the eiders can take care of the saddlebacks all right. Undoubtedly they were doing so long before Leif the Lucky sailed the Labrador coast while searching for Vinland.

The Basin a Kettle of Fish

From Gull Island we continued our cruise in the *Alca* to Thomas Tickle, a beautiful steep-sided harbor which lay that night under a full moon. The next morning a rough run of three hours brought us to Bradore Bay. How that boat did roll! We were glad to get into the sheltered retreat of the Basin, even though it was the rendezvous of fishermen having a successful season with their cod traps.

One of the schooners, we were told, had taken 100 quintals of fish from its net one morning and found it equally loaded at night. A quintal is 112 pounds of salted, sun-dried codfish; it represents about 50 six-pound fish.

In other words, the fishermen took approxi-mately 10,000 six-pound fish from their net in one day. That was, of course, unusual, but catches of 3,000 fish were frequent dur-ing our stay.

Stay we did for five days, because, when the wind was not whipping up the sea, the fog was so thick that it would have been madness to venture forth. There was nothing we could do but read or write, but the fishermen had a full-time job and went right on cleaning their fish into the harbor.

The Basin is very shallow and the water is clear. For acres about us the bottom was white with the heads and viscera that poured overboard in an endless stream from the three schooners anchored near by. The livers were collected in hogsheads to make vitamins for pale people; the fish themselves were split, salted, and stored away in the holds, to be dried later at Harrington or at home ports in Newfoundland.

White Flags Mean Full Fish Sheds

About the Basin are a couple of "summer homes" with their stages and fish sheds, but most of the fishermen come here from else-where, as their forefathers did long before Audubon's day. The two fish sheds had bars nailed across their doors, and white flags were flying from their roofs to indicate that they were full.

Elsa took one look at the bottom of the harbor and two whiffs of the air before she again sought refuge in the *Alca's* cabin.

But the Bradore Bay area had its pleasant side also, for, though the weather prevented moving the *Alca*, we could go ashore in the

Madam Puffin Keeps a Clocklike Schedule

At a definite time each spring, puffins give up their carefree lives at sea and nest on islands from Maine to Greenland and from Portugal to Norway. They dig burrows, carpet them with straw pallets, and lay single large eggs. On certain English islands they invade rabbit warrens, driving out the rightful tenants or living with them. This moon-faced mother dug her home beneath a Quebec boulder (page 246).

dinghy and tramp the island in which the Basin is located. We could row the mile to the mainland, when it was not too rough, steering by compass when we could not see through the fog.

We found a little trout stream with a couple of youngsters fishing. My first cast hooked a richly colored 10-inch speckled trout; and the boys who were using improvised lines and bits of bacon for bait yelled, "That's a good hook you've got, mister!"

It didn't take long to fill the creel with small trout up to 15 inches in length, and we felt a bit set up, thinking back on the puny 7- and 8-inch ones at home. We did not know what was in store for us at our next stop at Blanc Sablon, where we were again marooned for three days.

The Blanc Sablon River is a much larger stream, stemming from a fair-sized lake some two miles inland and meandering down through the scrubby spruces and muskeg over a sandy bottom to the sea.

The tide is not strong at this point, but it did not look like a trout stream to me. Nevertheless, we were shown a pool near the village, where it was said the fishing was good at the change of the tide.

Sure enough, when the stream began to flow out with the tide and the water was littered with bits of seaweed, the trout began to rise— not 10- or 12-inch fish, but 2- and 3-pounders. Elsa hooked a 4-pounder and by careful maneuvering slid it up on the sandy beach without a landing net. For two hours she lorded it over me. Then I hooked one that weighed four and three-quarter pounds on the Hudson's Bay Company scales, and my ego returned (page 240).

Fish Too Big—Quits Fishing!

The next day the storm continued, and Ollie Hewitt and I explored the river as far as the lake. On the way back we discovered a small pool, at the foot of the first rapids, in which lay a half-dozen of the largest fish I had ever seen in a trout stream. They were probably salmon, but I shall never know, because the tackle in my inexperienced hands was too light for them.

The first one took the same fly that had landed the big trout the day before. He

Auks, Caught in Nets, Help Feed a Lonely Jan Mayen Island Garrison

Technicians who man a meteorological station on this Arctic island welcome flesh and eggs of razor-billed auks as a change from canned provisions. A supply ship from Tromsø, Norway, reaches the storm-swept island once a year. Recent years have seen a sharp decline in razor-billed auk numbers. The great auk died out almost a century ago.

started up the rapids some 10 yards until I knew I had him well hooked.

What I should have done at this point I do not know, for the fish certainly had things his own way. With a rush he cleared the water—a yard long if he was an inch! My only heavy leader parted in the middle. For the first time in my life I quit fishing because the fish were too big!

The following day the weather cleared somewhat, and we were able to see the northern tip of Newfoundland across the 20-mile Strait of Belle Isle. We headed back toward Perroquet Island in Bradore Bay Sanctuary, easternmost of all the sanctuaries.

A cod net was anchored a couple of hundred yards offshore, and puffins in a large flock were having an amusing time balancing on the floats. We feared for their safety, but when we circled the net we could find only one bird that had become entangled.

A worse tragedy had befallen a half-dozen of the birds that had ventured into a seal hunter's shack from which most of the roof had blown off. Apparently the door had closed while they were inside, and they were unable to rise abruptly enough to fly out through the open roof.

Puffins Have Big and Little Foes

Ollie Hewitt estimated that 48,000 puffins were nesting on this island, which for hundreds of years has been honeycombed with their burrows. But on the day of our visit most of the birds were away fishing or incubating in their burrows; there were no more than two or three thousand of them in the water about the island.

While waiting in a blind for the return of the puffins, I became unpleasantly aware of armies of ticks crawling around the rocks, apparently waiting for the same birds that I was waiting for. We became well acquainted, if not intimate, during the ensuing wait. I

National Geographic Photographer Maynard Owen Williams

Dovekies, Plentiful in the Far North, Furnish Food and Clothing

Huge numbers of these quail-size birds remain, despite tremendous quantities eaten by humans, foxes, ravens, and gulls. Here natives of Etah, Greenland, prepare a dovekie feast. Only the breasts are eaten; average serving is eight per person. Greenlanders store thousands of birds for winter, using holes in the ground as home freezers. Dovekie eggs also are eaten, and the birds' skins make warm shirts.

have often counted the minutes while waiting for a tardy friend, but this time I counted the ticks, and if someone had told me there were sixty ticks a minute, I could readily have believed it.

How the puffins have survived the attacks of these hordes of bloodsuckers through the ages, and, indeed, how the ticks can thrive in this Arctic climate, are matters difficult to understand.

Nor are the ticks the puffins' only enemies. When Audubon visited Bras d'Or (as the bay was called in 1833), his son John collected a pair of gyrfalcons whose nest revealed remains of puffins. From my blind I watched a peregrine falcon strike down one of the puffins near its burrow, and before we left the island we found evidence of six other fresh kills.

The sanctuary is well protected now from "eggers," but the natural destruction of these charming, quizzical little birds continues and keeps them from overpopulation (page 245).

Many razor-billed auks and common murres were nesting under the gigantic jumble of stone slabs that line the shore; on top of the island were several pairs of horned larks and pipits. Elsa found a beautiful pipit's nest, with six brown eggs, built in a curious triangular cavity in the reindeer moss atop a small boulder.

As the weather again became threatening, we left this interesting island and headed back to St. Mary Islands. The number of gannets cruising back and forth seemed to have increased since we traveled eastward. We heard Hudsonian curlews passing overhead, already started southward on their fall migration.

Black Flies a Scourge at Mecatina

At Mecatina Bird Sanctuary the black flies were unbearable. In spite of our efficient deterrent, they attacked our eyelids and ears and crawled down our necks wherever we neglected to smear the fly dope. At St. Mary

Islands, fortunately, they were comparatively scarce.

Here two other passengers joined us: Ollie Hewitt's brother-in-law, Tom Barry, an ardent fisherman looking for a rest from his strenuous paper business in Madawaska, Maine; and Louis Le Mieux, a student at Laval University, Quebec, who had been left at St. Mary Islands to study the great black-backed gull (page 254).

The following day Ollie and Tom went jigging for cod, while Elsa and I photographed guillemots. Ollie explained to Tom that the harder he jerked the line the larger the fish he would catch.

Tom gave the line a mighty tug and hooked one of the largest cod caught on that part of the coast—60 pounds, ten times the weight of the average cod.

With six on board we scarcely rattled around, even when the sea was rough. Two had to sleep on the tiny deck and pray it would not rain. Drying out sleeping bags was next to impossible.

Continuing our journey westward, we alternated bird islands with trout streams, putting in the good days in blinds with the birds and the foggy days with the fish.

Between Wolf Bay and Romaine is the Fog Island Sanctuary, low-lying rocks exposed to the storms of the open Gulf. Landing here is often dangerous or impossible. We were lucky in having a couple of fairly quiet hours so that we could visit a colony of murres and cormorants nesting in a much more accessible place than most, on broad shelving rocks where we could easily walk among them.

Young Murres Grow Up at Sea

The young murres were now nearly one-third grown and about ready to go to sea. Although they nest in dense colonies (pages 261 and 262), the murres, like the auks and the puffins, are rather solitary during the rest of the year. When the young are two or three weeks old, each family with its one chick goes off by itself to the open sea, where the youngsters finish growing up.

On an adjacent island was a fairly large colony of Caspian terns (page 260) and ring-billed gulls (page 249), with young now well feathered, scampering over the rocks and even swimming out to sea.

The wind freshened while we were there, so we had to pull anchor and start for Romaine in a rough sea. Held up here for a day and a half by high winds, we explored the Olomane River, a beautiful salmon stream, and visited an encampment of Montagnais Indians on high rocks overlooking the bay and village.

From Romaine to Natashquan is a dangerous part of the coast for small boats, with no shelter from the sea. We covered these 60-odd miles in fairly good time, however, and before dark slid into a beautiful little harbor at the Little Watshishu River.

At Mingan, which we reached the next day, we were cordially entertained by Lt. Col. E. P. Kern, of the U. S. Air Force, who built and operated the modern airport there. Mingan was an important landing field on the main northern route to Goose Bay, Labrador, and thence to Iceland. Now under Canadian administration, it still is used by the Northeastern Air Command of the USAF as a transport stop.

Expedition Counts 99,000 Birds

Dr. Hewitt's inspection trip was now completed. We had visited all of the sanctuaries along this coast and counted 99,000 birds using them for rearing their young. The *Alca* could now be put up for the winter; Sam Robertson would return to La Tabatière and Ollie Hewitt to Ottawa. Elsa and I would circle the Gaspé Peninsula before returning to Cornell.

What a different country this proved to be from Audubon's Labrador! The highway followed close to the long, smooth shore. Except in a few places, the rocks were concealed by luxuriant hayfields, gardens, or forests.

Thrifty homes, neat villages, horses, cows, sheep, and all those things which we had not seen for over a month enchanted us after the wild north coast. We were bound for picturesque Percé and Bonaventure Island.

Lying two miles offshore, Bonaventure Island presents to the sea a series of ledges formed when its soft conglomerate rock heaves off in huge blocks during winter (pages 132-133 and 239). These ledges, since time immemorial, have been the summer home of the strange and spectacular sea birds known as gannets. As large as some geese, they are snow-white in plumage, with black tips to their wings and an orange-buff wash to their heads (pages 134–136).

Not shy, the gannets permitted close approach and proved to be the answer to a bird photographer's prayer. Their black-faced youngsters were still covered with long, fluffy white down which gave them the shapeless appearance of giant powder puffs with black handles.

Gannets spend the greater part of the year on the open sea, plunging like animated javelins from high in the air at the luckless mackerel or other fish that dares venture close to the surface. As they glided past us at the edge of the cliff, they turned their heads and surveyed us with a cold gray eye encircled by blue. They gave an impression of abstract power that is perfectly at home in storm or fog or whatever the wild sea has to offer.

249 Photographed on Gull Island, Quebec

Whether to Sit and Warm the Eggs or Stand and Face the Camera—That Is the Question

Six feet away, the author's blind poses a problem for this **Ring-billed Gull.** Fish are her daily bread, but when migrating across prairies she accepts grasshoppers caught on the wing.

250 Photographed near Provo, Utah

Mormons Honor the California Gull for Its Aid to Early Settlers

By devouring crickets which threatened crops, **California Gulls** are said to have averted starvation among Utah's Mormon settlers. A Salt Lake City monument commemorates the event. These gulls nest on inland lakes.

251

Short-billed Gull Travels Inland to Raise Its Family

Though found near salt water most of the year, the Pacific coast's **Short-billed Gull** retires to inland Alaska and western Canada in breeding season. Late summer finds it winging westward over prairies and mountains to reach the sea. This species is the American representative of Europe's common gull.

Nesting Among Rushes, a "Prairie Dove" Tends Three Eggs

In summer **Franklin's Gull** is a bird of the prairie States, hence its nickname. It often follows the farmer's plow, dining upon worms and grubs exposed in the furrows. Most flocks migrate to Latin America; a few prefer the Gulf coasts of Texas and Louisiana. Nests are built in prairie marshes.

252

ʌ **Robber Barons of Isla Raza**

Heermann's Gulls, aristocrats of the gull family, breed on Raza, migrating later to California or even as far north and south as Vancouver Island and Guatemala. Usually shy, they are tame on Raza.

ⱴ **Robber Gull Steals Tern Eggs**

The photographer was making tests to learn how birds recognize their own eggs. Before he could get out of his blind, gull (right) had eaten every egg not guarded by the **Elegant Terns.**

"Who's That?" Puzzled Kittiwakes Eye the Author →

Atlantic Kittiwakes are year-round seashore residents. Even in breeding season they disdain the protection of sheltered inland areas. Seaweed nests are built on rocky ledges above the surf. When fishing expeditions take them far from land, these graceful little gulls often settle on the waves for a peaceful nap before returning home. They are found in northern climes on both sides of the Atlantic.

Kittiwakes derive their name from a characteristic call, "Kitta-aa, kitti-aa" (page 237).

253

↙ Sabine's Gull Nests on Arctic Tundra

Named for its discoverer, Sir Edward Sabine, Arctic explorer, this gull is seen but rarely in Atlantic coastal areas. Preferring Alaska, it breeds in scattered colonies near the Bering Sea. In winter **Sabine's Gull** migrates to the coast of Peru.

This tonsorially correct specimen shared its Alaskan tundra with short-billed gulls, whistling swans, spectacled eiders, and little brown cranes.

254

ʌ   He Can't Make Both Ends Meet   ⌄   Pious-looking Pirate Nurses Brood

The curious bill is a tool for the **Black Skimmer;** he drops the long lower mandible to snap up shrimps and killifish along the warm shores of the Americas.

Lacking fish, this bold **Great Black-backed Gull** steals the eider's eggs and young. This is largest gull on our eastern coast. He prefers a hermit's life (p. 244).

255 Photographed near Monterey, California

"How About Eggs for Breakfast? Let's Rob a Neighbor's Nest"

When sea food and refuse are scarce, **Western Gulls** ravage the nests of sea birds, devouring eggs and young. These large gulls are seen everywhere along the California coast, where they haunt rocky shores, breaking reefs, and harbors. This pair is perched on a headland above the surf at Monterey.

256 Photographed by S. A. Grimes near Corpus Christi, Texas

One Good Tern Was Once Mistaken for Another

Forster's Tern once was thought the same as the common tern, which it resembles, except that it has the outer web of the longest tail feather white. It breeds on coasts of Virginia, Louisiana, and Texas, and inland from Oregon to Manitoba. On migration it appears in other parts of the United States and south to Guatemala.

257

⋏ Young Common Tern, Still Hungry, Demands a Second Helping

The **Common Tern,** or "sea swallow," hovers and plunges for its food instead of alighting on the water, gull fashion. It is a numerous species found in many lands. Full-grown youngster (right), having downed a minnow, cries for more.

⋎ This Polar Resident Is the Greatest Traveler of Them All

Arctic Terns hold the bird world's championship for long-distance migration. They winter in the Antarctic and summer in the Arctic, flying some 22,000 miles round-trip. To keep their schedule, they must average about 150 miles a day.

Photographed near Churchill, Manitoba

Herring Gulls Return Each June to Nest on This Wind-swept Boulder in Arctic Wastes Adjoining Hudson Bay

With thousands of more hospitable nesting sites available, this familiar gull of our ports and beaches picks a lonely frost-cleft "rock of ages," in Isabelle Lake, near Churchill. Revisiting the site after 10 years, the author found **Herring Gulls** using the identical spot. Old gulls sometimes practice infanticide.

Screaming Elegant Terns and Heermann's Gulls Raise a Blizzard of Wings as the Photographer Invades Their Nesting Ground

Photographed by Lewis W. Walker on Isla Raza, Gulf of California

259

© National Geographic Society

260

Photographed by Cleveland Grant on the Labrador Coast

↑ Walt Disney Creations? No, These
Birds Are Atlantic Puffins

Though their huge beaks suggest the parrot family, **Atlantic Puffins** are sea birds and adept swimmers. They nest on rocky islands from Maine northward.

↓ Proud Parents Guard a Newly
Hatched Caspian Tern

Caspian Terns, largest members of the tern family, nest in Northern Hemisphere countries. This couple shared their sandy island with California gulls (background).

Photographed in Bear River Refuge, Utah

Photographed on Fog Island, Quebec

↑ Atlantic Murres Wear Formal Dress in Their Rock Nursery

To this barren island off Quebec a colony of **Atlantic Murres** returns every May, each pair to raise a single chick. Nests they disdain; eggs go on the bare rock. Each egg is pointed so sharply that, instead of rolling away, it pivots in a circle. Mix the eggs; each pair restores its own. "Murre," the alarm cry, named the bird.

Guillemot, Alias the "Sea Pigeon," → Sun-bathes on a Rock

"Sea pigeon" is a popular name suggested by the **Black Guillemot's** dovelike form and its habit of billing and whistling like a squab. Rocky headlands and sheltered bays of the North Atlantic are the guillemot's home.

For at least 10 years this female returned to St. Mary Islands, Quebec, in nesting season. Her eggs always were laid in the same spot, a crevice between rocks. Observers identified the bird through a numbered band, here barely visible on the right leg (page 240).

© National Geographic Society

Photographed on St. Mary Islands, Quebec

Photographed on Cliff Island, Quebec

Some Murres Wear Glasses, but No One Knows Why

Only few **Atlantic Murres** acquire spectacled appearance, caused by white feathers, of bird in foreground.

A Heron Visits
Her Downy Chicks

During its first year, the adolescent **Little Blue Heron** wears white feathers. In this stage it sometimes is mistaken for the snowy egret, although distinguished from that bird by greenish, instead of black, legs and bill. Adult plumage is slaty blue. Little blue herons nest from Delaware and Arkansas to the Gulf coast and Central America.

Photographed by S. A. Grimes
near Jacksonville, Florida

263

This Dove Prefers
Desert Terrain

Common in Mexico, **Western White-winged Doves** are declining in the United States. Along the border they are shot as game. Certainly not the dove of peace was this cactus haunter, which pugnaciously drove other birds away from the photographer's feeding station.

© National Geographic Society

Photographed by R. J. and Florence Thornburg
near Tucson, Arizona

264 Photographed by Alfred M. Bailey near Tampa, Florida

White Ibis, Deep in a Matted Swamp, Turns Its Startled Gaze to the Camera

In earlier years the **White Ibis** was hunted ruthlessly in Florida, its favorite State. Thousands were killed by gunners along the Shark River. Bodies were salted in barrels and shipped to Habana and elsewhere for food. Thanks largely to efforts initiated by the National Audubon Society, these handsome birds are now protected.

White ibises breed as far north as South Carolina and winter from Florida and Louisiana to Brazil and Peru. Mating season finds them gathered in large colonies. Nests, crudely made of sticks, are placed close together in trees or mangrove thickets.

Unlike the heron, which it resembles, the ibis has a curved bill and flies with its neck extended. It often indulges in graceful soaring maneuvers and glides after a few strong wingbeats, as no heron ever does. One of the fairest winter sights in Florida is an ibis flock returning at eve to roost. The birds advance in long ranks, wave after wave. When above their homes they rise in unison before scattering to spend the night.

Touring for Birds with Microphone and Color Camera

A FLUTTER of wings close behind me, and a low, growling call. Quickly I turned and nearly slipped from my precarious perch when my gaze fell upon the crimson breast and iridescent green head of a coppery-tailed trogon. It was less than 10 feet from my incredulous eye (page 11).

The wonderfully beautiful bird was obviously disturbed by my ascent of the tree, and for a moment my heart pounded as if I had been caught red-handed at the secret door of some ancient Aztec treasure.

For 50 years ornithologists better acquainted with Arizona and more familiar than I with the ways of trogons had been hunting unsuccessfully for the home of this exotic bird. Now, perhaps, the discovery was to be mine.

We had been told of these strange birds in Madera Canyon, Texas. The late Maj. Allan Brooks* had seen them while studying and painting the birds of the Santa Rita Mountains of southern Arizona.

Indeed, the presence of this bit of tropical sunshine, not far from a recently completed road up the mountains, seemed to be so well authenticated that we began to hope we might capture its voice with the sound camera.

But as for finding its nest, this was beyond our fondest hope; and when our good friend, the late Dr. Charles T. Vorhies, of the University of Arizona, directed us to the spot where the birds had been heard calling and promised to treat us to a good dinner if we found the nest, we jokingly acquiesced.

Improbable as it all seemed, in less than 12 hours we had succeeded in recording the trogon's curious song, a song which has a strange resemblance to that of a hen turkey with a jew's-harp. Now I was on the verge of finding its nest.

Ten feet above was an old woodpecker's hole, a little irregular in outline from exposure to wind and weather and from claws of departed *carpinteros*. In such places other species of Mexican and South American trogons had been known to nest.

Watchful Waiting Is Rewarded

I had climbed to several other promising holes that morning without even so much as a squirrel scolding me. Moreover, since even in South America I had been unable to stalk trogons closer than 30 yards without their taking wing, I felt sure that the close scrutiny I was now receiving portended that I was either in the nest tree or very close to it.

Not wishing to disturb the bird further, I descended the tree and set up an observation blind on the ground. Within an hour the male trogon returned and flew directly to the hole toward which I had been climbing. For five minutes he clung to the edge of it, like a woodpecker, cocking his head very deliberately and looking down inside with seeming admiration.

I thought the female was probably within, but 10 minutes later she appeared from somewhere in the forest and, after pausing at the entrance for an interminable moment, slipped in and remained for 20 minutes. Perhaps she was laying an egg; or was she feeding her young by that curious and lengthy process known as regurgitation?

The next day, with the aid of a mirror and flashlight, we settled the great question, for there, 14 inches down from the opening and with no sign of nesting material, were two shiny-white eggs. The first authentic nest of the coppery-tailed trogon in the United States had been discovered.

Trogons Disregard Grass-mat Blind

When we found that the birds were not afraid of the grass-mat blind on the ground, we raised it to a scaffolding in the tree above and soon were observing the birds on their own level, about 20 feet from the nest opening. Sometimes they perched on a near-by branch within arm's reach. The large eyes and trusting behavior gave the birds a friendly appearance.

We could not remain in Arizona long enough to record the hatching of the eggs and the feeding of the young; so we showed the nest to William Proctor, one of Dr. Vorhies's students who lived not many miles distant, and he kept it under observation until the young left. During this time it became the cynosure for all resident and visiting ornithologists, while we, unfortunately, had to depart.

Touring for birds with a microphone and color camera is somewhat more complicated than merely setting out to see how many kinds of birds one can observe.

Before we returned to our "base camp" at Cornell University, we had in less than a year seen nearly 600 different kinds of birds, if we include the various geographic races; by the end of the year a new record of 681 was established. However, we had recorded the songs

* See "National Geographic Magazine Cumulative Index" for listing of the 19 series of bird paintings by Major Brooks in issues from 1932 to 1939.

U. S. Navy, Official

Firm but Gentle Is the Launching Hold of the Seasoned Pigeoneer

About to release the bird from the rear door of the Navy's nonrigid airship K-2, this sailor holds it in the approved manner—thumbs over the back and the bird's legs held between the first two fingers of the right hand. Pigeons survive at altitudes where humans would die without supplemental oxygen. During the war, blimps engaged in antisubmarine patrol over coastal waters of both Atlantic and Pacific Oceans carried homing pigeons on their missions as a matter of course. In non-powered free balloons, pigeons often are the only source of communication with the home base.

"Canadian" Birds Are Comfortable in California

Cool and foggy summers in the vicinity of Berkeley permit the russet-backed thrush to nest on the campus of the University of California, whereas the eastern race of this thrush, the olive-backed, is strictly a Canadian bird. This russet-backed thrush family poses on a spruce branch after a meal. A number of northern birds extend farther south in coastal California than in the East (page 286).

or calls and secured satisfactory color films of only slightly over 100 different kinds.

It would be possible to study the check list of North American birds, wherein is given the distribution of each species and subspecies, and plan a trip in which one might see, in one season, at least 1,000 of the varieties listed.

But not much time could be spent in any one locality, and one would have to enlist the cooperation of many local observers to point out the exact spots where many of the birds of limited distribution are found.

Some of our North American birds, especially among the water-loving species, are found during the summer from coast to coast and from the Gulf of Mexico to Alaska, and the individuals from California are so similar to those from Maine that no one has ever been able to tell them apart. Such are the spotted sandpiper (page 213), killdeer (page 209), and Wilson's snipe (page 118).

On the other hand, a wide-ranging land bird like the song sparrow (page 109) has been broken up into 26 different geographic races, and it would be almost impossible to find them all in one season.

Birds Migrate along Fixed Routes

It is interesting to contemplate the present distribution of North American birds when we plan a vacation with them. It may be a new idea to some who have not given it much thought that creatures so free-moving as birds, which travel thousands of miles on their migrations, should so restrict their movements during the summer and so direct their travel routes on migration that many common species are entirely absent over large parts of our country. We look in vain for water ouzels along the streams of the Alleghenies; we never see nutcrackers on the mountaintops or magpies in the valleys of eastern United States.

On the other hand, wood thrushes are never heard singing in California, and the number of warblers found there is small indeed.

The reason doubtless lies in the fact that North American birds have come from two different sources and have not yet completed their conquest of the entire country.

The ouzels, nutcrackers (page 33), and magpies probably came into North America by way of Alaska; their closest relatives still live in similar habitats in Asia and Europe.

The warblers, on the other hand, invaded our country from the south. Many species have not yet found their way west of the Great Plains, and none has extended its range to the Old World.

Just why one species like the Kirtland's warbler should restrict its summer activities to a few counties in northern Michigan, while another like the yellow warbler (page 60) should occur, with slight variations, practically all over the North American Continent, is not always clear; but such problems help to make

Thick as a Feathery Snowfall, Birds Blanket South Florida's Cuthbert Lake Rookery

Wood ibises soar on black-tipped wings over the island. With them, aloft and on the ground, are egrets, water turkeys, and cormorants. This nesting ground, one of the largest in Everglades National Wildlife Refuge, once was a favorite haunt of plume hunters (page 72).

Charles C. Ebbets

There's More Excitement Here Than at Coney Island on the Fourth of July

Squalling, fighting, pushing, and chattering, thousands of birds keep the nesting ground buzzing with activity. Flights of winged adults continually come in with food or to give nest relief to their mates. Other flights go out on foraging expeditions.

A. E. Stewart

Flushed by Camera Plane, a Regiment of White Pelicans Casts Batlike Shadows on the Mississippi's Mouth

Winter visitors to the Gulf coast, these birds were engaged in a community hunt. Lining up in a semicircle, white pelicans beat the water and drive fish into shallows to be scooped up in their immense beaks (pages 129-131).

This May Be the Entire Population of Atlantic Snow Geese

Summer habitat of these birds is northern Baffin Island, Ellesmere Island, and Greenland. Every October they congregate at Cap Tourmente on the St. Lawrence River, remaining there until cold weather drives them south.

This flock, migrating, settled on the Fortescue marshes of Delaware Bay in March, 1946. Before the picture was made, aerial reconnaissance failed to reveal any other geese in the neighborhood. Then the flock was driven out into the bay and photographed.

Using an enlargement of the photograph, Charles L. Slaughter of the Bombay Hook National Wildlife Refuge, near Smyrna, Delaware, gratified a lifelong ambition by making a count of the flock. His total: 13,494. Experts say the figure represents at least the vast majority of the Atlantic snow goose population, if not its entirety.

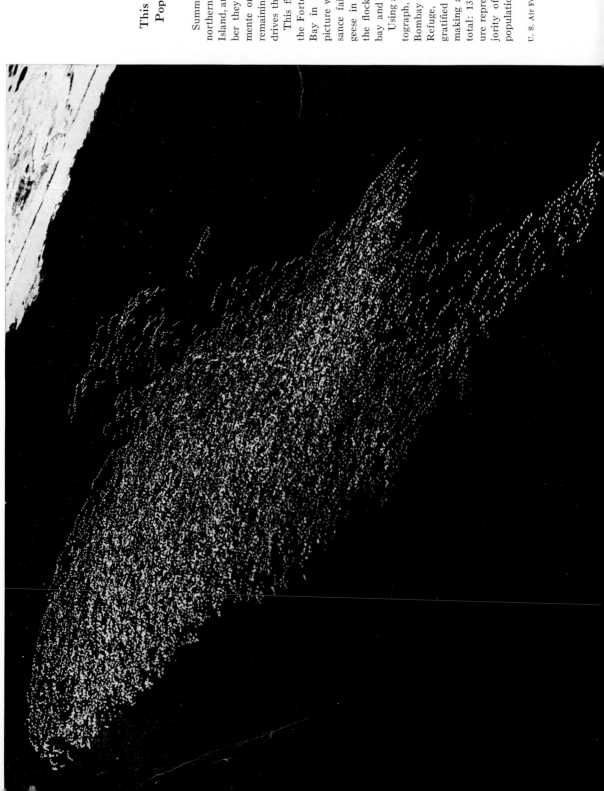

271

ornithology the fascinating study that it is.

Touring for birds with open eyes and listening ears drives home the subject of distribution. The bird student realizes when he leaves the range of one species and enters upon the range of another even more clearly than he recognizes the crossing of the Continental Divide or the various State boundaries.

For a number of years the Cornell Laboratory of Ornithology, through the sponsorship of the Albert R. Brand Foundation, has been engaged in recording on film the songs and calls of birds (see footnote on page 307). This has made possible an accurate study of the voice and hearing ability of the various bird species, in addition to providing a new approach to the study of birds through phonograph records of their songs. This method trains the ears in a way comparable to that which previous methods of bird study have provided for the eyes.

The song period of each species is comparatively short, and the difficulties encountered in recording some of the commonest species are so numerous that it has taken years to secure even a moderately complete collection of the songs of birds of the eastern United States.

Extinction Threatens a Prairie Chicken

Our first objective on the western trip of 1939 was to be the Attwater's prairie chicken of southern Texas. Though it still occupies a portion of its previous range along the Gulf coastal prairies, it threatens to follow its close relative, the heath hen, into extinction.

Thomas Waddell, the local game warden at Eagle Lake, seemed to know the whereabouts of every chicken on the prairie in that part of Texas and directed us to several "booming grounds." He warned us, however, that there was little chance of their becoming active unless it rained.

That afternoon he showed us about a dozen of the birds sharing a large pasture with several hundred cattle, including a few awe-inspiring Brahman bulls that glowered menacingly at us.

The next morning we arrived at the booming ground long before daylight. The cattle were still asleep, and five or six male prairie chickens were already there, though we heard no calls from them. The placing of our blind and microphone frightened them away, and they did not return that morning.

A mile or more to the southwest, however, we could faintly hear a few "boom-booms," as if there might be chickens courting in another pasture. Knowing the extent of some Texas pastures, I thought it might be a long hunt, but an hour's exploration showed us where the birds had been.

We planned, therefore, to set our blind and microphone in the evening and to sleep there, in order not to disturb the birds should they come to the booming ground during the night.

The top of the truck was equipped with a flat platform of such dimensions that we could use part of it as a base for a blind, or two of us could sleep very comfortably on it with air mattresses and sleeping bags.

With all equipment set, our sound technician, Charles Brand, slept in the truck so that he would merely have to turn a switch from his bunk if the chickens should start calling during the night.

My son David and I slept on top, under the stars. But it so happened that the stars lasted only until 3 a.m., when, with little warning, it rained!

Nocturnal Concert: "Um-boom-boom"

But it's an ill wind that blows no good, for, true to Waddell's prophecy, the rain touched off the chickens. Inside of an hour, the "Um-boom-boom" of a male bird in action was sounding across the dark prairie.

Soon a half-dozen ardent suitors were puffing out their air sacs and calling with almost the fervor of early spring.

None of the chickens approached the blind very closely, and their activities ceased by 7:30; so, although we got a good record of their voices, successful color photography was out of the question.

It was interesting to watch the air sacs on the sides of their necks swell out like small oranges as they shook their heads and stamped on the ground preparatory to giving their resonant calls. Curiously, these calls sounded no louder at 30 feet than at a distance of a quarter of a mile (page 197).

Occasionally a bobwhite could be heard in the distance. From time to time a wonderfully graceful scissor-tailed flycatcher (page 15) hovered over the booming ground, and one actually alighted on the blind.

Trees are scarce on the prairie, and one small knoll, with a dozen oaks and acacias and one pine, was the gathering place for five pairs of these birds, as well as great-tailed grackles and mourning doves (page 273).

The scissortails were chasing one another around one particular oak, hovering above it, opening and closing their long swallowtails, and flashing the rosy lining of their rapidly vibrating wings against a deep-blue sky.

In the lone pine the grackles were executing their courtship, accompanied by such sounds as shatter an adult's nerves but delight children. These sounds resembled the effect created when you draw your fingers over a toy balloon and let the air out at varying speeds: first, low squeals, then high squeals, followed

273

⋏ This Dove Sometimes Mistaken for Extinct Passenger Pigeon

Although the last known passenger pigeon died in 1914, the **Eastern Mourning Dove** (above) is sometimes mistaken for its larger and extinct cousin. These familiar doves are found in the United States, Canada, and Mexico. In some States they are hunted in fall as game birds by sportsmen.

⋎ Ground Dove Builds Its Home in a Jasmine Vine

But the fragrance is doubtless wasted, for birds have little sense of smell. **Eastern Ground Doves** are not much larger than sparrows; yet, with their mincing steps, small heads, and chunky bodies, they are typical doves. The bird gets its name from nesting and feeding on or near the ground.

Photographed near Ithaca, New York

274

With Canny Foresight This Yellow-billed Cuckoo Reared Its Brood Close to the Family Larder

An empty web of tent caterpillars and green leaves on the apple tree indicate that the young fared well. Deep-yellow mandible and guttural chirping quickly identify the adult bird with its long, white-spotted tail. In contrast to the European cuckoo, the **Yellow-billed Cuckoo** does not lay its eggs in other birds' nests, but hatches and rears its own young. During the winter these cuckoos benefit our good neighbors in Colombia, Venezuela, and Brazil by destroying hairy caterpillars.

A "Currant" Event in the Garden Has Brought an Ugly Fellow Out of a Lovely Blue Shell

This **Black-billed Cuckoo** built her nest in a currant bush, and the first of the eggs has just hatched a youngster that only a mother could love. The species is a fairly common nesting bird in northern United States and southern Canada, less common southward except in mountains. It winters in Colombia and Peru.

Photographed near Ithaca, New York

275

Photographed near Ithaca, New York

Valentine Greetings! Barn Owl's Heart-shaped Face Aids Hearing

Frill-like feathers border the facial disk, a fold of skin serving as the outer ears' sounding board. It is tuned to rodents' high-frequency squeaks. For night vision, eyes have extra rod cells. The **Barn Owl** hunts over dark meadows and city dumps. Often dubbed "monkey faced," it is one of our most useful birds and should be protected.

276

When Danger Threatens, Big Sister Horned Owl Spreads Her Wings and Almost Conceals Little Brother

These **Western Horned Owls** near Tucson, Arizona, will wear head tufts of feathers, resembling horns, when fully grown. Among owls, as well as most hawks, females are larger than males. One of the fiercest and most powerful of birds, the horned owl is found throughout North America. "Tigers of the air" sometimes strike fearlessly with their claws at men approaching their nests. They will attack any bird or mammal not too large; even house cats and skunks are not immune. Poultry raisers are their worst enemies. When rabbits, squirrels, mice, and other rodents are scarce, the owls turn to fowl, wild and domestic.

277

Photographed near Tucson, Arizona

278

↑ Here Is the Largest and Fiercest of Owls

The **Pacific Horned Owl** poses with his "horns" laid back. Like the tiger, he strikes unheard, his talons dealing death to birds and mammals. Though despised by farmers when he takes poultry, this owl feeds usually on rabbits, squirrels, mice, and even skunks.

↓ This Owl Has Its "Horns" Alerted

Having appropriated material left 30 feet up a beech tree by a red-shouldered hawk, this **Great Horned Owl** sits on three large white eggs and a Norway rat saved for an evening snack. In addition to crying "Whoo," it can make noises resembling dogs and cats (page 48).

Day Owls Adopt → Hawk's Habits

Ferruginous Pygmy Owls inhabit river valleys from southwestern United States to Panama. They nest in woodpecker holes and feed upon large insects and an occasional small bird. Like the hawk, this little predator hunts and calls in broad daylight. Its tail, relatively long for an owl, is flicked about in the same manner as the sparrow hawk's. Big yellow eyes, however, are typical of the owl family.

Photographed near Tamazunchale, Mexico

279

↓ Pet Owls Eye Their Host

These **Northern Barred Owls** were pets of the author for more than 10 years. One, brought to him as a downy youngster, became quite affectionate; the other, nearly grown when acquired, remained rather sullen throughout its life. Barred owls, also called hoot owls, are found in moist woodlands east of the Rockies. Westward they are replaced by the similar spotted owls (page 187).

Photographed in Ithaca, New York

280 Photographed by A. M. Bailey and F. G. Brandenburg in Colorado High Country

⅄ "Who's That Knocking at My Door?"

When a photographer whacked a pine tree with a stick, this startled **Saw-whet Owl** popped its head from the nesting cavity. Also in the hole were found four homely nestlings. This owl utilizes for its home an old woodpecker hole or other tree hollow. It feeds on mice and insects, occasionally taking small birds.

⅄ Babies Are Brought Out for an Airing

A hollow in a tree stump was the home of this family of **Pasadena Screech Owls,** smallest of the eared owls. The mother laid three white eggs deep inside. Her gray owlets, barely tufted, were growing fast. The sound of this bird in parts of the South is a "sign" of death or trouble (page 47).

Photographed by Lewis W. Walker in California

281

Nature's Mousetrap—a Young Saw-whet Owl Lunches near Grand Canyon, Arizona

Its mother had cached a white-footed mouse on a branch while teaching it to hunt. The **Saw-whet Owl,** a friendly bird, may sometimes be captured by hand in daylight as it sits quietly in a thicket. In adult plumage the breast is heavily streaked. Its rasping cry sounds like a saw being filed.

282

↑   **Mother Brings Another Gopher**

Forty gophers and 42 rats and mice were brought to this **Long-eared Owl's** nest in a 114-hour period.

↓   **Downy Young Await a Handout**

These **Short-eared Owls** vary in size, indicating mother began incubation before all the eggs were laid.

↑ Gravel of Schoolhouse Roof Serves as Home

Strangely, the **Eastern Nighthawk,** resting on the flat roof, is not a hawk at all but is related to the whippoor-wills. The common name derives from its hawklike appearance when on the wing. Nighthawks do aerial acrobatics at dusk when catching insects.

Nocturnal D.D.T. → of Bird World

Chuck-will's-widow becomes active at dusk, and woe to the insect that comes too near! Although large beetles compose over half its diet, dragonflies, moths, locusts, and roaches are welcome morsels. A large edition of the whip-poor-will, it is found in the southeastern States from Maryland and Missouri to Florida.

Photographed by S. A. Grimes
near Jacksonville, Florida

283

284

⋏ **Rescued from California Highway,
Owl Becomes David's Pet**

Taken from its cage, it becomes playful in author's Ithaca home (page 288). **Western Burrowing Owls** live in prairie-dog holes in western States, and feed on lizards, grasshoppers, and small snakes. The Florida burrowing owl, slightly darker, frequents Florida prairies and digs its own burrows.

⋎ **Saguaro Manor, Perfect Home,
Leased from Woodpeckers**

Fifteen feet above the hot Arizona desert, a female **Whitney's Elf Owl** looks out of her doorway. The woodpecker cavity is lined with a stiff shell of hardened cactus juice. The elf owl has a rounded head with no tufts. It ranges from southeastern California and southwestern New Mexico into Sonora State, Mexico.

by a crashing sound as if the bird were beating his wings on dry twigs.

All this accompanied a display of plumage that was equally ridiculous.

Grackles Display Plumage

The bird first threw his head back on his shoulders and inflated himself until he appeared twice his normal size, his feathers standing on end and his enormous tail spreading. In the bright sun the brilliant iridescence of otherwise black feathers shot out gleams of purple and green.

Next, he threw his head forward and, as he collapsed, he rapidly fanned the air with his wings, producing the crashing sound already mentioned.

We drove the truck up to the pine, set our blind on top, and recorded the whole performance in color and sound.

That evening we accompanied Mr. Waddell to Eagle Lake to watch the fulvous tree ducks make their nightly excursion to the rice fields. I had always thought of this tropical species as rare in the United States, as indeed it is in most places; but here was a concentration that would give palpitations to a veteran duck hunter.

Yellow-crowned night herons (page 287) began to move about at dusk; also egrets. Then flock after flock of the tree ducks rose up and circled the marshy lake until the air was full. There were thousands of them, all squealing in an unducklike manner, "Kill-deah, kill-deah," as they headed for the rice fields, which were flooded but showing green above the water.

We decided to accept the late Mr. E. A. McIlhenny's invitation to visit his "Bird City," on Avery Island, Louisiana. This is one of the most unusual and picturesque spots in the South and one that lends itself so conveniently to color photography that it has become a mecca for bird observers from all over the world.

Thousands of snowy egrets (page 139) and Louisiana and little blue herons (page 263) nest within arm's reach of commodious observation blinds built by Mr. McIlhenny. These the birds have accepted as part of their security in a man-made environment.

So spectacular are the herons that the average observer forgets completely some of the other birds that have even more interesting habits or more colorful plumages.

For instance, there was a tree full of anhingas, or snakebirds (page 286), at the opposite end of the lake. They intrigued us immensely, especially when the youngsters began rummaging inside their mother's throat for polliwogs and killifish.

The little fellows, with their long, slender,

featherless necks, looked even more serpentine than their parents and spoke convincingly for the evolution of birds from reptiles.

If you wish to study the birds of the desert at close range, you should offer them a drink, or, better still, go where someone else has been providing their much-needed water for some time prior to your visit. Drinking tanks for the cattle and bird baths lure the desert birds from far and near.

In Tucson we met a most interesting chap, an apiculturist, who has helped many ornithologists get acquainted with Arizona birds. Mr. H. E. Weisner seems to divide his friendship between the birds and the bees. More than a dozen species were frequenting the shallow pan of water which he refilled several times a day.

We set up our blind a few feet from this watering place, and I amused myself for several hours studying birds I had not seen before except at a distance through binoculars.

There were two families of Gambel's quail (page 199) with young about two weeks old; cañon and Abert's towhees; ash-throated and Arizona crested flycatchers; Palmer's thrashers; phainopeplas (page 51); pyrrhuloxias; western mockingbirds and Arizona cardinals; Bullock's orioles (page 80); Mexican ground doves and white-winged doves (page 263); Gila woodpeckers (page 14) and gilded flickers.

Apiculturist Bakes Cake for Birds

In addition to offering them water, Mr. Weisner bakes a cake for them, using cornmeal, suet, and honey. Even the woodpeckers are keen about this bird biscuit, and a beautiful pyrrhuloxia would take it from his hand.

There was one discouragement to nest hunting about Tucson, and that was the heat. The sand over which we tramped averaged about 150° F., although the air was not much over 100? Early in the morning, however, it was cool, and then we added rapidly to our collection of bird songs.

In the evening we visited the groves of giant cactus and recorded the calls of the elf owls (opposite page) that utilized the higher nesting holes dug by woodpeckers.

From Tucson we journeyed northward to the Grand Canyon, Bryce and Zion Canyons, and southwest to Hoover Dam. The grandeur of these natural wonders absorbs one, and even birds must wait. But a profound change in bird life, as compared with that of southern Arizona, is evident. The canyons are farther north and of much higher altitude, the rims of Grand Canyon and Bryce Canyon being from 7,500 to 8,000 feet.

Our bird fauna is so intimately associated with differences in temperature that the late

Allan D. Cruickshank, from National Audubon Society

Snakebirds Build Untidy Homes of Sticks and Twigs

Long, slender anhingas swim with their bodies submerged and only the head and neck above water; hence their reptilian nickname. Males are a rich iridescent dark green with white markings; females have light-tan heads, necks, and breasts. Hatched naked, the young soon grow a woolly coat of yellowish down. Anhingas are found from the Gulf Coast States southward.

Dr. C. Hart Merriam, a former chief of the U. S. Biological Survey and member of the Board of Trustees of the National Geographic Society for 54 years, 1888-1942, conceived an explanation, based almost entirely upon temperature, for the many variations in distribution of plants and animals in America. He called it the "Life Zone Theory" and he formulated the "Laws of Temperature Control."

Temperature Differences Affect Bird Life

According to this theory, each species has certain basic requirements of temperature, or "a physiological constant." Its northward distribution is controlled, therefore, by the length of the growing season and its southward distribution by the temperature of the six hottest weeks of the summer. This corresponds roughly to the period of reproduction.

Those species which cannot stand the heat of summer when rearing their young either go north or else find the same conditions on the tops of the mountains. Those which require a long season to raise their young and don't mind the heat populate the southern areas.

Wherever we find a locality where the heat of summer is not extreme and yet the growing season is long, as on our Pacific coast, we are likely to find a great intermingling of northern and southern forms.

In the San Francisco Bay region, for example, where the fogs of summer reduce the heat, one finds northern or mountain birds almost at sea level. Chestnut-backed chickadees, russet-backed thrushes (page 267), juncos (page 108), brown creepers (page 34), and kinglets live almost side by side with such hot-country birds as mockingbirds (page 37), California woodpeckers (page 10), bush-tits, California quail (page 199), wren-tits, and road-runners.

Of course some birds and some plants are much more adaptable than others to ranges of temperature. It is only those that have definite limitations that make good "indicators" of life zones to the faunal zoologist or to the touring ornithologist.

Thus the rim of the Grand Canyon is in the Transition life zone, with such indicators as Steller's jays, black-eared (pygmy) nuthatches, red-backed juncos, Cassin's purple finches, and mountain bluebirds.

A Yellow-crowned Night Heron Stands Lonely Vigil

Like the green heron, it prefers a hermit life, although occasionally it consents to nest in the company of a few other herons. This species is most common in the Tropics, but it wanders northward and occasionally nests as far north as Long Island or New England. In immature plumage the yellow-crowned night heron is streaked brown and is almost indistinguishable from the black-crowned night heron in the same stage (page 141). Both look remarkably like bitterns. When alarmed, this heron creeps from the nest and then, at a safe distance, springs into the air with a hoarse call.

The floor of the Canyon, on the other hand, a mile below, is in the Lower Austral zone, with such birds as Say's phoebes, ash-throated flycatchers, desert sparrows, and long-tailed chats.

Life zones are particularly conspicuous in the Rocky Mountain region. However, since many other factors there, in addition to altitude and latitude, affect temperature, there is a great deal of irregularity about the zones that is confusing even to an experienced observer.

The trees, however, are usually good indicators. When you pass from the Digger pines into the yellow pines, you know you are passing from the Upper Sonoran into the Transition zone; and when the yellow pines give way to the red fir and the Jeffrey pine, you know you are passing from the Transition to the Canadian zone, without having to wait for hermit thrushes (page 41), kinglets, solitaires, or dusky grouse to tell you so.

In similar manner, when the whitebark pine replaces the Jeffrey and the mountain hemlock the red fir, you know you are entering the Hudsonian zone and you will be listening for nutcrackers and white-crowned sparrows. Finally, when you leave the trees behind and enter the Arctic-Alpine zone, you will start looking for ptarmigan (pages 195, 196) just as surely as if you had traveled to Hudson Bay and started hiking across the tundra.

From Desert Lands to Rich Farms

But after viewing Bryce Canyon even a flamingo might seem colorless, and certainly the rest of the landscape for several days seemed very drab.

So we hurried on toward Pasadena, passing through groves of the curious Joshua trees, between Las Vegas and San Bernardino. These in turn gave way to oranges and lemons when we left San Bernardino and irrigation became possible.

With the change from desert to rich farm land there was just as distinct a change in the bird life, blackbirds and orioles and grosbeaks replacing thrashers and cactus wrens.

From Pasadena a half day's drive took us to the Sequoia National Park in the mid-Sierra, where we were soon driving among trees that were giants when Columbus was a little boy. What we could see of the sky through a lacework of branches 300 feet over our heads was deepest blue.

It was summer in the San Joaquin Valley below, but here it was spring, with the dogwood in bloom, white against the red-brown trunks of the sequoias. But spring is hardly the word. Despite the date, June 13, that night clouds rolled in and it snowed. Next day the clouds hung so low that we could see only halfway to the tops of the trees.

The following morning it cleared at daybreak, and we recorded the cheery song of the fox sparrow (page 109), the chirping of a pair of evening grosbeaks (page 104), the twitter of the junco, the scolding of a white-headed woodpecker, the wiry song of the Calaveras warbler, and the conversational warbles of a Cassin's vireo.

It was then that we heard our first sierra grouse tooting from the top of a red fir near one of the campgrounds. Despite the noise of chopping wood and the tinny rattle of meal preparation, we secured a fair recording of its low, rhythmical hoots.

Once more the clouds came, and we decided to move down to lower altitudes.

Bird Haunts of Berkeley

A sojourn at Berkeley for six weeks, while I was teaching at the University of California, gave us opportunity for recording birds of the campus and for week-end excursions to favorite bird haunts.

Monterey, with its nesting western gulls (page 255) and black oyster-catchers, occupied us first. Near there we were shown a nest of the rare white-tailed kite in the top of a blue oak, with an unusual second brood.

Another interesting week end was spent at Los Banos in the hot San Joaquin Valley, with its multitude of water birds. Flocks of white pelicans, white-faced glossy ibis, black terns, stilts, and avocets fascinated us most.

One Saturday was spent in Muir Woods with its giant redwoods and midget birds— chestnut-backed chickadees, kinglets, brown creepers, and winter wrens; another at Point Reyes, where hordes of murres, cormorants, and guillemots were nesting.

Near Stockton we saw a colony of blue grosbeaks (page 101).

Near Mount Diablo we located a nesting tree, convenient for study, of the California woodpecker. This strikingly marked bird lives in colonies wherever the blue and valley oaks occur in sufficient numbers to supply its staple food of acorns. The birds drill holes in the bark in which to hide these treasures and give them constant protection against marauding jays and squirrels.

Even more interesting than storing of provender, however, is its communal way of life. There were several nesting holes dug in the tree where we set up our blind on top of the car, but we soon discovered that in one there were young of differing ages and that they were being fed by two pairs of parent birds.

After considerable waiting I managed to get several shots which showed three birds at the nesting hole at one time, as well as a quantity of stored acorns around it (page 10).

Most woodpeckers have a keen sense of territorial rights and will not permit intrusion near the nest by any other woodpecker. Such a social arrangement as we found among these woodpeckers, therefore, came as something of a surprise to me.

The birds of the University campus at Berkeley are interesting and friendly but not very colorful. Brown towhees hop around the grass like robins, which, by the way, are much less numerous than our eastern robins. Spurred towhees (page 107) whine from the shrubbery and forget the first two syllables of the "Drink your tea" song that the familiar eastern towhee gives (page 106).

Our return from California by the northern route was marked by several interesting stops, although, since it was now August, the song season was over. We did, however, secure some calls of the mountain quail and the chukar partridge near the Lava Beds National Monument, and of the nutcrackers (page 33) at Crater Lake, where they have become nearly as tame as the ground squirrels and have learned to drink from the bubbling fountains.

On our way to Carson Pass, in the Sierra, late in July, we had acquired a baby burrowing owl. It had ventured out of its mother's cyclone cellar near Stockton a little too soon for its own safety and stood in the middle of the highway defying traffic.

Speo, as we christened him, shortened from his generic name of *Speotyto*, became David's special pet and care for the rest of the trip. And now, as I write this in my study, he watches my moving pencil with apparent fascination, ready to pounce on it should I lay it down, as if it were a slender lizard or a cricket.

When we let him fly about the study at night, he becomes as sportive as a kitten. His little curtsies, his inquisitive gestures, his intimidating postures when he discovers something strange, and his mock ferocity in pouncing on an eraser keep us amused and bring to mind the golden days spent in touring for birds (page 284).

289 Photographed by Lewis W. Walker in Kofa Mountains, Arizona

Sitting on Its Snack Bar, an Elf Owl Feasts on a Grasshopper

No bigger than a sparrow, the **Whitney's Elf Owl** snatches nectar-hunting insects as they are attracted to the yellow blossoms of a century plant. This smallest of North American owls nests in a giant saguaro in the Kofa Mountains. The tiny night flyer, in contrast to his bigger cousins of silent flight, wings through the blackness with a noisy swish. It feeds almost exclusively on ants, beetles, and grasshoppers.

© National Geographic Society

290

Photographed near Ithaca, New York

↑   **End of a Successful Fishing Trip**

The **Eastern Belted Kingfisher** makes a rattling call, like the clicking of a reel. Diving from 20 or 30 feet in the air, it seizes its finny prey with javelin bill. It winters as far south as British Guiana or Trinidad. This bird lives a solitary existence except in the mating and nesting seasons.

↓   **Seven Little Fishermen**

Here the young **Eastern Belted Kingfishers** have been posed at the mouth of their 5-foot tunnellike home. Unlike those of most young birds, their feathers will remain in the casings until the fledglings are nearly full-grown, thus protecting them from the sandy walls of their burrow.

Hummingbird →
Inspects a
Glass Feeder

The hummingbird family (Trochilidae) is strictly American; none of its members is native to the Old World. More than 600 species and subspecies make up one of the largest avian families in numbers.

This **Anna's Hummingbird** is a Californian. The bottle of sugar water has six holes in its metal cap, permitting hummers to thrust in their long tongues.

Photographed by Harold E. Edgerton near Orange, California

291

↓ Chimney Swift
Bends Double

With her viscid saliva, the **Chimney Swift** glues twigs in cup form to the inside of a chimney or barn. So small is the nest that this female must press against the wall and bend backward while incubating her eggs.

© National Geographic Society

Photographed near Bay Pond, New York

This Male Hummer Wears a Rose-red Bib

Broad-tailed Hummingbird, whose notched wing tips make a clattering sound, is generally heard before he is seen. Viewed from a different angle, his brilliant red throat might appear dark maroon. Light's diffraction accounts for flashy colors. Rays striking the dark grating formed by feather fibers break up into glittering spectral hues.

292

Hungry Sword Swallowers Take Food

With a series of deep, convulsive thrusts, the female **Broad-tailed Hummingbird** pumps regurgitated food. Usually she feeds each youngster in turn, but sometimes the stronger shoves his nest mate aside and grabs a second helping.

Eggs hatch in two weeks. The young emerge black, blind, naked, and as small as honeybees. They attain full size and feathers in three weeks.

Photographed by Walker Van Riper near Denver, Colorado

293 Photographed by Robert J. Niedrach in Ramsey Canyon, Arizona

↑ Blue-throat, Tiny but Tough, Warns Rivals Off His Flowery Domain

Males often monopolize tasty blossoms, driving off competitors. Dive-bombing, they may chase hawks a hundred times their size. Columbine and Mexican campion conceal this **Arizona Blue-throated Hummingbird's** syrup feeder. High-speed photography freezes wingbeats too rapid for the eye. Hovering wings beat 55 strokes a second, on the average. In courtship dives the count may rise to 200. Hummingbirds in flight have been clocked at 55 miles an hour.

↓ Rufous Hummingbirds Gather Lunch Heedless of the Cameraman

Males, jealous of food supplies, may clash head on in mid-air; dropping, they may continue combat on the ground until the exhausted loser flies away. These three migrating **Rufous Hummingbirds** stopped on the rim of Arizona's Grand Canyon for a thistle-blossom lunch. They nest from Montana to Alaska and winter in southern Mexico. Darting males (center and right) sometimes sparkle like live coals; the female (left) is plainer.

Photographed by Harold E. Edgerton in Grand Canyon, Arizona

Photographed by H. E. Edgerton in Holderness, New Hampshire   294   © National Geographic Society   Photographed by R. J. Niedrach in Ramsey Canyon, Arizona

Glittering in the Sunlight, Elegant Males Seem Daubed with Fresh Paint

Rivoli's Hummingbird (right), five inches long, is a veritable giant compared with the **Broad-billed Hummingbird** (upper left), whose length is only about 3¼ inches. A colored vial holds the promise of sugar water for the **Ruby-throated Hummingbird** (lower left), only species occurring regularly east of Nebraska.

Photographed by R. J. Niedrach in Madera Canyon, Arizona

Color, as Well as Nectar, Attracts Hummers. Ruby-throats Favor Red Flowers

So well developed is the hummingbird's color sense that individual birds are known to have mistaken women's gaudy hats for delicacies. Left: Male **Ruby-throated Hummingbird** feeds from a cardinal flower; right: the female draws nectar from a scarlet mint.

Photographed near Ithaca, New York

296 Photographed by Robert J. Niedrach in Ramsey Canyon, Arizona

Timid Black-chinned Hummer Shares His Banquet Table with a Bumblebee

In flight the little **Black-chinned Hummingbird** hums like the nectar-sipping bee (center). He is found in semiarid terrain from Texas to British Columbia. Glancing light occasionally reveals a violet throat band.

Freezing the Flight of Hummingbirds

By Harold E. Edgerton, R. J. Niedrach, and Walker Van Riper

IF hummingbirds were human, they might well have wondered why lightning was flashing all around them on summer days of cloudless sky and brilliant desert sun.

Flashes several hundred times brighter than Arizona sunlight blinked among the darting birds but disturbed them not a bit. Each of these man-made flashes lasted only 1/5000 of a second. They came from our high-speed flash equipment, developed for what might have been called "Operation Hummingbird."

This project had a dual purpose: first, construction and testing of new lightweight equipment especially designed for motion-stopping natural-history color photography in the field; second, recording on film the flight of species of hummingbirds new to our cameras.

Wings whirring 55 times a second wear a cloak of invisibility. All one can see is a tiny darting ghost in a blur of wings. Hummingbirds are literally as quick as a flash— but not as quick as a modern high-speed flash.* Used with today's color film, it can penetrate the mystery that hides the incredibly rapid movement of hummingbird wings from human eyes. Thus we were able to "freeze" the flight of several species of American hummingbirds in color for NATIONAL GEOGRAPHIC MAGAZINE readers.

Hummers Cooperate with Science

These Kodachrome and Ektachrome photographs (pages 291-296) are examples of a special kind of photography requiring elaborate apparatus, much hard and patient work, thousands of miles of travel, and the cooperative antics of one of the most interesting and beautiful of birds.

Dr. Edgerton had pioneered in this work. He took the first high-speed flash pictures of hummingbirds in black and white in 1928. Picturing the ruby-throated, only North American variety found east of the Mississippi, the photographs proved the hummingbird a most absorbing subject.

So courageous that it sometimes tackles hawks, the little creature is so unafraid of man that it can easily be enticed within close-up range of camera and lights.

Later, with more powerful lights, Dr. Edgerton made the first flight photographs of hummingbirds in color and presented the remarkable results in the NATIONAL GEOGRAPHIC.†

To picture additional species, Dr. Alexander Wetmore, Secretary of the Smithsonian Institution and Vice-chairman of the National Geographic Society's Research Committee, suggested that we travel west and photograph the dozen or so species commonly found in the Rocky Mountains and other western regions.

Such a task called for a mobile form of high-speed flash photography, sometimes called the "strobe" (for stroboscopic). This brief but amazingly brilliant flash, synchronized with a camera shutter, had found many important uses. It "stopped" whirling wheels in industrial plants as effectively as it froze hummingbird flight. In World War II, night-reconnaissance planes carried extremely powerful sets, weighing more than a ton, for taking photographs behind enemy lines.

For natural-history field work, however, the device had to be light in weight and independent of electric power lines.

"Suitcase Set" Makes Flash Mobile

Working with a grant from the National Geographic Society, Dr. Edgerton and his associates designed a battery-operated, remote-control flash unit that packed into a 50-pound suitcase. With this "suitcase set," Dr. Edgerton photographed four species of hummingbirds in the West in 1947.

In late May and June of 1950, four of us spent three weeks in the field in Arizona under the joint sponsorship of the National Geographic Society and the Denver Museum of Natural History: Dr. Edgerton, Professor of Electrical Measurements at Massachusetts Institute of Technology; Robert J. Niedrach, Curator of Ornithology, and Walker Van Riper, Curator of Spiders, Denver Museum; and O. A. Knorr, student ornithologist.

By then we had even lighter equipment. Flash units for each of our three cameras had been engineered down to seven pounds.

Expert advisers who contributed to both our projects included Dr. Gilbert Grosvenor; Dr. Alexander Wetmore; Dr. Arthur A. Allen; Henry B. Kane of Massachusetts Institute of Technology; Gjon Mili, noted photographer; and the eminent ornithologists Herbert Brandt and Roger Tory Peterson.

* See "A New Light Dawns on Bird Photography," page 21.
† See "Hummingbirds in Action," by Harold E. Edgerton, NATIONAL GEOGRAPHIC MAGAZINE. August. 1947. See also "The Hummingbirds," by Crawford H. Greenewalt, NATIONAL GEOGRAPHIC, November, 1960.

Harold E. Edgerton

A Hummingbird, All Motion Stopped by the Camera, Seems Big and Fierce as a Hawk

Hundreds of times brighter than sunlight, a stroboscopic flash lasting 1/5000 of a second reveals intimate details of this Anna's hummingbird fluttering close to the camera lens. His wings whir 55 times a second.

A hummer flying at top speed is too fast for even the speed flash's brief, brilliant imitation of a lightning bolt. When wings beat 200 times a second, they appear slightly blurred on film.

Working with a National Geographic Society grant, the authors in 1950 developed new electronic flash equipment to record habits of several hummingbird species in Arizona.

On a similar expedition in 1947, Dr. Edgerton and his associates used a 50-pound flash unit packed in a suitcase. For the later studies, lighter and more convenient equipment was developed in Dr. Edgerton's laboratory at the Massachusetts Institute of Technology.

Ornithologists and scientists took part in the new project. Denver Museum of Natural History was a co-sponsor.

Walker Van Riper

Impossible to Fly Backward? The Camera Shows How It's Done

Reverse flight once was dismissed as an optical illusion. Here a multiple exposure by stroboscopic light catches a female broad-tailed hummingbird backing away from a feeder (page 301).

When Harold Edgerton started west on his 1947 trip, his first objective was the broad-tailed hummingbird *(Selasphorus platycercus)*, abundant in the Rocky Mountain region from southern Idaho to Mexico.

The male's red gorget (page 292) resembles that of the ruby-throat. His jewellike throat patch flashes its brightest when seen head on, with light at the right angle; otherwise it appears dark red to black. Some pictures indicate that the gorget flash may depend in part on erection of the throat feathers.

Broad-tail Gently Pushed from Nest

On the Evans Ranch in Colorado, Mr. Niedrach and Mr. Van Riper showed Dr. Edgerton his first broad-tail nest.

"May I go closer without disturbing her?" he asked from a distance of 20 feet, looking doubtfully at the brooding female.

He was assured that he might go as close as he wished.

Shortly we had three cameras, as well as a collection of lights, aimed at the nest from a foot away. Even then, to get the mother bird to leave the nest, we actually had to *push* her off! Not until completely dislodged did she "rev up" for the take-off (page 300). Then she circled the tree once, but came back immediately and resumed her duty of keeping the two miniature eggs warm (page 305).

The male broad-tail has one characteristic that distinguishes him from other North American hummers: his flight is accompanied by a strange trilling or vibrating sound. He is nearly always heard before he is seen.

The sound has been variously described as "a shrill trilling," "a shrill screeching noise something like that produced by a rapidly revolving circular saw when rubbed by a splinter," or "a curious, loud, metallic, rattling noise."

Close observation reveals that the intensity of the sound correlates with the vibration rate of the wings. When the bird hovers before a flower, his wings beating about 55 times

Lights! Action! Camera! Pushed from Nest, a Feathered Star Performs Reluctantly

Inquisitive humans and their gear failed to disturb this nesting broad-tailed hummingbird. Poked gently by R. J. Niedrach, she took off on a short flight. Walker Van Riper operated the camera (page 299).

a second, there is little or no sound. The chatter becomes distinctly audible in level flight when the beat rises to 75 or higher, and is loudest in the "dive-bombing" courtship display, when the wings reach a rate of 200.

Our pictures of male and female broad-tail wings in actual flight reveal the source of the sound for the first time. When flying, the female makes only the usual buzzing, or humming, sound. The photograph of her spread wing shows that all the primary feathers are normally shaped (page 299). Not so with the male; his first two, or outermost, primaries are uniquely modified, narrowing at the tips to produce the slots shown in the picture (page 303). Air fluttering through these slots produces the rattling whistle.

In migration male broad-tails usually precede the females, arriving in Denver about the middle of May. This species (and apparently a number of others) is highly matriarchal. The late Frank Bené's observations indicate that the female black-chinned hummingbird selects her nesting area and begins to build the nest before searching for a mate. When she finds him, she completes the nest, lays the two white eggs, incubates them herself, and cares for the young until they are ready to fly and feed themselves.

Our observations of the broad-tail, while limited, seem to show that it follows the same schedule.

Nests of the broad-tail average a little over 1½ inches in outside diameter and somewhat less in height. The inner cup, about an inch in depth and diameter, is lined with soft plant down, often from willow and cottonwood seeds; feathers are rarely used. Lichens, dry leaves, and fibers, bound together with spider webs, form the outer shell. Always the outer layers of the nest are camouflaged in color and texture to match the supporting limb (page 292).

This hummer nests not only in the mountains up to 10,000 feet but—conveniently for picture takers—also in the cities.

Hummingbirds Have Twins

Hummingbirds lay only two eggs. Those of the broad-tail hatch in about 14 days. The young, born helpless, naked, black, and blind, are about the size of honeybees. They are fed by regurgitation, the mother thrusting her bill down the baby's gullet with a convulsive spasm (pages 292 and opposite).

Besides nectar, the food consists of small spiders and insects gleaned from flowers or caught in the air.

Walker Van Riper

Dinner Is Served! Few Other Birds Feed Their Young While Hovering, Like Hummers

Wings beating rapidly, the broad-tail thrusts her long, sharp bill deep into the youngster's gullet. Feeding by regurgitation, she supplies a diet of nectar, spiders, and insects.

In about three weeks, the expanding bodies of the young have pressed the little nest out of all shape. They are now as large as the parents and wear a full covering of feathers. For a time they exercise their wings at the nest, then take off in flight. Though they still are fed by the mother for a few days, they soon have mastered the art of hummingbird flight—up, down, forward, sideways, and even backwards.

Backward Flight Is No Illusion

In 1867 the Duke of Argyll, in *The Reign of Law,* stated that no bird could fly backwards. He conceded that the hummingbird might appear to do so as it left a flower, but held that this was an optical illusion; that the bird really fell away, turned, and flew ahead. Undoubtedly the noble author never watched a hummer fly, because it is easy to see that the bird *does* fly backwards.

To demonstrate the performance photographically, we contrived a switch to set off three flashes in extremely rapid succession, so that the hummingbird would appear in three positions on the same film. The first flash showed the bird's bill leaving the feeding bottle; the second and third proved actual backward flight (page 299).

This photograph shows graphically another hummingbird feature, the long, protruding tongue, the organ that distinguishes the hummingbird sharply from other bird groups. A sort of double-barreled tube, split and fringed at the tip, the tongue can be extended beyond the bill tip nearly as far as the bill's own length. This remarkable implement acts as a sucking tube to extract nectar from flowers and also as a probe or sticky brush for collecting small insects found there.

Since our pictures were made at varying distances from the subject, it was not possible to make the reproductions to scale. To give some idea of relative size, here are significant dimensions of the broad-tail: length from tip of bill to tip of tail, 4½ inches; length of bill, ¾ inch; over-all diameter of nest, 1⅝ inches.

In mid-July we returned to the Evans Ranch in Colorado to look for the rufous hummingbird *(Selasphorus rufus).* During a lull in the rain, Van Riper and Niedrach went to the meadow behind camp to look for birds. Suddenly Van Riper shouted to his companion, "Come quick, the rufous are here!" Three adult males, with fiery throats and copper-colored backs, were darting about, sipping nectar from the common mountain flower, the pentstemon.

George A. Lewis

Her Nest Is "Wired for Electricity"!

A female black-chinned hummingbird feeds her babies in a tiny nest attached to an electric cord on a porch in Independence, California. Small insects and nectar comprise the menu. Birds nested in this spot for 20 successive years.

One male took possession of a pentstemon patch by perching on a tall weed from which he could see and attack all intruders. From his high perch the rufous power-dived on interlopers, chased them away, then returned to the weed with the boss hummer's peeping cry of possession. Periodically he went over his patch to collect the nectar and insects that had accumulated in the flower cups.

On the rim of the Grand Canyon we studied and photographed a boss rufous for two-and-a-half days. He liked to perch on a branch just above six thistle bushes. We were successful with close-up photography of this bird, probably because he was used to throngs of Canyon-viewers and therefore tolerated our lights, cameras, and background (page 293).

Early one morning Edgerton observed two young males contesting the ownership of a large and desirable thistle bush. Whenever one of the evenly matched contenders attempted to glean nectar from a flower, the other attacked him from the rear with beak and claws.

After many rear attacks and aerial dogfights, the two tiny adversaries faced each other in mid-air, hovering with beaks belligerently thrust out like miniature fencing foils and with tails spread in fury.

Together the birds rose vertically in the air, only five inches apart. When 30 feet up, they came together with a shock, then dropped to the ground, where they remained quiet except for an occasional flutter. The hummers did not appear to use their beaks while on the ground; instead, one grasped the other by the back with his claws and held on with bulldog tenacity.

The aerial maneuvers alternated with wrestling matches on the ground for more than an hour. Eventually one bird gave up and flew away. By now the victor was so tired that he did not give chase in the characteristic rufous manner. He did manage to fly to his perch and announce to the world that he was the owner and would defend his holdings.

Rufous hummingbird lives as far north as Alaska, migrating to Mexico for the winter. This brilliant bird is seen over the entire western region during the southward migration in summer. His polished gold gorget glistens like metal.

Anna's Is a Handsome Redhead

Our next quarry was Anna's hummingbird (*Calypte anna*), California's most typical member of the Trochilidae. Californians know him well because he frequents populated places. Incidentally, he is the only hummer that spends the entire winter mainly in the United States.

To those who know only the ruby-throat of the East, the adult male Anna's is impressive, his entire head a sheath of rose-red metallic feathers. We wanted to find an adult male that would show his gorgeous head by posing 15 inches from our lens (page 298).

Walker Van Riper

Frozen Flight Reveals the Source of a Hummer's Sound

Primary feathers of this male broad-tail's wings taper at the tips, producing slots. Air fluttering through the openings results in a distinctive rattling whistle. Female broad-tails, with normally shaped feathers, fly with a buzzing sound like other hummingbirds (page 300).

A letter from Mr. Benjamin F. Tucker, of Long Beach, California, decided us. "There is no better place," he wrote, "than Santiago Canyon."

In memory of his wife, Mr. Tucker had donated a site in the canyon to the California Audubon Society. At the Dorothy May Tucker Sanctuary we found many Anna's and black-chinned hummingbirds.

Here visitors sit comfortably on a screened porch to watch hummingbirds going and coming along a row of feeders. These are glass containers of sweet liquid, enormous compared with feeders elsewhere, each with six feeding holes. Mr. Tucker had devised an ingenious metal plate, half an inch above the liquid, to prevent bees from feeding. Hummingbirds, however, can thrust their long tongues through holes in the plate to sip.

Huachucas Home to Many Hummers

In the Huachuca Mountains of Arizona, where we worked in 1950, we established headquarters at the Carr Canyon Ranch of Maj. and Mrs. John H. Healy, who provided every comfort and expert field assistance.

The profuse and varied animal and plant life of the Huachucas includes species found only here, or rarely elsewhere in the United States. At lower levels, yucca, cactus, century plant, and ocotillo grow on the warm slopes. All of these bloom and attract hummingbirds in season.

On our list were six species of hummingbirds—Rivoli's, blue-throated, black-chinned, broad-billed, white-eared, and broad-tailed. We hoped to see Costa's and counted Allen's and Anna's as remote possibilities. We probably could not find as many kinds in a small area anywhere else in the country.

The dominant hummingbird in the Huachucas is the blue-throated (*Lampornis clemenciae*, page 293). Its specific name was bestowed in honor of a Frenchwoman, but by a happy coincidence the Latin meaning of *clemenciae* is "tame" or "domesticated." It is an apt name, for the blue-throat likes to make its home close to the dwellings of man.

Early records report the blue-throat as building its nest in ferns and other low plants along canyon streams, but of late years nearly every nest found is under a bridge or a water tower, beneath house eaves, or in outbuildings.

Blue-throats use the same nest over and over, building it higher each time. One nest we found had evidently been used five times, doubtless by the same bird and probably in two successive years.

In Mrs. Wallace G. Haverty's garden in Ramsey Canyon, Arizona, three species—blue-throated, Rivoli's, and black-chinned (page 296)—fed constantly on masses of yellow columbine and other blossoms and at syrup bottles provided by their hostess.

In the Haverty garden the top sergeant was Pappy, a male blue-throat who first appeared in 1939 as a mature bird and was, therefore, at least 12 years old. Though this statement cannot be verified in any manner satisfactory to science, it is entirely possible.

Pappy had his own lookout perch, his way of flying at other birds, and other idiosyncrasies by which Mrs. Haverty could confidently identify him. From his perch Pappy lorded it over blue-throat, Rivoli's, and black-chin alike. He watched both feeding stations at opposite sides of the garden. When a rival flew to a feeder, Pappy dived and drove him away. This left the other station unguarded, and another bird would seize the opportunity to feed for a moment in peace.

When we thought to vary the routine by setting up another feeder out of Pappy's sight, the move brought on a mild disaster. Pappy at once discovered the new feeder and began to guard all three. The additional work appeared to excite and upset him, and he hit one Rivoli's male so hard that he actually knocked it out. Under Mrs. Haverty's expert care, the victim eventually recovered, but we tampered no more with established order.

A Feathered David Routs Goliath

One evening at Carr Canyon Ranch Albert Knorr sat watching a young male blue-throat through binoculars. Suddenly a commotion broke out in the farmyard. Through the glasses Knorr saw a young Cooper's hawk attacking a guinea hen.

Junior, the young blue-throat, saw the hawk too and valiantly dive-bombed to the attack, hitting the raider from above and behind. Finally the hawk gave up.

Junior streaked back up the hill, came to a hovering stop in front of Knorr's face, and uttered the high, squeaky "peep, peep" characteristic of excited blue-throats Then he returned to his perch to ruffle and preen his feathers as he watched for new victims.

In addition to the "peep," male blue-throats sing a low, gurgling, contented sort of warble, feeble but sustained, a pleasing song for ears close enough to hear it (within 50 feet).

Hummingbirds have been said to have every avian gift—fast flight, extraordinary homing faculty, strength to cover long distances, ability to fly up, down, sideways, forward, and backwards, and incredibly magnificent color—every gift, that is, except that of song. As a matter of fact, several species besides the blue-throat have pleasing little songs.

Writers have questioned whether hummingbirds may not produce songs that cannot be heard by human ears. Sir D'Arcy Thompson has pointed out that there might be some relation between the size of animal vocal cords and the pitch of the sounds produced. He concluded that hummers might well sing at a level too highly pitched for human ears.

With this in mind, we watched singing blue-throats carefully through binoculars. Movements of the throat coincided with the singing, but now and then the sounds ceased while the throat continued to vibrate, seeming to indicate that some of the passages were pitched too high for our hearing. It would not be difficult to record this song and to analyze its characteristics in the laboratory.

Dr. Wetmore once wrote in the NATIONAL GEOGRAPHIC of Rivoli's hummingbird:*

"The first sight of this species is not likely to be forgotten, as among its small fellows it appears a veritable giant, with handsome coloring enhanced by its size. It is one of the most attractive birds of a region noted for interesting species."

Rivoli's hummingbird *(Eugenes fulgens,* meaning the "shining one") is mainly a Central American species, ranging as far south as Nicaragua and northward through the highlands of Guatemala and Mexico. It barely crosses our southern border into the mountains of New Mexico and Arizona (page 294).

In slow flight the actual wingbeats of the Rivoli's become distinguishable, not a blur, as in smaller hummingbirds. The sound of the slower wings is softer. When photographing the three species—Rivoli's, blue-throated, and black-chinned—in the same location, we quickly learned to identify each by the wing sounds.

Black-chin Buzzes Like a Bee

The little black-chinned hummingbird *(Archilocus alexandri)*, only $3\frac{3}{4}$ inches long as against 5 inches, looked to be half the size of the other hummers (page 296). By actual weight, he should be much less. The buzzing of his wings sounded like a bumblebee.

When the blue-throats appeared, the little black-chinned became timid and hard to photograph. The smallish gorget, a purple patch between the black chin and white collar, flashes only when the light is right.

The black-chinned covers an unusually wide breeding range, from southern British Columbia and western Montana to northern Mexico and western Texas, Colorado, and New Mexico. In the Huachucas at the time of our visit, the black-chin males fed mostly on

---

* See "Seeking the Smallest Feathered Creatures," by Alexander Wetmore, NATIONAL GEOGRAPHIC MAGAZINE, July, 1932.

Walker Van Riper

Mom's on Her Nest; All's Right with the World

From defiantly cocked bill to rakishly tilted tail, this broad-tail presented a picture of maternal devotion. Cameras and lights a foot away failed to disturb her slumber. Pushed from her nest, she flew briefly, then returned to warming tiny eggs (page 299).

pink thistles at the canyon mouths; while females built their second nest or fed youngsters. We found many nests along stream beds and low in the sycamore trees just out of the mountains.

Casualty rates for nests seemed high. For example, we found three nests within a stretch of 50 yards in lower Ramsey Canyon. We marked them down for night observation, as we wished to find out whether the male took his turn at night incubation. We never learned, for within a week we found the nests all destroyed, possibly by other hummers in search of nest-building material.

Though unable to observe other black-chin nests, we made night checks of the blue-throat twice. Both times she, not he, sat on the nest.

We regretted not having the opportunity to become better acquainted with *Cynanthus latirostris,* the broad-billed hummingbird. Though this charming bird undoubtedly visits the Huachucas and probably breeds there, we saw none during our stay. We found it only at Arizona's Madera Canyon, where we obtained a few pictures of the male (page 294).

The broad-bill is a little bird, about 3¼ inches from tip to tip. A broad, bright-pink bill distinguishes the male. He wears bluish green on his gorget, green on the upper parts of the breast, head, and back, and has white posterior underparts and a glossy blue-black tail. In the United States the rare broad-

bill lives only along the border in Texas, New Mexico, and Arizona.

We had hoped to photograph Costa's hummingbird in Arizona. Records indicated that it was not likely to occur in the Huachucas. So we spent a day in the San Pedro Valley and another in Tombstone searching for the bird, but without success. Eventually Dr. Edgerton found and photographed a fine male—in New York City! This specimen, at the Bronx Zoo, was taken in Death Valley National Monument and had lived for five years in captivity in perfect health—a record.

Costa's *(Calypte costae)* belongs to the same genus as Anna's. The males of the two species are somewhat similar, both having colored foreheads and throats. On the Costa's the color is purple or amethyst; on the Anna's, rose red.

We have now recorded all but four of the 13 hummingbird species that come regularly to this country to breed: ruby-throated, black-chinned, broad-tailed, Costa's, Anna's, Allen's, rufous, calliope, Rivoli's, blue-throated, buff-bellied, white-eared, and broad-billed.

Still missing are Allen's, calliope, buff-bellied, and white-eared. These four, as well as the hundreds of kinds in Mexico, Central America, and South America, leave us plenty of scope for future operations.*

* See also "Holidays with Humming Birds," by Margaret L. Bodine, NATIONAL GEOGRAPHIC MAGAZINE, June, 1928.

N. J. Berrill

Double-crested Cormorants Nest High in Deadwood Skyscrapers

Although most breeding colonies are on treeless islands, these birds occasionally take to lofty homes. If a tree is not already dead, the toxic excrement of the birds will soon kill it. New nests are built in about four days by the females. The males bring in materials but take no part in actual construction. Shown here are young birds. The four subspecies of the double-crested cormorants range from Alaska and Newfoundland to Florida and Mexico. European or "common" cormorant is shown on page 241.

Mexican Detour

"MEXICAN Detour" we called it because the Mexican part of the 1946 National Geographic Society-Cornell University Expedition had all the earmarks of a glorified detour. There were road constructions, tire troubles, interesting people, and hazy directions. There were exciting moments and unexpected panoramas—and that final exaltation felt when one finally rolls out on the smooth road after a long, circuitous passage to avoid some obstruction.

We spent in Mexico only six of the 16 weeks devoted to sound recording and bird photography. Yet the combination of mental and physical hazards and the satisfaction of overcoming them dominated the christening of this story; so "Mexican Detour" it is.

Late in February we headed south from Ithaca, New York, in two cars.

Our son David drove the station wagon, which housed photographic and sound-recording apparatus. He was to be the chief sound technician in our efforts to add to the recordings of jungle sounds which we had started in Panama the year before for the Office of Scientific Research and Development with Dr. Paul Kellogg, associate professor of ornithology at Cornell University.

We planned also to continue recording songs of North American birds, on which all of us had worked for more than 10 years.*

Elsa (Mrs. Allen) and I took turns driving the "red rabbit," which held our camping duffel. It was a rough ride, for, owing to war shortages, the car had no shock absorbers. Both vehicles were so heavily loaded that they were destined to give us trouble, especially in Mexico where we left the smooth roads.

Our first stop was Mattamuskeet Lake, North Carolina, to record the whistling swans which winter there. Willie Cahoon, refuge manager, showed us a spot on the south side of the marshy lake where we could drive the sound truck to within 200 feet of the water's edge. With our 350 feet of cable it was possible to set up the "electric ear" beyond the fringing bushes and to aim the microphone's parabolic reflector at the dozing birds.

Whistling Swans Didn't Whistle

In spite of the several hundred yards intervening, we secured an excellent recording of their sonorous notes whenever they sounded a welcome to another flock joining them from some other part of the marsh. We never heard anything from the swans that could be interpreted as a whistle.

From Mattamuskeet we headed for Tampa, Florida, with a short detour to Bull Island, South Carolina, where we photographed waterfowl and wild turkeys with the help of Waring W. Hills, refuge manager there. We could do no recording, as there was no way of getting the station wagon to the island.

In Tampa we found Charles Broley still up to his old trick of banding eagles. This retired banker took up eagle banding as an avocation when he attained 60, and at 73, had climbed more than 500 lofty trees to band more than a thousand of our national birds (page 309). Most young men hesitate to climb the tall pines where the eagles build their nests, usually over 100 feet above the ground, but Mr. Broley thought nothing of it.

I was satisfied to photograph his eagles from the ground with long-focus lenses and to do all my banding by proxy (page 180). It was thrilling, however, to watch this young man, then nearly 70, stand on a branch 60 feet from the ground, toss a rope over a limb six feet above his head, catch the end and go up, hand over hand, to the branch above, and finally reach the nest.

Sometimes the young birds would throw

* Recording songs and calls of wild birds was started by the Laboratory of Ornithology at Cornell University in 1930 under the sponsorship of the late Albert R. Brand. With sound recording in its infancy, apparatus was bulky and crude compared with present standards.

At first, activities centered about Cornell, in central New York State, but in 1935 the first of a series of expeditions took the author and his colleague, Dr. Paul Kellogg, from Florida to Montana in search of vanishing birds. A report on this expedition appeared in the NATIONAL GEOGRAPHIC MAGAZINE for June, 1937.

Since that time, in a series of expeditions to all parts of North America, an effort has been made to record voices of as many species of birds as possible. More recently, the voices of amphibians, insects, and mammals have been added to what is now designated as the "Cornell Library of Natural Sounds." This work has also been described in the April, 1950, NATIONAL GEOGRAPHIC MAGAZINE.

Two volumes of phonograph records that include songs of 121 species of birds, and a volume of 26 amphibian calls were published by 1950. Among a dozen more recent special records are two that include songs of more than 300 species of the birds of the eastern United States. Records of the songs of African and Mexican birds have recently been published by the Cornell Press from field recordings of collaborators.

The sensitive microphone is supplemented by a 40-inch parabolic reflector, aimed like a gun, which brings the bird 15 times closer to the recorder (page 310). Bird voices are recorded on magnetic tape.

During World War II the author, his son David, and Dr. Kellogg took part in an Office of Scientific Research and Development project for the study of jungle acoustics and recorded and identified the sounds that came from the Panamanian jungles by day and by night. In the recording project they were assisted by many Cornell students, including Charles Brand, son of the original sponsor.

themselves on their backs and strike at him with powerful talons; sometimes they would take off on a long glide and land in the brush a quarter of a mile away. Nothing would do then but to hunt them out and carry them back to the treetop in a bag, because the parents never feed their young on the ground.

It would be far safer and easier to climb to the nests when the eaglets are smaller, but at that stage the leg bands would not fit so neatly.

New Facts from Banded Eagles

What has Mr. Broley gained by this effort besides the satisfaction of doing something few others have dared to attempt?

For one thing, he has ascertained from the returns of his bands the unexpected fact that all the immature eagles in Florida migrate north in summer, even as far as New Brunswick and Prince Edward Island, Canada; also that the bald eagles seen passing Hawk Mountain, Pennsylvania, and similar places in the fall are Florida eagles returning to their homeland. By the relatively high percentage of band returns he has shown the dire need for protecting the comparatively few eagles left in this country.

The municipal pier at St. Petersburg, across the bay from Tampa, is a mecca for bird photographers. Here in the bright sunshine pelicans panhandle for fish; three species of gulls catch bread thrown into the air; and lesser scaup ducks (page 175) come flying to meet one and dive for rice in the clear water at one's feet.

From Tampa we headed southeast to Lake Okeechobee and Kissimmee Prairies in hopes of recording the sandhill cranes (page 201), which sometimes assemble in large flocks in winter. We got Mose Lanier, an old-time gator hunter, to guide us to the "goose ponds," where as many as 600 cranes had gathered.

It was now the middle of March, however, and the winter flock had disbanded. Only two nesting birds came in to have their voices recorded. Their nest was still empty, but on the way back to Okeechobee, David found another containing the customary two eggs. Unfortunately, incubation had just started, and the birds were too wary to accept a blind.

That Fantastic Bird—the Limpkin

Not far away Mose showed us an American egret colony in a palmetto hammock on the dry prairie, at a spot where we could drive the sound truck right under the nests. We secured a good recording of the egrets' nonmusical voices, though the wind in the palmettos sounded at times like castanets and made more noise than the egrets.

The following day we started for Wakulla Springs, an eerie spot about 16 miles south of Tallahassee and the home of that fantastic bird, the limpkin (page 201).

A giant spring comes out of the ground 175 feet deep and so crystal clear that the fish seem suspended in mid-air. The long ribbons of wild celery grow to tremendous size and support snails as large as golf balls. These are the food of the strange limpkins.

All about the spring are great moss-covered cypress trees housing barred owls and pileated woodpeckers. Herons, egrets, coots, and snakebirds are numerous, and ospreys build their bulky nests along the stream that flows from the spring. Schools of mullet that have made their way up from the Gulf of Mexico are continually jumping and making life interesting for these fish-eating birds.

There is a hotel there now offering jungle cruises in glass-bottomed boats and everything to make one comfortable, but the weird calls of the limpkin give this beautiful spot its real distinction.

Another ornithological attraction in this part of the United States is the home of Herbert L. Stoddard, all-time authority on the bobwhite quail and a gentleman of the old school. His Sherwood Plantation near Thomasville, Georgia, thronged with birds from titmice to turkeys, is a paradise for song recorders and photographers. Our first morning there found me in his turkey blind with my camera, while Elsa and David recorded the small birds about the house.

Frogs Chorus After Cloudburst

The following day a cloudburst brought out the spadefoot toads as I had never seen them before—hundreds, all hopping in one direction toward a shallow pond. Soon the piny woods resounded with their explosive brayings. Whenever a toad felt the urge, he would suddenly inflate his snow-white throat, sound one blast, and deflate just as quickly, so that at a little distance the pond seemed covered with bobbing ping-pong balls.

David secured an excellent recording of the chorus for our phonograph album, *Voices of the Night,** together with the calls of the ornate chorus frog that came out with the rain in equal numbers.

Usually these amphibians are active only at night, but some were still calling at noon when the sun came out, and I was able to secure an unusual film of both species singing. By afternoon all was quiet. They had found their mates, the eggs had been laid, and they could now rest for another year.

Our next stop was the Aransas National

* See "Voices of the Night," by Arthur A. Allen, NATIONAL GEOGRAPHIC MAGAZINE, April, 1950.

Charles Broley Bands His Thousandth Eagle

Usually he bands young bald eagles in their nest, 100 or more feet in the air. Here he demonstrates his technique on the ground, for the benefit of the author. Over 70, Mr. Broley could find no nest so high or so inaccessible as to deter him from his work (page 307).

Wildlife Refuge near Austwell, Texas, where we hoped to record the whooping crane, one of the rarest birds in North America. Seventeen of the known 26 birds had been reported wintering on this refuge. Differing from the sociable sandhill cranes, which winter there in large flocks, the whooping variety scatters singly or in pairs, or in family groups of three, over widespread areas that are difficult to reach by car.

Whooping Cranes Uncooperative

Mr. Charles A. Keefer, who managed the refuge, had no difficulty showing us in the distance three pairs of whooping cranes. He made every effort with his tractor to get the recorder out to the wet prairies where the birds might fly by, but they were not cooperative. Occasionally they flew within recording range, but they never let out a whoop unless they were a mile away, and the wind never stopped blowing.

Other birds, however, behaved better, and we left with good recordings of lesser Canada geese, little brown cranes, Rio Grande turkeys (page 200), and several lesser fowls. We also secured some colorful photographs, especially on Carroll Island, located about one mile off shore, and now considered a part of this refuge.

This low-lying island, reached by shrimp boat in an hour and a half, is the summer home of the spectacular roseate spoonbills (page 145), as well as brown pelicans (page 129) and several species of herons. On March 29 only the Ward's herons (page 143), American egrets (page 140), and reddish egrets (page 142) were nesting, but flocks of spoonbills, snowy herons, and white ibises (page 264) were loafing about, awaiting the urge. A hurricane a few years before had swept most of the bushes from the island, so that the few that remained were full of nests, and many birds were building on the ground.

From Austwell we continued southward to Harlingen, home of those keen field naturalists, Mr. and Mrs. Irby Davis, who had offered to lead us along some of their favorite bird-

California Gulls Give a Concert on the Bear River Marshes of Utah

The microphone is set in the parabolic reflector at right; the recorder is in the car. The author and his colleague, Dr. Kellogg, with the assistance of David Allen and other Cornell students and collaborators, had by 1961 recorded the voices of more than a thousand species of birds and other animals, of which 514 represent birds of the United States and Canada.

Within This Blind on Bear River Marshes the Author Waits for Winged Performers to Come Within Camera Range

Several species of ducks swim in the open water. At right is the nest of a black-necked stilt; at left, the nest of an avocet (page 233); in foreground, the nest of a pintail (page 174). It was possible to photograph all three nests without moving the blind (page 316).

311

Hugo H. Schroder

Half Falcon, Half Buzzard Is This Baby Caracara

This tropical species, popularly called "Mexican eagle," which has found its way north to southern Texas and central Florida, usually nests in the cabbage palms. It feeds largely on snakes, lizards, and turtles, but is not adverse to joining with the buzzards to feed on carrion. This bird is so strong and aggressive that it can force large vultures to surrender carcasses on which they are feeding.

were charming, the view over Monterrey was magnificent, the jagged peaks above us inspiring, and the birds did their best to entertain us.

Sennett's thrashers sang like the brown thrashers at home; Lafresnaye's tanagers, with their buzzy songs, reminded us of scarlet tanagers; Audubon's orioles sang like small boys learning to whistle; and the beautiful painted redstarts sang like cerulean warblers.

Occasionally we heard the coppery-tailed trogons twanging their jew's-harps, and the songs of chestnut-backed solitaires floated down the mountains like tinkling glass. Cedar waxwings and migrant warblers from Canada were numerous, and never have I seen more pileolated warblers in a single morning.

We could have enjoyed birding here for a week, but unfortunately had to be on our way the next day.

We continued on the Pan American Highway to Ciudad Victoria, Ciudad Mante, and Antiguo Morelos, where we detoured westward on the San Luis Potosí road, heading for a favorite birding spot of the Davises in the humid oak forest on the mountains.

Here we found blue mockingbirds, crimson-collared grosbeaks, Mexican trogons, motmots, chestnut-backed solitaires, Veracruz ivory-bills, and ivory-billed wood hewers. Each day before dawn we were awakened by the continuous song of a Coues's flycatcher, similar to the wood pewee at home in that it did not stop to catch its breath for 20 minutes at a time.

Camping in this place had its disadvantages in ticks and chiggers, and recording was hampered by wind and rain. But it was delightful to renew acquaintance with beautiful green jays and the red-crowned and yellow-cheeked

ing trails near the Pan American Highway before we should head for Durango.

For many years they have been spending their vacations in eastern Mexico, and I doubt that anyone has achieved a better knowledge of the field identification and of the songs and calls of these semitropical birds than is enjoyed by the Davises. Their skill saved us many hours, first for a few days around Harlingen and in the Santa Ana Refuge, and later along the highway as far as Tamazunchale.

New Birding Trails in Eastern Mexico

One of the most unusual spots was Chipinque Mesa, a few miles south of Monterrey, up a winding mountain road. The cottages parrots, always competing over nesting holes. Here too we added two military macaws' raucous voices to our sound records and made several attempts for the song of the chestnut-backed solitaire.

This wood, loaded with moss, epiphytes, and orchids, was rich in bird life, and we resolved to return to "Irby's Mesa," as we christened it, on our return journey.

Breaking camp and returning to the Pan American Highway, we continued south to Ciudad de Valles, where we stopped to recharge the batteries so necessary for sound recording.

Breaking Trail in a Quarry

An abandoned quarry 20 miles farther south was a favorite birding spot of the Davises, and for this we headed next morning at daybreak. The quarry road was overgrown with climbing bamboo beset with large thorns, so it took us two hours to clear a trail far enough into the brush in order to get the sound equipment away from the noise of the highway.

Here a great chorus of chachalacas resounded across the valley. The chachalaca is the smallest of the guans, a group of New World tropical game birds related to the turkey. It is about the size of a grouse, but has a much longer tail and lives in the dense brush.

At dawn these birds fly to the tops of small trees and greet one another with an amusing raucous chorus. One bird seems to call, "Keep it up, keep it up"; another screeches, "Cut it out, cut it out." This keeps up until the hills re-echo.

Passing flocks of parakeets were nearly as noisy when they flew overhead, but were silent when they alighted in trees.

The Hole Fills the Bill, and the Bill Fills the Hole

The old nest of an ant-eating woodpecker was a snug fit for this emerald toucanet, smallest of the toucans. A fruit-eating, tropical American family, these birds have very large, although light, beaks. Beaks and feathers are usually brilliantly colored. This one was photographed near Tamazunchale, Mexico, the northern limit of its range (page 314).

When the chachalacas and parakeets were silent, we noticed an all-pervading undertone of low-frequency notes that soon resolved itself into the songs of white-winged doves and red-billed pigeons.

Apparently they were at the height of their courtship season. At close range one could interpret the white-winged doves' call, "Who cooks for you, and you and you?" The red-billed pigeons, with equally soft voices, called, "Whooooo kicka de ball?" Together, however, and by the dozen, they merely added a murmuring background to the more striking calls of other birds.

One of the most appealing was the plaintive whistle of the Mexican tinamou, calling, "Where are you?" in oft-repeated phrases.

The tinamous constitute another New World group of partridge-sized terrestrial game birds found from Mexico to Argentina. They are really more closely related to ostriches and have heavy bodies, small heads, and practically no tails. They seldom fly, but skulk in the thick undergrowth where they are not often seen, though their musical whistles are heard frequently.

Tinamous respond quickly to an imitation of their calls. I sometimes had them whistling within 10 feet of me in the wild pineapple thickets without being able to see them.

Becard Fights for Building Supplies

A pair of becards were starting their bulky nest of Spanish moss and fibers fastened to the tip of a mountain-mahogany branch. It was amusing to watch an Altamira oriole trying to sneak in and steal some of the fibers for its own nest. Just as often it was driven away by the much smaller becard, whose righteous wrath made up for its inferior weight and size.

Our next stop as we continued southward was just north of Tamazunchale at a tourist court, where we found comfortable quarters for 10 days while we explored the surrounding country for birds.

It was now the middle of April, and we were considerably handicapped in our recording efforts by rain. Even so, we found a number of new birds, since this area represents the northernmost extension of the tropical fauna along the Pan American Highway.

We were especially interested in the emerald toucanets, the smallest of that curious family of tropical New World birds, the toucans, which have such large bills and bizarre coloration. The toucanet is largely green, with a yellow and maroon bill; but other species, frequently seen in zoological parks, are black with yellow or white throats and splashes of red.

Toucans nest in holes in trees. We found one toucanet nesting in an old woodpecker hole (page 313) in which the aperture was so small he had to alight with his bill in the opening if he expected to enter. Apparently the cavity inside was much larger, for he had no difficulty turning around inside and putting his head out in a fraction of a second.

Not far from the toucanets David found the nesting burrow of the curious jaylike motmot. This bird preens the barbs from near the end of its long tail to give it a racquetlike form. The burrow was in a steep-sided ravine near the base of a waterfall, nearly dry. The burrow itself, however, was quite damp, and contained three white eggs at the inner end, with no sign of a nest or even a bed of sand. Instead, the floor was uneven and stony.

Parrot Backs Down into Nest

Here at Tamazunchale we found our first red-crowned parrot's nest in a natural hollow of a tree 20 feet from the ground. It contained three white eggs, but again with no sign of a nest except for dead wood at the bottom of the cavity. It was amusing to watch the slow-moving bird back down into its nest, using both bill and feet to hang on.

I started a feeding station outside our window, facing a wooded stream, and loaded it with bread and fruit. Early next morning I heard a sound at the shelf. Hoping to find it crowded with tanagers and thrushes and saltators, I sneaked to the window, but, to my dismay, found an itinerant black cow munching the last of the papayas.

Altamira orioles were hanging a long stockinglike nest to the tip of a bamboo in the garden. Curious heavy-billed anis sunned themselves on the tops of the shrubbery, and Tamaulipas thrushes sang and behaved much like robins. Cheerful little pepper shrikes sang and disported themselves in roadside trees, and a few catbirds and Lincoln sparrows, still on their winter quarters, reminded us of home.

One day we drove to Xilitla. The road left the highway about 22 miles north of Tamazunchale and wound up the mountain in hair-raising fashion to about 3,500 feet. Here in the moss forest we found the beautiful slaty solitaires, better known as "clarinas," as well as yellow-bellied trogons and Abbot's tanagers which we had not seen before.

Birds Beside a Waterfall

The Davises continued southwest to Jacala, whereas we returned to Ciudad Mante and Irby's Mesa with an interesting side trip to El Salto. Here is a magnificent waterfall, seven miles off the San Luis Potosí highway, west of Antiguo Morelos.

The falls themselves make a spectacular cascade over a limestone ledge. The water is a rich blue and as clear as that at Wakulla Springs, but so impregnated with lime that many little irregular conglomerate dams and innumerable pools have been formed below. The dams were covered with moss and ferns and dotted with cardinal flowers.

Interesting birds inhabited the fringing forest around this charming spot.

Over the enormous amphitheater made by the falls circled 10 large military macaws. They climbed the lianas that hung from the top, and several entered holes in the limestone cliffs, where they were doubtless nest-

In Vain the Author Waits for an Imperial Ivory-billed Woodpecker to Appear

With a 17-inch lens on his Leica camera, the author focused on the nesting hole. Mrs. Allen tapped on the tree, but the giant woodpecker was not at home. Nesting had not yet begun in this high pine forest near Durango, Mexico. Diligent search revealed only a single female bird, not yet nesting (text below). Larger than the ivory-billed woodpecker (page 2), it is similar in habits.

ing. A prairie falcon darted after white-collared swifts that often dived through the falling water into caverns behind. A spotted cañon wren nested in a small cave near by, and his cascade of whistles took us back to our own Rockies. Wild Muscovy ducks flew up and down the stream. A chestnut-backed solitaire tinkled away near the brink of the falls.

Seeking the Elusive Ivorybill

From El Salto we made our way to Durango where several of our fellow countrymen were most cooperative in helping us locate our objective—the imperial ivory-billed woodpecker. Mr. Chester Lamb, a veteran collector, had written me that he had seen this rare bird a few years before in the vicinity. We were hopeful of finding a nesting pair that we could study, record, and compare with the more northern ivorybills, which we had observed in Louisiana in 1935.*

Mr. John Zalaha had seen a large woodpecker two weeks before, and invited us to his lumbering camp, El Progreso, about 30 miles north of Coyotes. The trail led over a rough mountain road, up and down canyons, but ever rising to about 9,000 feet. Here the pines were much larger, and there was some evidence of large woodpeckers having worked recently over the dead trees.

We were much encouraged to note piles of bark at the base of some trees, because our more northern ivorybills feed by scaling off bark of recently dead trees for the beetle larvae beneath. We found nesting holes that looked too large for pileated woodpeckers, but we saw no woodpeckers themselves.

It was the middle of May, but still early spring in the mountains. Mexican bluebirds were just starting to nest, olive warblers were building, and trogons had not yet started. Thick-billed parrots that occasionally wander northward to Arizona were flying about, and David watched a pair going in and out of an old woodpecker hole. With their longer tails, more pointed wings, and very heavy bills, they look a good deal more like macaws than ordinary parrots.

* See "Hunting with a Microphone the Voices of Vanishing Birds," by Arthur A. Allen, NATIONAL GEOGRAPHIC MAGAZINE, June, 1937.

We saw many flocks of band-tailed pigeons, but they were not nesting. Pygmy nuthatches, however, and spurred towhees (page 107) already had young, so we were encouraged to think that the imperial ivorybills might also be nesting. On the evening of the third day David reported one ivorybill flying over the canyon to the west of the camp. It was headed for the mesa, where we all had been hunting.

The next morning we were out at daylight and, with two Mexican boys to help us, scattered over the level area, some two miles square, in the direction in which David had seen the bird flying.

Success! Author Locates an Ivorybill

It fell to my good fortune to locate the bird.

Several calls like a tinny nuthatch first attracted my attention, for they seemed identical with the notes I had become familiar with in Louisiana 10 years before. Slipping through the great pines, I soon had an excellent view of the bird near the top of a dead spire, whacking off large pieces of bark, examining the trunk beneath, and occasionally giving those familiar tin-trumpet calls. With my binoculars I could see its yellow eye and easily recognized it as a female imperial with no red on the head.

Except for the absence of the white "suspender" markings on the back, it was a carbon copy of the Louisiana birds, and not until it flew did its much larger size become apparent.

Its straight, direct, ducklike flight, without the undulations typical of the pileated and most other woodpeckers, was also very similar to the flight of our ivorybills. The large white patches on the wings were the same as noted in Louisiana; and finally, when it took off through the forest, it repeated the other bird's habit of going so far without stopping that I never found it again.

Later in the day, however, David saw what was probably the same bird flying over the canyon near where he had seen it the night before.

For several days we haunted this spot, but we never saw it again, nor did we find any fresh cuttings. Regretfully we decided it must nest later in the season and gave up our quest.

In easy stages we reached the Bear River Migratory Bird Refuge near Brigham, Utah. Set up by Congress in 1928, with the cooperation of the State of Utah, its original purpose was to stamp out botulism, a disease which annually killed thousands of waterfowl and shore birds on the shallow alkali ponds and flats at the north end of Great Salt Lake (page 160). It was possible to divert water from the Bear River to this area, and by the use of dikes and dams to control the water levels. In this way, part of the polluted areas could be dried up and the water deepened in other areas, thereby largely eradicating the disease.

Now it is a paradise for a great variety of waterfowl, marsh, and shore birds, and a boon to bird observers and photographers as well as to sportsmen.

The ponds, which are three miles long, are arranged like pieces of a pie, with dikes radiating from the headquarters building in the center. One can drive along the dikes without unduly disturbing the birds and watch them at their nests from car windows. In some places colonies of western gulls have set up housekeeping right in the middle of the dike, and these parts have to be closed to traffic. Avocets, stilts, and Wilson's phalaropes (pages 233 and 235) join the gulls.

On the gravel road leading into the refuge we found five pairs of snowy plovers (page 207) with eggs just inches from the tracks made by our tires. Gadwalls, pintails, cinnamon teal, and mallards (pages 168-175) nest in the weeds by the roadside and even close against the foundations of the headquarters buildings.

Pelicans Wary of Big Carp

On the apron of the dam, a few feet from the office windows, Brewster's egrets vie with night herons and white pelicans for the small carp that try to ascend through the shallow water. The huge grandfather carp, however, mill around unmolested among the pelicans, which seem wary of overloading their pouches.

White-faced glossy ibises (page 144) stride about the edges of shallow ponds and join with the herons to form a sizable nesting rookery in the cattails. It was quite a comedown to photograph night herons (page 141) at water level in the West after the treetops of the East. At one spot along the dike (page 311), without moving my blind I photographed an avocet nesting on one side, a black-necked stilt on the other, and a pintail on her nest in front (pages 174 and 233).

By the middle of June large flocks of male pintails and mallards had appeared on the marshes to finish their molting; many of the females were still incubating or brooding small young. Since waterfowl lose all their flight feathers at once, it is necessary for them to assemble where there is an abundance of food close to shelter, for they cannot fly to escape danger. Males always start their molt ahead of the females. By the time we left, on June 17, there were thousands of males along the dikes.

Author's Acknowledgments

MOST of the photographs in this book represent experiences which the author has shared with some congenial person. Some of the photographs represent days of effort, some only a few minutes; but, in reviewing them, the author finds himself indebted to a great many friends who have assisted him in various ways. He would like to relate just how each one helped to make the photographic project successful, to acknowledge his indebtedness, and to express his thanks for the pleasure of their companionship.

To some he is indebted for showing him the bird or nest to be photographed later; to others he is grateful for assistance in transporting equipment, building blinds, etc.; to still others for kindly hospitality in unfamiliar places.

The long hours spent in the blinds have given the author new insight into the lives of birds and plenty of time to reflect on the virtues of friends who have been so universally kind and understanding.

In recalling those who have been most helpful, the author thinks first of a sympathetic mother, who enabled him to purchase his first camera in 1907 and who followed his adventures with a camera for half a century.

The one who has been called upon most frequently, however, to sacrifice comfort and personal desires to the whims of a writer or bird photographer has been his ever-considerate wife, Elsa (pages 129, 240). Through the years, she has never failed at home or in the field to be ready with assistance and to subjugate her own affairs to the needs of the moment.

Their son David has accompanied the author on most of the expeditions recounted in this book, from Panama to Alaska, and has been most helpful in finding birds' nests, in setting up blinds, carrying equipment, doing camp chores, and attending to all the amenities that determine the comfort and success of a long trip.

To his colleague, Dr. Paul Kellogg, the author feels deeply indebted for unfailing advice and assistance in maintenance of equip-

ment in good working condition and for relieving him often of other duties when an unexpected opportunity for camera work arose.

To Dr. Gilbert Grosvenor, long the President; to Dr. Alexander Wetmore, Vice Chairman of the Research Committee; to the Board of Trustees of the National Geographic Society; and to members of the National Geographic staff, the author feels unusually indebted for equipment and financial aid on the various expeditions and for the encouragement which the careful publication of his photographs and articles in the NATIONAL GEOGRAPHIC MAGAZINE have given him. To Mr. Andrew Poggenpohl, for the careful editing which the published material has received in making it into this book, he is very grateful.

He is indebted, likewise, to Dr. Harold E. Edgerton (pages 21, 297) for supplying him with a much improved speed-flash equipment, by means of which some of the latest and best pictures were obtained. In 1947, working with a grant from the National Geographic Society, Dr. Edgerton and his colleagues designed a battery-operated, remote-control flash unit which produced man-made flashes of light lasting only 1/5000 of a second. With this equipment, Dr. Edgerton made the outstanding series of color photographs of hummingbirds in this volume, which were first reproduced in the August, 1947, and August, 1951, issues of the NATIONAL GEOGRAPHIC MAGAZINE.

To Dr. Herbert Friedmann, Curator of the Division of Birds, Smithsonian Institution, he would express appreciation for assistance in checking accuracy of color reproductions.

To the Trustees of Cornell University and to members of the administrative staff he is likewise indebted for making it possible to arrange his vacation periods from the University, during the month of June, when bird activities are best suited for study and photography.

He would like also to thank the following friends, some of whom are not mentioned specifically in the text, for services rendered which have made the collecting of material for this book such a pleasant

National Geographic Photographer John E. Fletcher

318

"Are You Still There?" Mother Gannet, Coming In for a Landing, Looks for Baby

As she back-pedals with broad wings, she spots her offspring with unerring instinct. Youngsters at right look like black-handled powder puffs; at 13 weeks they will outweigh their parents. Cliff-top nests here at Bonaventure Island off Canada's Gaspé Peninsula for the most part are crude bundles of sticks and seaweed (pages 123, 132-136 and 239).

task: Prudence Allen, Jack Arnold, Harold Axtell, Guy Bailey, Marguerite and Fred Baumgartner, Albert and Charles Brand, Myrtle and Charles Broley, Stephen Bivins, Allen Benton, Harold Bryant, Walter Browne, David Canfield, Stephen Collins, Anna May and Irby Davis, James Dickerson, Theodora Cope Fletcher, Lawrence Grinnell, Lloyd Gunther, Oliver Hewitt, Sally and Southgate Hoyt, Frances and Frederick Hamerstrom, Merrill Hammond, Cordia Henry, Joseph Howell, Robert Johnson, John Keefer, Brina Kessel, Henry Kyllingstad, Edna and Arthur Lane, Claude Leister, Harrison Lewis, Olive and Sam Lloyd, Charles Lueder, Edward Mc-Ilhenny, Heinz Meng, Alden Miller, William Montagna, the Misses McKeel, Robert Niedrach, Fred Osborne, Lucy and Miles Pirnie, Roger Tory Peterson, Warren Petersen, Allan Phillips, Mary and William A. Rockefeller, Arthur C. Smith, Ada and Herbert L. Stoddard, Lyman Stuart, James Tanner, Edwin Teale, Phebe Travis, Fred Truslow, Malvina Trussell, John Vandernacker, Florence and Richard Weaver, H. E. Weisner, Cecil Williams, William Wimsatt and Mr. and Mrs. John Zalaha.

Included in this book are 67 color plates by 20 of the leading bird photographers of the day. Their names are printed under their contributions. To them, individually and collectively, the author feels deeply grateful for permitting their charming photographs to be included and thus add so much to the attractiveness of this volume.

Arthur A. Allen

Ithaca, New York
May 1, 1961

INDEX

Bold-face Figures Denote Color Plates

For additional reference see the National Geographic Society's *The Book of Birds* in two volumes edited by Gilbert Grosvenor, President, National Geographic Society, and Alexander Wetmore, Secretary of the Smithsonian Institution. These volumes, currently out of print but available in public libraries, were the first to present in full color all the major species of the United States and Canada. They include 950 color portraits by Major Allan Brooks. Volume I covers diving birds, ocean birds, swimmers, wading birds, wild fowl, birds of prey, game birds, shore birds, marsh dwellers, and birds of the northern seas; Volume II: owls, goatsuckers, swifts, woodpeckers, flycatchers, crows, jays, blackbirds, orioles, chickadees, creepers, thrushes, swallows, tanagers, wrens, warblers, hummingbirds, finches, and sparrows. The narrative is by Arthur A. Allen, Gilbert Grosvenor, Henry W. Henshaw, Francis H. Herrick, Frederick C. Lincoln, Robert Cushman Murphy, T. Gilbert Pearson, Alexander Wetmore, and others.